from Eddie

ECHOES IN GREEN

The Big Yellow Sun

(scenes from an early Tipperary childhood)

A memoir

To Elsie

by

Edward Forde Hickey

with every good wish

Edward Forde Hickey

Other books by Edward Forde Hickey

The Eary Morning Light (2015)

A New Day Dawning (2016)

Footsteps in the Dew (2017)

A Bunch of Wild Roses (2020)

Tales from Tipperary (2020)

Reflections (2020)

From Time to Time (2021)

Old Faces (2021)

Chattering at School (2022)

Gaslight Days: Book 1 – From Over the Sea (2023)

Gaslight Days: Book 2 – The Road Ahead (2024)

Gaslight Days: Book 3 – The Journey Goes On (2024)

These reflections are dedicated to

children everywhere –

a tapestry of what once was

Why should all the past be washed away as though
written on some little schoolchild's slate?

(author unknown)

CONTENTS

ESCAPE FROM THE RUINS

Between 1940 and 1941

It was September 1940 and the first week of the German Blitz on London. Some of the houses in our back street were turned into heaps of rubble, including St Luke's Anglican church near the Falcon Arms pub – 400 yards from our front door.

I was Nell and Patsy Hickey's firstborn child – a newborn baby just four months old. I had spent most of that time inside an oxygen tent following my premature birth in St Mary's Hospital near Paddington Station.

My mother knew she must save me from the next load of bombs that was surely on its way – maybe this very night. She hadn't a moment to look round for her hankie into which to shed a few tears. She lay her suitcase on the bed and started packing.

As always, my father, Patsy, could read her like a book. She must take me to her mother in Ireland where I'd be safe on the little farm with my grannie and her eldest son, Jack. I could spend my days in their little thatched cabin for as long as the war lasted.

After splashing the two of us with a few drops of holy water, Patsy pushed his precious Nell up the basement steps with me tucked firmly underneath her arm while he fussed over her and waved us goodbye.

We hurried to Queens Park Station and sped down the line to Euston Station. We took the six hour steam train to Holyhead in North Wales and crossed over the sea to Dublin. From there, we caught the train going to Limerick.

By that time, we were worn to a thread. We were hungry as well and I had already started howling like a banshee, keeping everybody awake.

We got off at Nenagh Station in Tipperary. My mother's brother Jack was there to meet us with Moll the Mare and her cart. He hadn't seen his sister since '37 and was more than happy to see her now and catch up with all the news about the war and the German bombing raids.

'Welcome home, Nell,' said he. 'Thank God the two of ye have got here safely. What with all the air raids, it's nothing short of a miracle to see you and baby Ned and both of ye alive and well.'

He could see how tired my mother was and he took her by the arm and carried her suitcase out to the cart. He lifted her up onto it and got up on the seat in front.

Before putting the whip to Moll, he kept turning round to make sure we were warm enough and that the tartan rug was firmly wrapped round us. By that time, I was fast asleep in my pile of woolly blankets.

There was still a journey of five miles to go before we reached Dolla and the little farm. Moll was anxious to get home to Lightning the Ass, her lifelong companion and she trotted briskly out of the station yard. Jack, too, was eager to get home. As soon as we left the town, he started puffing on his pipe and humming happily to himself.

My mother would have no peace of mind till we reached the end of our journey. She and Grannie had so much to talk about. There hadn't been a baby in the house since '26 when my mother's youngest sister, Winnie, was the last of Grannie's fifteen children to be born. Like all her brothers and sisters (barring Jack), Winnie had left home as soon as she was sixteen, heading for Dublin to work as a servant in a rich man's mansion.

My mother's hasty journey had taken her away from Patsy for the first time since the day they were married. As she neared her childhood home, she kept reflecting on what had now pulled them apart from each other: this blasted war. Was it ever going to end?

She kept on thinking – thinking of her neighbours racing to the underground railway station with their children and their few possessions – thinking of me above everything else. What a contrast my life was going to be on Grannie's farm compared to the dusty gloom of London and the ugly bomb sites that had ruined our street! Tipperary's hills and woodland were places where I would grow and flourish under the watchful eye of Grannie and Jack.

Her happy thoughts, however, were marred by something far less reassuring: how on earth was poor Patsy going to cope while she was in Dolla? Who would come in and cook his dinner for him?

These thoughts were soon interrupted. For, before the cart reached Grannie's little cabin, she was starting to nod off and was in danger of toppling herself and me from the cart and into the ditch. In the meantime, I continued to sleep – something I hadn't done for most of the journey since we left Euston.

The next few days at Grannie's place were filled with emotion. The thought of returning to her basement flat and leaving me with my grannie was a heavy load on my mother's heart. She knew she had to go back to Patsy as quickly as she could and look after him. This meant she couldn't stay more than a week on the farm – two at the most – nursing and looking after me.

Such sad thoughts continued to fill her dreams during the night. There was one thought above all others: when she was back in London, she'd no longer have the motherly joy of holding me in her arms and lulling me to sleep next to her.

To test her even further, something else was pressing on her. There was always some young Irish girl in London waiting to take her place as a nurse in the hospital. Jobs were scarce enough for people coming to the big city like Patsy and herself or for anyone who happened to be Irish. If she didn't get back to work soon, she'd almost certainly lose her position.

Where would that leave her? There'd be no more letters for her to write home with the little bit of money to help her mother put food on the table or keep herself in decent clothes for Mass and the odd visit to the shops. She knew that her mother had little enough money to keep things afloat. Her husband, Will, had been dead these past twelve years and was buried below in the graveyard.

There was a list of other matters too – each one alarming enough to cause her to worry: the lack of a proper lavatory, the lack of water from a tap and its hot water in which to wash me and bathe me.

To distract her from these gloomy thoughts, she spent a great deal of time gazing at me while I slept in the cot that Molly Hughes brought down for me. At night, she kept imagining that the sound of the German bombs was still ringing in my ears since my howls kept Grannie, Jack and herself awake for most of the night.

She hadn't set eyes on Grannie since leaving home. How shocked she was to see her mother's back so stooped – the result of sciatica. She was now over sixty and looked every inch her age. But what woman wouldn't look tired and worn after all the child-bearing she'd been put through? And now she had the unexpected burden of me and my babyhood needs to put up with. Who was going to give me my milk?

She prepared her suitcase – quietly and stealthily when neither Jack nor her mother could see what she was doing. But Jack was up and dressed an hour later and he drove her to Nenagh Station for her journey back to Patsy. It was a sad farewell for both of them. So anxious was she about Patsy that she didn't even have a thought of saying goodbye to Grannie.

As soon as she reached Paddington, she was determined to go on living as though nothing out of the way had taken place. She carried on preparing Patsy his sandwiches of bread and cheese and gave him his bottle of milk for his lunchtime break. He'd be tired after cycling the six weary miles from Harrow Road's Halfpenny Steps to Craven Park. He'd be hungry even before settling into the work of helping clear away the bomb site rubble.

In the evening, she and Patsy sat at the fireside, discussing their present crisis: the cruelty of the war, the loss of their new baby and whether my grannie, being so old, would be able to deal with my many needs.

If that wasn't enough, there was yet another unsettling thing coming their way and it would change their lives all over again. Patsy was now classed as too old to go soldiering on the front line against the Germans. Yet, when October arrived, he was informed he was to be sent to Lakenheath in East Anglia along with other older men, mainly Irish fellows like himself, to help lay out the runways for the American aeroplanes if the Yanks should enter the war.

My father was a healthy specimen and strong enough for this sort of work. He would need to be. He and his colleagues had to work at breakneck speed around the cement mixers, with only the infrequent let off to get back home and see their wives at weekends.

Worst of all – midst so many uncertainties – was something which neither of my parents could possibly know: that the fight against the Germans was going to last far longer than anyone had imagined – or that I would be forced to stay with Grannie and far away from them for the next five years – and that when I returned to them in September '45, I wouldn't have the foggiest notion who they were. Gone would be the rivers. Gone would be the woods and the hills and the meadows. Gone would be the children with whom I had grown used to going adventuring. Above all, gone would be Grannie and Jack, the only parent figures I had ever known. All gone forever. Oh dear!

Grannie's house is an old, thatched cabin built 300 years ago and embraced by hills studded with pine trees stretching to the sky. There's no artificial lighting in the house – just the light from the half-door and the front windows.

Throughout the evenings, there are two smoky candles and an oil lamp to keep the living room bright and cheerful. There are no radiators for heating the rooms – just the big open fireplace, which is brilliantly ablaze and heaped high with logs and turf throughout the day. After the evening meal, Grannie and Jack sit round its warmth and are as hot as toast.

Jack saves his turf in the bog out in Glown, three miles away. He gets his logs from Clonmore Wood which bounds Grannie's farm. He cuts it at certain times of the year agreed on by Lord Dunally. The lord owns the wood and likes to see Jack getting rid of its fallen trees and branches.

Jack also saws down trees on the ditches round the farm, especially the blackthorn and whitethorn, as they make the best blaze. He stores the logs on a woodpile outside the back wall of the pig house and stacks the turf inside the cow shed. This ramshackle affair consists of eight sawn-off telegraph poles and a number of galvanised sheets nailed down on top to keep Grannie's cows safe from the rain while she and himself are milking.

Whenever the rain comes (and it often comes in fast and furiously from Kerry), he puts a potato sack round his shoulders and makes a quick dash out past the pig house to cover his logs with the tarpaulin sheet that lies on top of it. He keeps his axe and bowsaw up there for sawing the timber and chopping it into logs to put on the woodpile. On the pig house roof also are the pitchfork and rake, as well as the mallet and sledge for fencing. There are some horseshoes and nails there and a few wooden handles – as well as the yard brush for Grannie to sweep away the goose-droppings when she has nothing better to do.

From my second year onwards, I watch him with a fascinated eye as he chops his logs into quarters. In my third year, I make feeble attempts to help him build up the woodpile and I bring in small armfuls of logs to help put a smile on Grannie's face. By then, she has begun teaching me to count them one by one whilst throwing them into the tea chest next to the fire. Aren't I the manly young fellow, carrying logs into the house in my bowed elbows and learning to count them with my crafty old Grannie!?

She has several other ways of teaching me to count, especially when the two of us are searching for hens' eggs in the little field known as the haggart next to the house. She lets me place them carefully in her apron whilst I'm counting them to her.

Water comes from the spring well in our neighbour Fiddler Joe's stream. It lies on the far side of Sam's Grove across the lane. Its water isn't good enough to drink – only for Grannie to boil the pink spuds in for our dinner as well as the white ones to give to her two pigs and her fowl.

It's also in my second year that I get used to walking with Jack to reach this well, he with his two big buckets and me with my little sweet-gallon. We watch our steps as we make our way down the slippery slope before reaching the well.

For Jack's daily mugs of tea, we walk as far as Brindley's spring-well. It's a hundred yards down the lane and lies in a grotto hidden behind a laurel hedge. It's worth the walk, as its water is pure crystal. When we go there, it is often bathed in sunlight, the sun's reflection sparkling up at us. Grannie also uses this water for boiling the Sunday joint of mutton, which Jack brings home from town every Saturday on the handlebars of his bike. It's a five-mile ride there and back. 'It keeps his legs firm and trim,' says Grannie.

I get used to going with Jack to this other well and watching him as he removes the stone slab and skims off the dead flies from the well's surface. He fills his buckets and half-fills my sweet-gallon so that I can carry my load of water back to Grannie.

By the time I'm three, I'm beginning to feel quite important. I not only bring the logs in to her, but I am able to bring back water for her. No wonder she calls me her little man!

With no indoor lavatories, each person has their own discreet place for easing themselves – either behind the bushes or deep in the dyke. Dock leaves are used for cleanliness.

Like most country people, we wash only the upper part of our body. This happens on Saturday night in preparation for Mass. Mass is held in the little wooden church at the upper end of the Silvermines village. It lies hidden behind the huge Protestant church, which still dominates the main street.

Saturday is also the night when Jack shaves his face. It's a weekly ritual, which he performs like other men, sharpening his cut-throat razor on the leathern strop. It's yet another occasion when he requires my help. He lets me hold the broken bit of looking glass in front of him so that he can see how well he is shaving himself. 'Hold it steady, Ned,' says he, 'in case I let the razor slip and cut my throat.'

Jack whitewashes the outside walls of our thatched house every few years. In the front, on either side of the half-door, are two small windows. Their frames have been painted an emerald green. They are never repainted but have been enlivened by boxes of red geraniums, under one of which, Grannie hides her door key when she's going to town or when she's calling on a neighbour (like Fiddler Joe's wife, Gret) to give her some duck eggs in exchange for a few cooking apples to make us a tart.

From as far back as I can remember, I have looked out the window and one of the first things I've seen are these red geraniums shivering before me in the morning sunlight.

Outside the half-door is a square flagstone where Rose, our sheepdog, likes to squat on sunny days after she's done her morning's work bringing back the cows from the Bull Paddock.

The haggart below the house is surrounded by tall trees. I've got used to listening to them groaning in the wind. The smoke from the house fire spirals up over the thatched roof, twisting momentarily before sailing off through the trees and vanishing in the sky. It's a fascinating start to each day – the smoke, the wind and the trees – all coming together with the morning to greet us.

Between the pig house and the lane lie the ruins of an ancient forge, which belonged to the Darmody family in days of old. Between the ruins and the pig house grows a purple, fuchsia bush. It masks the smell of the dung that Jack cleans out from the pigs. Behind the pig house and bordering the back cart track stands Old Tim's ditch. He's a crotchety old man at times. His ditch is full of alder and aspen as well as holly, which Jack calls the king of the woods.

At the upper end of the cobbled yard, Grannie keeps two creamery tanks, resting on a stone slab. She gives the tanks a good bit of her elbow grease every day with the scrub brush.

The thatch at the back of the house sags a bit and behind the broken back window stands an elm tree. I sleep in Grannie's bed for the first two years. This tree is another of the things I see when she holds me up, its huge branches swaying back and forth.

The shed for the cows lies beyond the elm tree. In springtime, it's the home of the wagtail family. I have nothing to do but listen and look all round me and there are times when I hear them chattering against the wind.

15

At the lower of the house stands the hen house. Overarching it is a wrinkly old hawthorn, whose branches continually bang off of its tin roof. The door of the hen house is so small that Grannie, even though she is stooped, has to bend down low to get inside.

When I am able to take my first few steps, I will make my morning trip down there with her and peer into the tea chest to look at the fluffy chicks chirping round their proud mother's wings.

Next to the hen house (and before we reach the haggart) stands the hen's dung heap, on top of which our young cockerel, Rusty, crows raucously to greet each day. The further end of the haggart is covered in nettles and dock leaves. There's also a bed of spearmint which perfumes our nostrils on our morning trips for eggs.

A low hedge runs down the centre of the haggart. Grannie places the bedsheets down its length on Monday mornings, turning them over from time to time with Jack's help to make sure both sides are getting dried and aired.

It's here in the haggart that the threshing of Jack's oats takes place in September. A man called Mitch comes from Templederry with his noisy thrashing machine. We hear its engine and iron wheels from miles away as it slowly makes its way up the hill, the steam rising out of its funnel. It's such a rare sight that children come running across the fields to take a look at it. For the men who come to help Jack, it's a devil of a job to get its wheels into the haggart. They run to the ditch and cut down a number of small branches from the trees. They lay them along the haggart gap so that the wheels can get a grip. After that, a much happier Mitch drives the thrasher in through the gap.

A day of lively work follows with scarcely a break for the men working round the thrasher. Jack kneels on the thrasher's roof and fires the sheaves of straw into its gaping mouth while the noisy machine keeps puffing away and the team of workers keep filling up sack after sack with the separated oats.

On these occasions, Grannie is as busy as a wasp, continually bringing out mugs of water to the men. During a well-

16

earned break, she brings them their gallon of tea. Jack is something of a humourist and tells me to ask Grannie to hurry up and bring the men more tea. He knows what I'm going to say as I am very young and innocent and still learning to speak properly.

'Grannie! Grannie! Why haven't you brang us weer tea?'

On hearing these words, the men smile and laugh at the sight of the little fellow from England complaining about the tea to his grannie. She and Jack smile at each other and they laugh too.

Next day, Jack loads the sacks of oats onto Moll's cart and takes them down to Maher's Mill in Happy Grove.

In the top right-hand corner of the yard, Grannie keeps her little garden. It's filled with gaily-coloured flowers like Sweet William and purple asters. She calls these flowers her jewels. In the centre – and towering above all other flowers – is a plant she calls American grass.

All round the garden runs a low privet hedge which Jack keeps trimmed. It's planted there to keep out the ducks. Grannie is kept busy chastising these little devils, driving them out of the garden with her stick as soon as she spots them coming in to search for snails. They sometimes break the stems of her flowers.

On the hedge, if the day is sunny, she lays out her rinsed tea towels after she washes the dishes and cutlery.

A stream runs down the length of the yard just inside the lane. It has three big flagstones across it, which form a low bridge for Grannie to drive her ass and cart across when going to Gerry's shop for her provisions or further off to the post office when she is posting a letter to my mother in England. The flagstones are each 6 ft long and 3 ft wide. They must have been there since the Stone Age (says Jack), for no one knows who put them there.

The lower one is cracked across its middle after an accident many years back when Mick-the-Devil (a hearse driver from Nenagh) drove his mare, Betsy, wildly into our yard. He was always late (says Grannie) and usually drunk. The heavy wheels of the hearse toppled him and his wagon into the stream, taking this flagstone in with him and causing it to crack.

This happened in 1903 when Jack was just three. He had to get to Nenagh Hospital to have a growth removed from his neck and Mick came to drive him there. It was an unpleasant experience for a child as young as Jack since the hospital was also used as a poorhouse where sick people and poor people alike were lumped together – adults and children side by side.

Luckily, it was a temporary measure and young Jack soon hurried off to Dublin where he made a speedy recovery and was soon as right as rain and sent home – but not in Mick-the-Devil's wagon.

In rainy weather, the stream is full to the brim and pours swiftly through Grannie's garden before peeping out under the flagstones on its way to the haggart.

Bordering the stream is a row of boulders on which the ducks like to stand and wag their tails – especially on rainy days when Grannie's hens hop quickly over to the house wall and hide matronly under the thatched eaves.

On the lane side of the stream is a hedge of prickly holly where, unlike the hawthorn tree at the haggart gap, no bird is ever heard singing.

From my pram near the window, I hear an army of noisy crows each evening as they fly over the lane to their nests in the trees in Sam's Grove. I hear them muttering to themselves as they settle down to roost after filling their bellies in Bill Corcoran's cornfield. When I'm a year or two older, I will make my way over to the flagstones and spend time gazing up at them. Oh, to see them so high in the sky and peering down at me!

Draped along the front of Grannie's house and stretching from the half-door to the hen house is a line of pink-blossomed rosebushes, fragrant throughout the summer. When the window is open, their scent pours in, contrasting with the smoky smell of the burning turf and logs.

Below the rosebushes is Jack's old bike for his quick rides to Gerry's shop to get his pipe tobacco. He doesn't smoke much as he rarely has the price of tobacco unless on market days when he might sell a calf or two, or on the day when the creamery cheque arrives for the milk from Grannie's cows.

Jack has painted the half-door the same colour as before – emerald green. But it isn't the smell of his paint that greets a visitor's nose. It's the pungent burnt-paper smell of the logs burning in the fireplace amid the crackling twigs that Grannie collected the day before. The smoke from the black sods of turf is another of the first things to greet my eyes from my pram once Grannie has lit the fire and when women come in to peep at me.

The floor is usually cluttered with sacks of meal as well as the feeding buckets for Grannie's fowl or for Jack's pigs and his four calves. At times, one or two adventurous hens tiptoe in through the half-door to see what they can steal from the bucket or (braver still) make a grab for a few spuds from the burner next to the fire.

Between the front door and the window ledge hangs the holy water font in the shape of a statue of the Infant of Prague. Above it are a few nails: one for Jack's cap when he comes home from the fields and one or two for men to hang their caps on when they come in to take a shy look at the baby from England and offer their merry greeting of 'God bless the child and God save all here!'

In among the meal sacks are a few hooped hurleys. They have been there since Jack was a young hurler. The bigger of Grannie's two skillet pots is also kept there for special occasions when she's cooking a hen or a goose for Easter or Christmas.

Hidden in there also is the unlicensed gun belonging to Tom Hayes. Jack makes use of it whenever the days get a bit hungry and he needs to shoot a rabbit in the hills around Mucklin.

'Mucklin is the kingdom of all the rabbits,' he says.

On the back of the door is his greatcoat. Next to it hangs the latest rabbit he shot, its blood dripping down onto the floor. Once I am able to walk, I stand there admiring our latest dinner-to-be, puzzled by the blood left in a dark puddle at my feet.

On the front table, Grannie prepares her week's supply of soda bread and two apple tarts – that is, if she gets a few cooking apples from Gret. An hour later, Jack is seen standing on the

19

flagstones and shaking his head as he watches her racing up the lane to give the second tart to Gret.

On the days when Jack has brought back two rabbits, Grannie skins both carcasses on the front table, making sure not to damage them. She is a dab hand at this sort of work – a skill handed down to her by her mother, Ellen. She knows she'll get sixpence for each rabbit-skin if she hands it in undamaged to Gerry at the shop.

In my second and third years of life, I am better able to take in what's around me and on evenings when Grannie has skinned her rabbits, I watch her pull out the pink and silvery entrails in a twisted ball and separate the meat from the rest of a rabbit's insides. All this is done in her grey enamel pan. After that, she cleans the pan and the oil cloth around it with boiling water before settling down to other tasks like writing one of her many long letters to my mother or darning one of Jack's socks with the needle from her pin cushion.

Between the table and the door leading into Jack's bedroom hangs a framed verse of the well-loved poem by Thomas Hood with the words that everyone seems to know and love, having rote-learned them at school, 'The little house says stay and the little road says go'.

Ever since the black days of the famine, many of their forebears left the hills and headed for foreign parts, never to come back.

High on the back wall are Jack's two rabbit traps next to the press cupboard. When fetching the cows from the Bull Paddock, he sometimes sees the little black rabbit droppings on the rabbit runs leading from the wood towards his cabbage field. He hates using these traps, but sometimes he has to. He spaces them out on the path along with a few snares that he made by sharpening hazel-wands and fixing a noose of wire round them to choke any rabbit on its way to do mischief in his fields.

Millet's picture of the Angelus hangs in the centre of the wall. All farmers stop work – Grannie and Jack too – when the middle of the day arrives and the church bells ring. Everybody then starts praying the Angelus in memory of the angel who came to see Mary to give her the good news that she was to be the mother of God.

The half-sized pendulum clock hangs next to Millet's picture and on the righthand side of the back table, rests the Roscrea bacon box filled with well-worn records. Behind it, Grannie keeps her tea tin. She keeps a row of willow-patterned plates in the press cupboard and next to the plates is her jug of sour milk for baking and the well-thumbed playing cards.

On some Wednesday evenings, the back table is pulled onto the centre of the floor for the card players. There's Mikey (Old Pat's son) from the house below Brindley's stile. There's Gret and her husband, Fiddler Joe. No records are played these Wednesdays and a heap of pennies lies on the table. Tobacco smoke quickly rises to the rafters and there is absolute silence except for the ticking of the clock. Suddenly, someone shouts, 'Big trump!' and gathers in the winning heap of pennies. This is followed with a few muttered curses from the other players.

In the bottom of the press cupboard, Grannie keeps the boot polish for blackening Jack's Sunday boots as well as her own long lace-up boots. Jack keeps his shoe-last in there, which he uses when putting new leather on his boots. Stored behind the polish-tin is his jar of pink poison paste and a few feathers for dabbing it on the bread. In cold weather when the rats come near the house, he smears it on a few slices. In the morning, he throws the dead rats into the bushes and burns the bread in the fire before the hens and ducks can get to it.

In one of the two drawers are Grannie's knives and forks and her apostle spoons with the words 'Shenley madhouse' stamped on them. Jack keeps a few bottle-corks in the other drawer. In a year's time, he will burn the top of them in the fire so as to blacken the three bald patches on the back of my head. These I unfortunately acquire after getting too close to his calves whilst he was feeding them.

On the upper side of the living room are two small bedrooms. The ceiling across both rooms is lined with elm boards that are sealed with light brown creosote. The partition between the living room and these two rooms stretches from the back wall to the front wall. It is painted in a light maroon colour, the same colour as the four wooden chairs that Grannie sets aside for visitors when they come in for a chat about the war.

In the centre of the partition is a large picture of the Sacred Heart with the face of Jesus gazing down on the three of us. He looks sad. His face is another of the first things I see each morning; that and the blazing fire. His head is pierced with a ring of cruel thorns.

One of these tiny bedrooms is Grannie's room. It is warm and cosy for me when I'm a baby beside her. It has the smell of smoky candles and mothballs – also a slight whiff of lily-of-the-valley perfume for special occasions given to her by Lady Dunally. Her circular po pokes out from beneath her bed.

She has a white dressing table with round knobs on its legs. In the drawer of the table, she keeps some old photos and a clipping of the white curls on my head in case she has to send me back to England in the near future.

She also keeps a stick of red rodden in there for sealing her parcels of shamrock on St. Patrick's Day or the Christmas goose that she sends each year to my mother and father. In the corner of the drawer is her bag of humbug sweets to give to Gret's children on Saturday mornings when they come down to do odd jobs for her.

On top of her dressing table, she has made an altar to her favourite saint – St Theresa of the Little Flower. On either side of St Theresa's statue, she has two small altar lights, which she lights up when she is saying her prayers before going to sleep. One of the prayers she says into my ear is the one to stop the Boodeeman from coming in through her little window.

Each Monday, once she has hung out her sheets on the haggart bushes to dry, she brings back from her garden a small nosegay of fuchsia flowers and arranges them in a glass jar next to the statue. She loves the smell of flowers.

The other small bedroom is called the visitors' room. At the door is a small nail on which Jack keeps the two hurling medals he won in the late '20s for the Dolla hurling team when they won the north Tipperary championship.

Between this small room and the half-door, Grannie keeps a stool with a white enamel bucket for the well-water. On Saturday nights, the stool is pulled out in front of the fire and she brings down the big tin bath and washes me from head to toe in readiness for next day's Mass.

On the end wall of the visitors' room hangs a framed copy of Grannie's last child, Winnie. She is wearing her First Holy Communion dress and has white shoes and white gloves. She is ten years old and is a picture of health and beauty.

As soon as I am able to walk, I creep into this room while Grannie and Jack are in the cow shed milking. The room is warm and snug like Grannie's room.

A year or two later, I'll be able to count the narrow pine boards across the ceiling – twenty-two in all. Some of them are marked with black stains where the rain has managed to come in through the thatch. On these quiet mornings when I'm on my own and have no distractions, I listen to the scurrying feet of little mice racing each other above my head.

Behind the hob next to the hen house is a room even larger than the living room. Because of its darkness and dampness, I will later get to know it as the Big Cave. It reminds me of the grey caves that Grannie points out to me when she opens her Sunday prayerbook. It is a cold room and when I am two, I will be classed as a little man and will leave Grannie's warm bed and the nights I spent snuggling down beside her. I will join Jack in his damp bed under a nest of thick blankets instead. This will give Grannie a bit of peace. I wonder if she'll miss my gentle snoring?

In order to get my toes warm, Jack will rub his feet against mine until I'm as warm and comfortable as a winter glove. By then, the screeching noise of the German bombs will be nothing but a distant memory in my ears.

The damp floor beside Jack's bed is layered with potato sacks to keep his feet warm when he kneels down to say his prayers – the prayers that Grannie will one day teach me to say while she's dressing me before the fire.

Next to the sacks is a large tea chest in which Grannie keeps her flour along with a big metal scoop to shovel the flour onto the front table when she is baking.

Over the mantlepiece hangs a large picture of a pope wearing a red skullcap. He has a grizzly beard with some angels dancing round his head. Beside his picture is a photo of the Dolla hurling team with Jack standing in the back row and holding his hurley across his shoulder like the other hurlers.

Next to this is a picture of another pope wearing glasses, which is strange since nobody except the doctor wears glasses. When I get used to Jack's room, he tells me that popes are holy men – men higher up than the rest of us. Their serious faces are enough to frighten any child, me included. In the coming years, when I find myself alone in Jack's bed and he has gone off to milk, this fear often raises its ugly head.

Above the bed, there's nothing but the black rafters. When it's raining, I spend some of my mornings staring at the back wall next to me and watching the brown stains snaking down the whitewash in slow, droopy lines.

Each night, Jack sleeps in his shirt like other men. On the bedrails at the foot of the bed, he hangs his trousers – also his Sunday suit. A line of brass reindeer runs across the rails. Each morning, from beneath my blankets, I see beams of dusty sunlight streaming in behind the reindeer from the back window.

At the lower end of the room and in the deep recesses next to the hen house rests a piano known as Old Harpy. It's unadorned and is not admired by either Grannie or Jack. It's a mystery why this obstacle ever came to be here or how on earth it was carried in through the narrow doorway. It must have been a pair of giants who struggled in with it. Old Harpy is stifled from the lack of air. It was once a gift from a rich lady that I came to know as Miss Posh Frock. She lived some way down the hill from us. It was her daughter, Cecilia, who played Old Harpy in her mother's drawing room – a young English girl with dainty manners and slender fingers. That's what Grannie said. Sadly, she died of consumption while still young. But she left behind her a great deal of echoing music, now dead and buried inside the piano lid.

Nobody in the lane knows what sort of an obstacle a piano is. The only musical instruments known to Grannie and Jack are the concertina which my Grandfather Will played or Fiddler Joe's homemade fiddle or the button melodion of Nan Hayes.

Grannie still has a use for the piano. Inside its depths (and to her mortal shame), she keeps her day-to-day provisions like the icing sugar and the cloves for apple tarts, as well as her nutmeg. It's no wonder Old Harpy doesn't play any music for us! I take a peep inside her at times. Black and white are her keys, the colour of the magpies in the branches of the alder tree on Old Tim's ditch.

When I'm a toddler and able to walk a few steps, I get to know what's inside her lid. While Grannie and Jack are busy milking, I sometimes creep into the room (my ears cocked sharp in case I get caught) and steal a few pinches of delicious icing-sugar. Grannie will never miss it. It's my first big sin!

This room has a tiny window at the back, against which Lightning rubs his nose and starts braying as soon as the big yellow sun comes up to tell Jack to get a move on.

In wet weather, Jack brings his bike in to repair the tyres with patches from his repair box. The room then smells of gum and Grannie strolls in to watch him at his work.

At the front of the room is a slightly bigger window. On its ledge, Jack keeps his shaving-stick, his cut-throat razor and the leathern strop for sharpening its blade. There is the smell of stale soap there. That's where he also keeps the broken bit of mirror for me to hold up when he's shaving.

On a small shelf too high for me to reach, he keeps his toothache medicines, cloves and lozenges as well as animal medicines and bottles for stomach cramp. On a nail beside the window, hang a few striped ties and his best cap and hard white collar, which he wears for Mass and attending funerals.

At the far end of the room is a loose-leaf table on which are some red glasses in case Father Enright comes calling. They are very dusty and Grannie hasn't brought her goose quills in to dust the corners of this part of the room.

Near the front window and underneath the thatch, Jack keeps his treasured sets of cigarette cards, such as uniformed soldiers or racing bicycles. When I'm a bit older, he will bring them down – one by one – to show me. Together, we will kneel on the chairs at the front table in the living room and study the coloured details in each set – their newness and sheer beauty and sheen. Jack will talk about the cards with me, for it's not only Grannie who spends her time teaching me lots of new things.

Also beneath the thatch he keeps old photographs. His favourite is a haymaking day photo with almost twenty of his friends turning rows of hay in one of our fields. Those were the times when everyone took turns to help one another.

There is a fireplace in this huge bedroom but no fire has ever been lit in its grate. It is stuffed with laurel leaves that Jack's father, Will, once brought back from Brindley's well.

From the early hours of the day, there's the sound of droning bees swarming round among the laurels. The chimney must be coated with honey, says Jack. Their noisiness, coupled with the braying of Lightning, makes sure that Jack leaps out of bed the same way the brass reindeer are seen leaping across the bedrail at the foot of the bed.

At night, the bees return to the laurels, often as late as midnight once they've finished visiting the flowers in Grannie's garden.

In contrast to the darkness of the Big Cave, the bright pink rosebushes and their scent seem to smile in through the window. Like the braying of Lightning, they tell Jack there's a colourful life waiting for him outside the half-door.

The chores of the day are nearly always the same: the buckets of water brought back from the well, the cows all milked and sent back to the Bull Paddock in company with Rose the sheepdog, the milk strained into the two creamery tanks, the fireside tea chest stacked high with logs as well as Grannie's jam jar replenished with bits of old candles for lighting next day's fire.

In the early days (though I am still not a year old), I cry very little, not even when my first small tooth is about to arrive. The music from the gramophone's spinning turntable and the heartfelt sighs of Grannie and Jack keep my mind occupied. Grannie knows all the songs and can recite the verses when she's out milking her cows. Yet she cannot sing a note.

Jack sings well, though a bit nasally. In the mornings, whilst I'm sitting in my pram and he and Grannie are abroad milking, I can hear him lilting his latest verses into the cow's ear. He swears his singing will get more milk from the cow. It's a pity (says he) that his mother can't oblige him with her own few songs. If she could, they'd have even more milk to throw into the tanks and send to the creamery.

When the evening oil lamp is lit, it spreads a welcoming cheer, twinkling merrily and making huge shadows across the back wall. That's when Grannie and Jack take their ease. They love nothing better than seeing the fire tearing along and the kettle for their tea bubbling on the crook above the flames.

On some nights, Grannie sits with her candle at the front table reading her holy Messenger book with its stories of the African mission among the native folk. Jack's candle is on the back table and beside it is his latest book from his pile of Zane Grey cowboy novels. He'll surely get a squint in his eye from reading so much. Next to his elbow is the gramophone and a heap of records, all waiting for him to turn the handle and start the night's musical festivities.

In between changing the needle and putting on the next record, Grannie pokes at the fire with her wire tongs. Jack grabs the heavy metal tongs and fastens a few more sods of turf on top to increase the blaze. It's a miracle the chimney doesn't catch fire. The room is now fully aglow, with the windows fastened for the night and the front door firmly hasped

On the front of the chimney, the soot is as thick as the bark of a tree. Jack uses it to clean his mouth like his father, Will, used to do, rubbing his forefinger back and forth across his teeth before rinsing it out with a mug of water. It's his way to make sure that the countless mugs of tea he drinks will not turn his teeth brown.

He is a proud man and knows how to look after himself. His cheeks are ruddy and his hair is black and wavy. When his father was alive, he would stand on tiptoe, gazing out over the geraniums to admire him as he wheeled his bike out across the flagstones before cycling off to the latest hurling match. Watchful as ever, his mother would turn her eyes to her beloved Will and smile, seeing how much he loved the sight of Jack throwing his leg out across the crossbar of the bike before speeding downhill, a merry song in his heart echoing back and the wind in his hair.

While Grannie and Jack are enjoying the evening's music, their sheepdog, Rose, rests in her nest of blankets under the back table. Perhaps she's dreaming of recent days when frolicking across the fields to help Jack bring home the cows. Perhaps she's guiding them out through John's Gate and up the lane. Perhaps she's sitting beside the stream in the back lane, giving them time for a well-deserved drink before driving them into the cow shed. Maybe she's dreaming of the fine work she did this morning when she intervened in the fierce battle between the red-eyed gander and the fat pig before rushing the pair of them out of the yard and up onto the dung heap in the haggart.

Next to Rose, in the corner where the turf is stacked, there lives a family of black beetles. Grannie is forever racing across the floor when she spots them marching towards the front door for their evening ramble. Stamp, stamp, stamp. With her big boots, she kills them on sight.

Next to the turf is a leather seat. On Saturday mornings, when Gret's older children come visiting, they vie with one another for a perch on this cosy spot. To distract them, Grannie takes down her pack of playing cards from the press cupboard. Then they stretch out on the floor and play their games of Mug-and-Match 'em or else Beggar-me-neighbour before getting on with their jobs for her.

The stool opposite the leather seat rests on three good legs and one wobbly one. Gret's younger children sometimes come visiting too. They also vie with one another to see who'll sit on this wobbly affair and they start rocking it side to side, making a rhythmical sound on the cement floor.

More important still in the eyes of the children is what she's got hidden in her bedroom drawer: her bag of humbug sweets. After their jobs are done, she gives each of them one or two sweets, but with her finger on her lip so that they'll not let their mother know about this small treat.

They'll be sure to come back next Saturday and bring her all the week's news: what went on at school this week, which bold child got beaten with the strap and what was the reason for it. They'll tell her which of a neighbour's cows fell into a drain, which woman is in bed sick with the toothache, who died last Tuesday and who bought a pair of wellingtons last Thursday from Robinson's shop in town.

Most important of all, she hopes to hear if anyone has said a word about the war and which side is winning. Is it the Germans or the rest of the world? She's been waiting all week for a letter from Nell to see if there's any news about her seventh son, Tom, who is fighting abroad in Africa. She loves hearing their news. She has no newspapers and no radio. Only the priest, the doctor and the vet have such a privilege in these difficult times.

In the fireplace rests the metal crane with its swinging arms and the holes in them for hanging pots and pans on the crook when she's doing her cooking. Before bed each night, Jack takes off his socks and hangs them over the heat of the dying fire. They often have a sour musty smell to them, for he has a small hole in his wellington which lets in the water. He hangs his damp topcoat on a nail behind the front door. It'll be dry in the morning from the overnight heat left over from the fire.

The hearth is topped by a sloping hob which rises to the rafters. On it are a number of thick nails on which Jack hangs his fletches of bacon.

He leaves them there to smoke once he's killed his yearly pig. The second pig has a merciful escape and is loaded onto Moll's cart to be sold to the Limerick pig buyers when they next come to Nenagh.

Across the front of the hob stretches a long strip of leather. Grannie calls it the tapestry. It is patterned with a series of geometric shapes: yellow against a brown and gold backdrop. On the right of the tapestry hangs her oil lamp, the glass globe of which she cleans each night by circling brown paper inside it. What would the three of us do without the friendly glow from its lamp during the long evenings of my childhood?

To the left of the oil lamp is a time-blackened picture of Grannie's older brother, Padder. He hurled for the Commercials hurling team in Dublin when they twice won the county championship in the late '90s. Dublin was the place (said he) that gave him his bread and butter. He was a man who worked hard all his life as a building contractor in the city centre. It's said that hard work never killed anyone but it killed poor Padder and he died of a brain tumour before he was fifty.

No one knows what became of his hurling medals. All the hurlers in the photo are seen wearing long white hurling britches as well as identical caps and they each have a droopy moustache. The picture of Padder is another one of the first things I see – that and the Sacred Heart picture – when I'm sitting up in my pram.

Beneath the tapestry and on the lefthand side is nailed an apple box. It makes a handy bookcase with two shelves running across it. It holds a number of old schoolbooks and novels like *Black Beauty*. Both Jack and Grannie love reading them even though the print is often faded and the covers are sometimes mildewed. Some of them will turn out to be useful in a year or two when Grannie starts putting her finger on the words and getting me to repeat them after her. A few of them are prizes given to her children by the priest in charge of the school in Killeen. Her children were good scholars and Mr Flanagan said a few polite words of praise when the last of them (Winnie) was leaving school.

Among these books, Grannie has her favourite: *The Spirit of Tipperary.*

When she was a child travelling across the fields with Bridgee Meara, the two of them would recite some of the shorter poems to while away the three-mile journey before getting to their school in the Silvermines.

Many years later, Grannie's children from the age of six took their own three-mile walk to Killeen school in the opposite direction. It was an arduous trek, starting out even before the cock crowed. They had to put up with all kinds of weather: gusty winds, sleety rain, misty fog or bright sunshine. But the hills and valleys and the Dolla River were uplifting and they never tired of enjoying the scenery.

They had a few slices of bread in their bag covered by a smudge of blackcurrant jam. They took a sod of turf for the master to warm his bum over the classroom fire while his pupils went on shivering – especially on those days when they were soaked to the skin from the rain.

As Jack was the oldest, he carried a sharp knife with him to cut a few turnips from a farmer's field and cleaned them in the stream outside the school. A turnip was their main lunch before tucking into their bread and jam.

Grannie knew the reason why her children got on well at school: it was the mountainy air getting into their lungs and clearing the cobwebs out of their sleepy heads whilst they struggled towards the school door. Unlike their mother and Bridgee Meara, who practised their poetry, they recited their tables on the way instead, singing each table in a repetitive singsong.

On the lower shelf of the apple box are a number of brown, faded newspapers. Some of them have photos of great hurlers such as Martin Kennedy, the man who placed discreet feathers on the pitch, stationing them the width of the opposing goalposts away from each other. This helped him turn round quickly towards the goalmouth and make sure of his score without even looking at the goalposts.

There's also a photo of the battling Mick Mackey from Limerick, whose head was seen running with blood from the many slashes thrust at him by the hurleys of opposing players while he was making a dash into the goalmouth to score yet another goal.

Though Jack spent precious moments gazing at such photos and reading the commentaries on past hurling games, he also liked reading about the men who fought for Ireland's freedom and to gaze at the photo of Sean Treacy's body thrown unceremoniously into the back of a lorry during Tipperary's troubles.

Grannie hated to see the sadness in her son's face during these moments and she tried to distract him with yet another cup of tea or by taking out one of his favourite records from the bacon box and putting it on the turntable.

Moll's collar and hames – her saddle, harness and chains – are stacked on a ledge to the right of the hob and above the oil lamp. Also on the ledge is Grannie's earthenware jar to warm her bed at night. Jack's last job of the day, after throwing a mug of water on the fire, is to fill this jar with hot water and place it at her feet so that she'll be snug and comfortable throughout the night.

Next to her jar are her large goose quills for dusting the chairs and the legs of the tables as well as the press cupboard. She has some smaller quills for the delicate work she has to do on the cobwebs in the corners of the room.

Jack has his own soft, downy feathers for putting iodine on the many cuts he gets to his forearms when he's trimming back the briars with his billhook. Like his father before him, he always works with his sleeves rolled up. His feathers have the softness of an owl's wings – so soft and so silent (says he) that a little field mouse cannot hear the owl hurtling through the air before its claws grab her in a death grip.

'Watch out! Watch out!' he cries as he makes a pounce at me with his clawed fingers and I scream with fear and laughter at one and the same time when he throws me up into the air.

Such happy moments are pure joy to Grannie, who remembers her own childhood days back in Victorian times and how it contrasted with mine – days when many countryfolk were still feeling the hunger that their parents had suffered during the days of the famine.

Those were days when women spent their evenings repairing nets for the men to go hunting small blackbirds and catch them by throwing the nets round the bushes – days when children spent their mornings scouting the ditches for young nettles to cook along with the blackbirds. These little birds tasted succulent enough but a family like herself and her eight brothers and sisters would need the patience of a saint to catch the number they'd need to feed them all.

Grannie was born in Curragharneen. It's half a mile across the fields from our present house. Being the youngest child, she spent a great deal of time with the old men, listening to their tales as they puffed on their pipes – tales that she passed on to young Jack when he was old enough to listen to her.

Her brothers and sisters were born in the '70s and had tales that they, too, passed on to young Jack – not all of them about the famine. Tales of how their young sister (my grannie) was a beauty at sixteen with cheeks as pink and smooth as an apple and eyes as dark as sloes. Their words were like honey to Jack. And oh, the grace and charm of her as she whirled her way through the harvest dance at the crossroads of Mountisland! And almost fifty years later, this Grannie of mine has hair that's still as black as a jackdaw's wing.

Not many years passed (she was scarcely twenty) when young Will Forde came knocking at her father's door to ask could he walk with her over the fields after Mass. His wish was granted and from that day on, they would stroll together on Sunday afternoons: she in her one good flouncy dress and he in his boater hat, which was the fashion at the time.

The older neighbours have tales to tell too – how the dashing Will had charms of his own – enough to capture my grannie's heart: his fine singing voice and his rendering of songs unheard of before – songs that he'd learnt from the English ploughboys in Lord Dunally's fields while he was learning to handle a horse and plough. Added to this were his light fingers as

33

he played for her his concertina while the two of them sat on the ditch on those happy afternoons.

After her marriage, Grannie had more than a few shillings in her purse. Will was a tidy ploughman and tilled the little farm right up to the ditch. There were plenty of spuds and cabbages to grace the table from now on – plenty of oats for the mare. Will made sure to pass on his ploughing skills to Jack.

There was another side to their marriage – the years when my grannie found herself giving birth to children year in and year out and they were tearing the life out of her.

Jack was her first. The first child was always the hardest. After that, there followed one child after another until she was expecting Tom. The previous children had found their way into the world by themselves and without any hardship to her. But giving birth to Tom was a struggle and it was after this birth that she developed sciatica, which turned into the stooped old lady I came to know.

That wasn't her only sorrow. For, after Will 's untimely death in '28 – and in spite of the fine food that he'd supplied on the table – her life changed for the worse. She had no breadwinner now and had stacks of children to feed. It was hard for a growing lad like Jack to emulate his father's prowess.

Years of scarcity followed. Above all was the price of clothing for the children. She hadn't shillings enough to go to town and buy new clothes for them. What was she to do for the makings of dresses and britches or for coats in the winter?

In desperation, she had no resource but to use her imagination: maybe find an old greatcoat of Will's still lying idle on the back of the door – one she'd spend half the night cutting up to make a First Communion suit for one of her sons. She was determined to make every effort not to bring shame on herself or her children. She'd make use of a cast-off frock sent up to her by Miss Posh Frock and cut out a new dress for a daughter's confirmation.

When the latest dress from Miss Posh Frock's old discards was presented to her and she had turned it into yet another lovely dress, she marched her daughter (this time, Sarah) down to Miss Posh Frock's hall door. She made sure the little daughter did one or two twirls round the parlour to show the good woman how well her mother had used her cast-offs. From then on, Grannie would never go short of material for new clothes. Miss Posh Frock must have smiled and wondered on seeing how Grannie had made such miraculous use of her old dress.

She had learnt these dressmaking skills during her service to Miss Posh Frock's aunt (Lady Demurely) for whom she had worked since the age of eleven. The good lady taught her needlework and embroidery – taught her how to stitch together a cambric shirt in preparation for her own future marriage – showed her how to cook and make apple tarts and cakes. Better still, Lady Demurely taught her fine manners at the table, how to walk like a lady and how to curtsy in front of Lady Dunally and win her approval. She taught her enough politeness to ensure she'd always survive. And it is from such a background that I – the infant child from London – was about to have my enrichment.

Without Will, times were always going to be sad for Grannie, especially at night when she felt the coldness of her bed and the stillness and solitude around her. In the darkness of night, she imagined he was calling out to her to come and join him. There was nothing she could do to soften the edges of her tearfulness.

There was more sorrow to follow as, one-by-one, her children left her to go and find their way in the world. And, just as she missed her beloved Will, she found herself missing each of them as they bid her farewell – missed the comfort of them, the laughter of them around the place.

Jack was all she had left. She was always at his side to encourage him. There wasn't a day when he wasn't out in the fields attempting to put food on the table like Will had done. Witness him shovelling the heavy loads of dung into Moll's cart, spreading it over the fields before he went ploughing and harrowing the soil. Witness him saving the crops of spuds, cabbages and the oats to feed the ever-patient Moll before he went reaping and tramming the hay and thrashing the corn.

Better days lay ahead for herself and Jack when I came into their lives. Days of uncertainty turned themselves round and there was a new spring in Jack's step.

He had never married or had a child of his own. But the minute he laid eyes on me at the railway station, he felt those rich feelings that a young father might feel: joy and awe. He saw nothing but good days ahead: the adventures we would have, the hurling matches we'd go to, the fishing trips to the Dolla River and the raids on rabbits in the neighbouring hills.

In my babyhood years, however, it is Grannie more than himself who steers my days. Old though she is at sixty (and to the surprise of everyone), she finds she has a new lease on life. The neighbours see the sudden change in her and talk about it for hours on end. They gossip about it over the dinner table and when bringing back buckets of water from the well.

'Biddy Forde is like a new mother,' says Gret to her husband, Fiddler Joe, as she passes him a cut of bread and taps his egg for him. 'Can't any fool see what's happening to her now that her sons and daughters have fled the nest? She's no longer lonely.'

'Yes,' nods Fiddler Joe as he tucks into his egg and drinks his tea.

'It couldn't have been much fun rearing all those children on her own,' goes on Gret. 'Biddy was always worried sick over the lack of clothes for all of them – their shoes for school and whether there was food enough to help their young bodies grow healthy and strong.' And she races for the teapot to fill her man's mug again.

Fiddler Joe nods and goes on slurping his tea. 'I hear the little fellow's mother has been sending parcels and the odd few pounds from her nursing job in England,' he says. 'I think 'tis new clothes she's been sending for little Ned.'

What he says is true. Grannie had recently torn open a parcel of baby clothes and was excited beyond measure at the sight of a fluffy yellow set of infant togs to replace my swaddling outfit.

It isn't just the neighbours who take notice. Jack sees the way his mother's determination has brought her spirit back into her. He notices how her life is full of her little grandson, the child she refers to as 'my little man'.

'Ah, my little man!' That's what she says when lifting me out of my cot and settling me in my pram, making sure I am as close to the fire as she dares so that I don't feel the draught coming in from the half-door.

'How's the little man?' say the neighbours as they pass by with their ass and cart on their way to Gerry's shop. There wasn't any other baby like me from the bombed-out streets of London.

Inquisitiveness gets the better of other people besides the neighbours and one morning, Lady Dunally calls into the yard to inquire about me. How unlike the other women she is! Herself and her perfume, her cheeks as shiny as satin and as soft as the snow. She is wearing a brightly-coloured dress and she has a few bangles on her wrist and a pearly necklace round her neck.

It is good of her to visit me, thinks Grannie. The priest never pays her a visit. She wheels my pram out as far as the flagstone and makes Lady Dunally a low curtsy. She pulls back the hood of the pram to show me off in the sunlight.

The rich lady peers into the pram. 'A fine, intelligent child!' she smiles. 'He'll be heard tell of yet – mark my word.' She doesn't know what else to say but her words flatter Grannie.

'I hope so, ma'am,' says Grannie. She doesn't know what to say either. Herself and Lady Dunally have never had a conversation before this. The kind lady places a shilling in Grannie's hand before remounting her pony and heading out to the hills for her morning gallop. Grannie makes her another curtsy as she looks up the lane after her.

Whereas other wartime children like those back in London are surrounded by countless fears and anxieties during these war years, I know no life other than the warmth of Grannie and Jack, my two loving guardians.

When milking is finished each morning, Grannie hurries back and lifts me out of the pram. Then she sits me on her knees by the fire and jigs me up and down, whispering a few endearing words into my ear like she always does: 'How many miles to

Banbury? Three score and ten. Will I be there by candlelight? Yiss! And back again.'

And as she hisses out her 'Yiss,' she lets me suddenly drop between her knees, then laughs out heartily when she sees the shocked look on my innocent face.

END OF PART ONE

THE SUN ARISING

Between 1941 and 1942

It is early morning. I am nine months old. The window in Grannie's room is ajar and her curtains stream out to embrace the sunlight. I am awake and I'm listening to the wind from the haggart. It blows the curtains back into the bedroom.

Though it's early in the day, our ass, Lightning, is already tired out from eating his favourite food – the thistles in the Blue Button Field. He pokes his head through the open window in an effort to greet me. His voice is not a bit musical and he produces such a bellowing hee-haw that he wakes up the family of beetles sleeping in the pile of turf next to the fire. Besides that, he has woken from her dreams our precious sheepdog, Rose. She scrambles from her nest under the back table and makes a dash for the half-door to escape his infernal racket.

'Hee-haw. Hee-haw,' cries Lightning again and I am filled with fear. I can't bear it a minute longer. Where on earth is my grannie? Where is Jack? Grannie is sweeping the goose droppings from the yard for the second time this week. Jack has gone to the market in Nenagh to check the price of calves.

Lightning's wretched hee-hawing is too much for Grannie to put up with and she puts down her yard brush. Then she hears my faint whimpering and she rushes in to rescue me from Lightning's noisy roaring.

'What is it, my little chickadee?' she whispers and for a moment, I stop crying when I see the sad look in her eyes. Nevertheless, I am ready for another bout of whimpering – maybe a cry rising to a roar – in an attempt to out-roar this rascally ass.

Nothing escapes Grannie's eye and she goes on caressing me with her soft, lilting voice till she has hushed away my tears.

Her old eyes glisten with anger. 'God blasht you, Lightning! You and yer impudent antics,' she cries. She rushes to the window and raps a fist off his nose. That'll teach him his manners.

Lightning vanishes just as quickly as he arrived. He goes off and hides behind the cow shed where he can sulk for the next hour. He has learnt not to annoy Grannie.

She turns back to the bed and sweeps me up in her arms. Her anger has gone and she can't help but chuckle. 'There-there, my little man!' she whispers and with her fingers she makes a small river through my curls while carrying me slowly over to the half-door. From there, I can look out and listen to a far better type of music than Lightning and his damned hee-haws.

She jigs me up and down in her arms and carries me across the yard. She points out the white clouds high in the sky. She points out the big yellow sun that's already smiling down on the two of us. She points out the pink of the fuchsia bushes. She points out the shivering haw berries scattered among the branches of the hawthorn tree next to the hen house at the end of the yard.

'That's enough for today, enough for any babbling infant to hold inside a head like yours, my little man,' she murmurs. Then she carries me back to the fireside and places me in my pram. She waits awhile until she feels I am at peace. Then she tiptoes to the half-door. She has to finish sweeping the yard.

Time passes. I open my eyes. I am not yet a year old. I still drink from a bottle. The milk is from Grannie's Kerry blue cow. It is strained and boiled before cooling and bottling. I am crying with the pain of my new teeth.

Grannie, when she should be having a long rest in her late years, has the devil of a job dealing with my backside – and at the most inconvenient hours of the day. Nobody knows where she gets her energy from. She keeps a neat row of newly washed baby towels across the crane over the fire during the evenings.

For most mornings, I'm locked inside the soft arms of sleep, dreaming my life away. When I awake, Grannie is at my side, tending to my needs: changing my clothes, wiping my backside clean before moving on to my need for food.

This morning, I am sitting up in my pram and taking in my new surroundings. I can hear the noise of the twigs blazing on the fire in front of my pram. I can see the fire snaking clouds of smoke up through the black soot and into the chimney hole. I see the tapestry over the fire. This long stretch of leather catches the daylight as it comes in over the half-door. The faded picture of Grannie's older brother, Padder, in his Dublin hurling team shows him looking back at me. The oil lamp hangs unlit beside his picture. A few dusty sunbeams have filtered their way through the front window over the redness of the geraniums.

As soon as she has finished milking, she pours me my daily supply of milk out of the bucket until she feels there is enough. She boils the milk in her egg saucepan before letting it cool beneath her muslin cloth.

Though she has been feeding me from a feeding bottle until now, she starts feeding me from a small mug from now on. Whatever else she is doing, she always stops when she hears me crying. This goes on throughout the day: the feeding, the changing, the nursing of me with a great deal of tender emotion firmly lodged in her heart.

There are times when she is utterly exhausted, though no one (not even Jack) is aware of it.

One dark morning arrives when she acts without thinking. She wheels me and my pram across the floor to give me something else to look at.

She sits down on the chair and starts pushing my pram back and forth – all the time reciting one of her rhymes to calm me down and stop my incessant crying.

But I keep on roaring and she wonders if the German bombs are still ringing round inside my head. *Will this child ever stop crying,* she wonders?

The roaring seems to go on forever until Grannie loses all her softness. 'What on earth will the neighbours think of me as they pass by?' she moans. *Oh, the frustration of this child of mine! How on earth am I to going to cope with him?* At times like this, she is aware of her limits – of her helplessness.

Suddenly, she loses the last vestige of patience. This has never happened before and she tightens her grip on the handle of the pram. In a fit of temper, she pelts the pram across the floor where it bounces off the hob, almost landing myself and the pram in the fire! The pram's sudden vibration on the hob nearly knocks the oil lamp off of the tapestry.

'Now you have reason to cry, you little nuisance of a child!' she shouts.

But she alarms herself at this sudden lack of control. She leaps out of the chair and rushes towards the pram. She is scarcely halfway across the room when she is stopped in her tracks. The pram comes bouncing back off the hob and almost knocks her off her feet. For a moment, it takes her breath away and she loses any bit of composure she might still have left.

I stretch out my tiny arms towards her. All my noisy roaring has vanished and I start to chuckle. It's as though Grannie has started a new game like the game that Jack plays when he comes in from milking and lifts me up to the rafters to see if I can see Dublin.

From a smile to a chuckle and then to a laugh, I fill the room with this merry noise and carry on for as long as I can.

'Well now, if this doesn't beat the band,' cries Grannie, staring open-mouthed at me as I offer her one of my beautiful smiles. It causes her to laugh till her sides hurt.

'Aren't you the little devil,' she cries. Then she lifts me gently out of the pram and her old hands hang onto me protectively. All has been forgiven.

A moment later, she dashes to the press cupboard, searching for the boot polish tin that she uses for blackening the boots for Mass. The lid is green with a golden rim round it. It has a shiny picture of a black horse on it. She places it in my chubby hands. I revert to my earlier babbling and begin gurgling with infant joy. Her anger has gone. My anger has gone. Herself and her little man are as happy as a king once more.

It is time for her to breathe another of her cheerful verses into my ear. She lifts me out of the pram and heads to the heat of the fire. She sits me down on her knees and tucks her apron in around me. She starts to stamp her boots on the hearthstone and makes a steady rhythm. She begins pouring out the words that I know so well. I have heard them several mornings before now:

'There was a little man
and he had a little gun
and away to the mountains
he did run.

With his big, tall hat
and a belly full of fat
and a pancake tied
to his bum-ba-lum-ba-lum.'

As a result, I chuckle more than ever – so much so that she forgets she has a hundred jobs she should be doing and she starts off whispering another verse, accompanied by an even livelier set of rhythmical stamps of her boots.

'I went into a tailor's shop. I picked up a needle…

But before she can finish her verse, she sees Jack strolling in the half-door with an armful of logs. He tiptoes over to the fire and ends the verse for her:

I stuck it in the tailor's arse. Pop goes the weasel!'

The heathen! He has ruined the magic of her verse and she swears she will redden his hide with the tongs if he speaks a rude word such as this ever again – especially in front of me. Why couldn't this bold son of hers have used the word 'bum' instead of a crude word like 'arse'? Oh, the devil that's in a man's tongue! She shakes her head.

But it isn't long before she and Jack take a fit of laughing, in which I happily join in, though I don't know why.

It's time for her to lay me down in my pram and tuck me in. Then she wheels me over to the half-door and out into the yard.

I am bigger now and I will soon have my 1st birthday. I have ceased from my earlier babbling and bawling. These days, I

44

struggle in my attempts at more adult speech. I am able to say the word 'milk' when I need to drink. I can say the word 'jam' when I want a small piece of bread with some blackcurrant jam on it. I am aware that milk tastes better than water – that bread is soft and crumbly. I am aware that jam is sweet and sloppy and that the Sunday meat is slippery and tasty on my new teeth. I am aware that the little bits of green cabbage which Grannie forks up for me to taste are sour and bitter. I can see that the heaps of sugar which Jack spoons into his tea are bright and shiny. I almost cry again when the yellow custard for the apple tart is too hot for my mouth. Some of it remains behind in Grannie's saucepan and it sticks there.

Grannie teaches me more new words: names for colours, names for smells, names for sounds, words that I can utter to let her know when I'm hungry or when I'm sad or angry.

A sad morning follows when I'm sitting in my pram in front of the fire. I find myself soaking wet and soiled. It isn't the same as at night, the times when Grannie ('Hush, hush! my little man!') reaches out her arms to comfort me.

And now, I don't know what I am to say or what to do. For I am unable to appeal to Grannie or Jack. In spite of my many new words, I haven't words to explain to them my present discomfort.

Without a moment's thought, I reach out my arm and in a fit of temper, throw my mug of milk away, smashing it off of the floor. A bundle of new feelings has suddenly welled up inside me. I am sorry my mug has gone out of my hands – that it now lies smashed on the floor – that I have lost my milk and need to get it back.

Grannie rushes in from the creamery tanks she was cleaning. She sees the damage I have done. This time, she refrains from anger. She knows she cannot afford to get cross like last time. She stoops and picks up the broken pieces of the mug. She starts humming softly to herself. She will buy me a new mug tomorrow from Gerry's shop – one with a bunch of raised flowers on it – pretty and with the words 'made in China' stamped on the bottom of it.

The weather is good. To make up for her recent misgivings, she takes me and my pram away from our recent confrontation. She steadies it on the flagstone outside the half-door. The sky is full of the early day's sunlight and the yard is warm. Yet she makes sure that I'm wearing my knitted pixy-hat – the one my mother, Nell, sent across from England.

Grannie always dresses her little man as neat as a pin. The old men driving by on their ass and cart wave their ash plants in the air, saluting this new child from England. I can hear their loud voices echoing back as they retreat down past Brindley's stile and on towards John's Gate.

Grannie sits me up straight so that I can get a better look at all that's around me, starting with the two creamery tanks. And, though I have lately been learning to use my voice a bit more, I am silent for a while in awe of everything – especially of my grannie – for this one precious moment. No one else knows what lies inside her head or mine. I can hear the swish of the wind in the tall trees across the lane. I can hear the crows cawing in the branches before they go off to their work on Jack's fields. I can hear the ching-ching of my uncle's hammer out in the cow shed where he is tending to Moll and her shoes.

Grannie stays with me for the next half hour. She has her work to do and she never sits still. She darts away on tiptoe and takes the sack of spuds from behind the half-door. She picks out only the best ones, the Kerr's pinks. She counts out twenty of them. She and Jack will devour plenty of them and wash them down with a few mugs of milk. What's left over, she will give to the squabbling ducks.

For the past six weeks, I have been learning how to crawl round the living room floor under the watchful eye of my guardians. Evenings are the only time in the day that this happens for the house fire is raging hot at all times of the day and there is no time for me to crawl unless one of them is in the room to watch over me when they've finished their work.

I have an impulsive need to wander and I could be crawling all over the living room for the rest of my life if let to do so. There is the gap beneath both tables with all the paraphernalia beneath them. To tempt me there is the magic of the space behind the half-door with the sack of spuds ready to get in my way and topple me over.

Jack can see that I'll be crawling till I'm ninety instead of learning to walk if he doesn't intervene and come to my rescue.

He brings together our four good chairs. He lays them back to back – two facing the fire and two facing Grannie's bedroom. On each of the chairs, he places some small thing: the green polish-lid on the first one, the Chinese mug on the second one, a pudding spoon to bang and smash on the third one and my milk saucepan on the last one. He says nothing – just watches me and observes.

It doesn't take long before I am tired of seeking out new areas of the floor to crawl towards. The legs of the chairs keep getting in my way. I struggle to grab hold of a chair leg and, bit by bit, I learn to climb up it. It takes me a few days. A new horizon is waiting for me at the top. It takes me a further week or two to make my way round all four chairs. This new game is far better than enjoying a pram journey from Grannie's chair to the rattling hob and back.

This is my eleventh month of life and I, at last, achieve my goal. I find myself racing round the edge of all four chairs.

Jack removes each chair, one at a time, so as to change my route – until the great day comes when all the chairs have been taken away and I'm left standing alone in the middle of the living room floor, not knowing what to do next. I am a very puzzled child.

Now is the moment when I can either sit on my bum and start crawling round the floor again – or, if I am brave enough, find my way round the partition wall and on towards the half-door. Like any young foal or calf, I seem to know what's best to do.

After a week of Jack walking me over and back from the back table to the half-door, the evening of success arrives. He grips my two hands, all the time edging himself back an inch at a time, until I begin to feel that the world is standing still and that something unusual is going to happen.

He lets go of my right hand and walks me slowly onwards – holding his breath. He lets go of my left hand and does the same thing. Both he and Grannie dare not move and they wait. Jack lets go of both my hands. I am standing alone. He walks away from me, just a few inches, then a foot or two, slowly, and ever ready to grab hold of me if my wobbly legs let me down.

No, it's not going to happen. I feel strange in my new position – here in the living room, standing on my own two feet.

I urge myself forwards with the utmost difficulty towards Grannie who is standing with open arms in front of the half-door. She is less than four feet away. This journey – my first – is about to start. Finally, I almost dash to catch hold of her outstretched arms. I have walked my first few steps.

Clap-clap-clap and more clap-clap-clapping of hands and I see the absolute joy in the faces of my guardians. I realise that I'm free from my pram. I am free of my crawling. The big world is waiting for me to come visit it.

Grannie unwraps the parcel from my mother, Nell. She knows what's in it. They regularly write to each other, my mother forever full of anxiety over the war and the bombing – full of anxiety over me as well, the infant child she feels she has lost.

For the past month, Grannie has been watching me crawl round the floor. She has had the good sense to keep my mother informed, for she knows that Nell will ask her to measure the size of my feet before I take my first steps. And now that moment has arrived.

What's in the parcel? A pair of brown sandals. Grannie holds them aloft. She is full of excitement.

She sits me on a chair in the light of the half-door and gives me the lid of the boot polish tin to fiddle with.

While I am distracted, she puts a pair of new white socks on my feet. I have never worn socks before. She bought them recently in Robinson's shop in town. She takes note of my toenails to make sure they are not too long. The cutting of them is a job that Jack has always undertaken.

She slowly puts the new sandals on my feet, relishing the moment. I am a happy child. I have never seen such objects as these new sandals and the sheen of them. She hums quietly to herself. She can't wait to see me walking around in them.

She takes the polish tin away. She lifts me slowly in the air and holds me out from her. She stares at me with a new and serious look at seeing me wearing my sandals. She carries me back to her little bedroom to gaze at myself in her dressing table mirror. New sandals. New socks. A new little man. And I marvel at the sight of myself and my sandals in the mirror. The children in the neighbouring houses wear nothing on their feet unless on Sundays for Mass or when they are marching the long distance to school.

Jack tiptoes in the half-door. He has already filled the tea chest with a sack of logs. He has put a sack of turf in under the wobbly-legged stool.

He pops his head through Grannie's bedroom door and looks me up and down. He is well-satisfied with my new appearance.

He still has work on his hands to improve my walking. He is a cautious man and during the next few days, he leaves nothing unchecked to advance my latest skill.

He takes me from his mother's arms and gives her a smile and a wink before carrying me out into the yard. The cobblestones are too awkward for me to practice my walking on. The three broad flagstones across the yard stream are as smooth as glass – even the one with the diagonal crack on it, which the wheels of Mick-the-Devil's wagon broke long ago.

He lifts me down onto the flagstones and I quickly grab hold of his fists. Over and back across the three flagstones, I take my first long walk as far as Grannie's garden and back again to the cracked flagstone. Jack stands behind me, holding onto my fingers so as to guide me along. This will go on for the next week or two. He never wearies. Neither do I. It's as if I'm aware of the great effort required. By the end of the week, the two of us are able to take the first extended walk and back to where we started. There is

49

little or no noise from the birds in the bushes or from the ducks and hens nearby. It's as if they know something important is going on.

If they could clap their wings, they surely would, thinks Jack. He's ever the humourist and he smiles to himself.

He looks back towards the half-door across which Grannie has been leaning all this time, smiling her approval at him.

To see her son and myself doing our walking exercise is refreshingly new, yet another move forward in my slow development from the babyhood days when I emitted my incomprehensible sounds. This is the day that she feels she has lost her baby and has gained her little man. And her eyes are filled with a softness towards myself and Jack, which he in turn seems to bounce back towards her.

From today onward, the two of them will keep an eye on me with increasing intensity. It's as though they have nothing better to do, for, as my walking improves, so will their need to make sure I don't walk into danger – that I don't get myself knocked over by the gallivanting pig – that I don't forget to walk far away from the raging stream on the days of heavy rain.

Each morning after saying her prayers, Grannie continues to sit me on her knees as though I were a baby. She still fusses as she puts on my clothes, whispering her tender voice into my ear with the same wistful look in her eye.

Once I'm dressed, she never wearies of teaching me what's new. She takes time to teach me my prayers and imitate the sound of her voice. She starts off with a solemn list of blessing prayers, starting off with 'God bless our sheepdog, Rose.'

I end up with, 'God bless Grannie and God bless Jack and God bless me, little Ned.'

Jack is not only a humourist. There are times when he is full of mischief. He knows words that are good ones and he knows words which his mother finds unacceptable.

He remembers the recent day when Ned Needles (another humourist) came crashing through the half-door and threatened to steal off with our two precious pigs.

'God bless Ned Needles,' Jack now urges me as I get up off my knees and finish my prayers.

'We wants weer own pigs,' I cry, reverting to my baby talk as I did in previous times of stress.

'May the devil fill his britches with shite!' shouts Grannie.

She immediately puts her hand to her mouth as though trying to take back the filthy word she has just said. Once again, she realises she has lost her ladylike poise and good manners and the shame of it puts her into an even bigger rage.

Her rascal-of-a-son dashes out the half-door and heads through the pig house gap to get more logs before she has a chance to throw the tongs at him. She can hear his ringing laughter at the trick he has just played on her: getting her to lose her self-control and the way he has succeeded in making her very cross with herself.

But it isn't long before he is sorry for what he did. He knows his mother only too well, knows how she fears my future prayers will include one for Ned Needles and that I will use the same filthy word that she herself was forced to use, following her son's untimely interruption.

She finishes her praying lesson for today. She takes the hairbrush and gently strokes it though my curls. She can't help noticing the three bald patches on the back of my head. Will they ever go away? She'd like to be sure. She will get Jack to burn in the fire one of the bottle-corks from the drawer and apply the sooty end of it to these bald patches so that no one will ever see them through the black smudges. It's a pity (she thinks) that he ever lifted me in over the dividing wall in the cow shed to take a closer look at the calves that he'd purchased at Nenagh market – a pity he encouraged me to stroke their foreheads. For now he knows that this was the time I caught the ringworm marks off of them.

In spite of my bald patches, Grannie sees a bright future ahead for me. This is the year that sees me walking further and further, the year when I can say lots of new words to let her know what's in my head and she will move things rapidly along. She'll extend my counting from the simple counting of eggs that we did when we went searching for them. She will ask Jack to extend my counting of logs when he pelts them into the tea chest beside the fire. When I am almost two, she will engage me in a number of other new words from the pages of nursery rhymes in her children's prize books. All these words are waiting for me in the apple box beneath the tapestry.

As the year goes by, she will find more advanced stories up there to read to me, especially the ones in *Aesop's Fables*. The book her son, Joe, won as a school prize for learning the whole of the *Ancient Mariner* throughout his last year at school.

An hour a day on these fresh tasks is not too much to ask of her. By the time I'm three years old, I will have so much learnt from her, Jack is left scratching his head. Where on earth does his mother get time for all this?

But she is a woman on a mission, determined to ensure I am well prepared when the day comes for me to go to school – either in Killeen or back in England with my mother and father. The thought of this makes her shiver. She knows that to lose me would break her heart. For, by now, herself and Jack are bonded as close to me as two sides of a window-glass, though I won't realise this till I'm a good deal older.

Every day, life and work go on as usual for my two guardians, but they cannot give all their time to looking after me. They have to balance these moments with their own chores, too.

It is Monday morning and already the big yellow sun is slung across the lower edge of the sky and about to peer over the tall trees in Sam's Grove across the lane.

Grannie is always happy to welcome each new day. First of all, even before she has said her prayers, she must tiptoe out to the ash pit behind the pig house to empty her po. She will take this moment to ease herself once Jack has headed down to the well for the buckets of water.

Monday – always Monday – is the day for her to wash the sheets and pillowcases along with Jack's shirt and her own blouses and skirts – but only if the weather is right for her to get them

52

dried. Today, the yard stream is full after heavy rain and its water has settled down again. She can see her reflection and that of the blue sky and the white clouds that show how clear it is. It will give her enough clean water to fill her bathtub.

She gets on with the washing and is soon sweating like mad as she pummels the sheets with the upside down yard brush. It's amazing how strong her skinny arms are. Jack keeps a sharp eye on her as she twirls the sheets round and round in the bathtub. 'She has arms as strong as a wrestler,' says he to himself.

When she thinks she has washed the sheets well enough, she takes them down to the yard stream and floats them round in it. That's when Jack comes to her aid. They proceed to wring them out together, each of them holding an end and twisting each sheet while moving closer to one another. All this time, Grannie keeps whispering a prayer to God that the sun will stay big and strong – that the wind from the far west will go on blustering.

Then, the two of them hang the sheets on the bushes to dry. Then, they go back to tend to the pillowcases along with Jack's shirt and her blouses and skirts.

It's Tuesday morning and yet another diamond of a day with the sky already full of bloody sunlight. I am still in my dreamland when I hear the cows' milk hissing into the two empty buckets. I realise that Grannie and Jack are abroad milking – that they'll be there a good while yet. I crawl out from under the blankets and feel the morning chill across the small of my back.

There are other days when Jack doesn't let me sleep too long like this. Today, however, he must have forgotten. He usually takes me with him when he's going out, as he likes carrying me on his back. Sometimes, he likes to sit me on a sop of hay inside the cow shed door and watch the wagtails speeding to their nests and dropping insects into their chicks' mouths.

Today is not one of those days. From my bed, I can hear the wind howling across the thatch. I wish I was outside with Grannie and Jack. I could watch the cows chomping their hay and chewing their cud. I have always enjoyed the sight of these cows. I have loved watching Grannie and Jack sitting on their stools with their heads tucked in towards their cow's belly. On those days, Jack sometimes squirts milk into my eyes just to hear me curse him with one of the rude words that the wily card players have begun teaching me behind Grannie's back when they come to play their card games on Wednesday evenings.

As soon as I hear Grannie and Jack tramping back from the cow shed, I get out of bed and into my britches. I walk out into the living room and across to the half-door. I watch them straining the milk into the creamery tanks. One day soon, I'll be able to walk as far as the cow shed without being carried.

Jack walks the cows down the lane and into the Bull Paddock. Grannie takes her milking stool to the far end of the cow shed where she can get a bit of peace and quiet and where no one can see her at her latest task – that of making butter. She fills the little sweet-gallon with the skimmed cream after separating it from the milk. It's the same little sweet-gallon that I'll be carrying to the well from now on to fetch water with Jack for us to drink and make tea with.

She sits on her stool and her skinny arms now show their true power. For she spends the best part of an hour rhythmically shaking the cream inside the sweet-gallon. Shake. Shake. Shake – as fast as she can work – until the first signs of her butter appear inside the gallon. Not even Jack has arms strong enough for this hard labour. But Grannie has been doing this since her childhood under the sharp eye of her mother, Ellen. She prefers her own butter to the butter that Jack brings back from the creamery.

Once she has enough, she cleans it with a jug of water. Then she spreads a little rock salt into it and makes an oblong shape between two flat paddle boards. The cream that remains in her sweet-gallon makes fine buttermilk. I am sure that she'll give me some to drink to make me big and strong.

She gets a respite from this heavy work during the weeks when Molly Hughes passes her butter churn down the hill – house after house – until the churn reaches her own door. By then, it has been well-tested by a number of neighbours in the nearby lanes.

Wednesday comes along. Grannie gets out of bed as soon as she hears Rusty the cockerel crowing and long before Lightning decides to greet her with his hee-haw braying outside her bedroom window.

I hear neither the cockerel nor the ass. I am still firmly lodged in dreamland after all the fine walking I did yesterday. In my dreams, I am strolling among the heroes in Grannie's fairytale books or shaking hands with the saints staring out at me from her prayer book after she's finished dressing me.

Her main chore today is baking. She'll bake two soda cakes and they will last most of the week, even though Jack takes most of the bread for himself, cutting huge, thick slices. He eats like a horse and does it quickly, with oceans of butter on each slice, the juices of which run out onto his lips and down his chin.

Grannie will also make another apple tart from a bag of apples that Gret brought down to her recently.

She stamps her boots into Jack's bedroom and over towards Old Harpy, the disused piano, with all the dead music locked inside it. She takes from inside the lid a nutmeg or two, her bag of sugar, her cloves and whatever else she needs. She shovels out a good few ladles of flour from the tea chest beside Jack's bed and spreads it over the front table.

She is now ready to get into her baking and will spend a good deal of this morning humming softly to herself while she bakes.

Jack stands nearby, admiring her handiwork as she buries her floury fingers deep in the baking bowl. She puts the first soda cake into the burner. She selects the best red coals from the fire and makes a hot circle of them in the ashes round the edge of the blaze. She puts several more hot coals on the lid of the burner.

Later on, she will put a good deal of sugar into the apple tart. There are other days when she will make a rhubarb tart instead out of the little clump of rhubarb in her garden. While she is cleaning the flour off the front table, she asks me to keep an eye on

55

the burner and let her know when the hot coals are fading away so that she can replace them with fresh ones.

I sit on the wobbly stool, watching over her burner and the nearby fire. I can hear the crickets chirping among the turf sods under the stool. The room is so quiet that I can hear the wren birds and their newborn chicks chirruping away under the hawthorn tree outside.

Next Sunday, after we have finished eating our mutton – me as well, swallowing the squares of meat that Grannie cuts up on my plate – we will tuck into the sweet apple tart until we have devoured it all. 'I'm as full as a tick,' Jack will say and that's when Grannie will give the two of us her broadest smile.

Whatever the day of the week, it's always the same pattern. The night before Grannie's baking day, Jack fills the tea chest with an overflowing load of logs, each one the right size so as to get her fire going next morning. He brings in an armful of turf to apply to the fire once it has started.

He's not the only one preparing fuel for the fire. With Grannie prodding at me, I spent yesterday afternoon filling her jam jar with broken bits of candles. It was yet another chance for me to do my counting as I emptied them into the jar until it was full. Then, me and my walking sandals followed her out to the haggart to help her collect a bag of small twigs. She knows the good ones to pick up – those that catch fire quickly. This is one more chance for me to add to my counting skills.

One of Jack's greatest pleasures is to watch his mother lighting the fire each day. She crinkles up sheets of brown paper from the stack behind the half-door and crushes them. She pitches a few of my broken bits of candles in amongst the nest of twigs that she's laid out among the papers. She places three of the smaller logs at either end of her proposed fire and adds a few drops of paraffin to the top of the heap.

She turns to Jack and he hands her his box of matches. She attempts to light the fire, scratching and scratching at the box with a few of the matches.

It's all in vain and she curses the fire that won't light. 'The devil himself couldn't light these twigs,' she sighs and hands Jack the matchbox. He adds a few sprinkles of turf powder to the prepared fire. He takes a new match and promptly lights the fire for her.

She gives him a grateful look. She can now get things moving. She crouches down at floor level and takes a deep breath. She blows on the fire arrangement, waving the sweet-gallon lid like a fan to help encourage the flames. A few sparks spring up, weakly at first, in a roll of black smoke. At last, they spread out into an orange sheet of flickering light. The smell of the smoke reaches my nostrils and wakes me up from my dreams. The penetrating smell is one of my favourites, matched only by the scent of the roses outside the house or the flowers in Grannie's garden. It's hard to know which smell I like best.

For a while, Grannie stays down on her knees and gives the fire a few more puffs in case it goes out. But she sees that the flames are now rising and making several rivers through the twigs before streaking upwards in a fountain and vomiting out through the chimney like the genie in one of Grannie's fairytale books. Her task is finished. All has ended nicely and she smiles at Jack. By now, her cheeks are red from all the effort.

I cannot stay in bed a moment longer. I rush out to her and gaze at the merry blaze she has made. She folds me in her apron. 'Ah, my little man,' she whispers, 'what brings you out from your nest at such an early hour of the day?' She brushes my cheek with her lips.

Jack lifts me up in his arms and takes me out into the breezy yard to see how well his mother's fire is working. From the chimney, a huge feather of smoke spirals off into the sky. He smiles at me and I smile back.

It's still early the next day and it's dark outside. Grannie tiptoes back into her bedroom, holding a lighted candle. First it's her shadow and then herself. As always, a deep feeling of longing for her grandson fills her. She continues to look down at me,

57

listening to the gentle sound of my breathing. I continue sleeping soundly.

Oh, that I could sleep on like this little angel of mine, she thinks. For just another moment, she lingers. She has so much she should be setting her mind to. 'This won't do at all,' she sighs and she hurries away from my side.

'I won't be able to let him stay in my bed for many more nights,' she sighs. 'He's getting bigger by the day – too big to be sleeping next to me much longer. He'll have to go to Jack's room in a week or two as soon as I can get him a fresh pillow and some new night clothes. Oh dear! How I'll miss the warmth of him.' Somehow or other, she feels guilty but she can't explain why she should. It's as though she is about to abandon me. But she knows she must stop thinking like this. She can't let such thoughts as these hold her back from the rest of her work.

It won't be long now until I am two. I am getting stronger and stronger and am much more aware of my surroundings than I was a year ago. Yet, I still have my fears – like the fear of the Boodeeman – a fear brought about by Grannie a few months back while she was dressing me in front of the fire and teaching me my prayers. I imagine this horrible brute forcing his way in through her bedroom window and stealing me away from her. I wish she hadn't told me of his existence. One thing is certain: when I am saying my blessing prayers with her, I will never say a blessing prayer for the likes of this monster or for Ned Needles, who once tried to steal our pigs.

I am kneeling on one of the chairs at the front table and peering out the window. I can see Grannie at her work. She is sweeping the yard all the way down from the pig house to the carts for Lightning and Moll. Her head is bent forward and she is stooped down over the yard brush. She is pushing it fiercely in front of her. It's as though she were in a fight with it and hated the very sight of it.

I have grown used to looking after myself and being on my own while Grannie and Jack are busy milking. I am aware of the quietness of the house, just the sound of the ticking clock on the press cupboard and the crackling of the twigs in the fire. But I'm not afraid – not even of that old fairy, the Boodeeman.

I am perched at the front window, gazing out past the yard to see who might be passing down the lane. Suddenly, the rain comes pouring out of the heavens. I've never seen it as fierce as this before. It makes huge splashes that hop off of the yard. I don't think Grannie or Jack will dare leave the cow shed in this sort of weather. They are trapped in there with the cows, like me at the window. I continue gazing at the savage rain. The ducks don't seem to mind a bit. I listen to them quacking merrily. Most of them are paddling around in the stream and wagging their tails as they spin round in circles. There's no sign of the hens. I know where those faint hearts are: standing in a row underneath the thatched eaves of the house or hiding beneath one of the carts. I have seen them doing this sort of thing before, even when there were just a few miserly drops of rain, when Jack was taking me out for another one of my walks. They always look so sad, peeping across the yard at the ducks and envying their high jinks in the stream.

The rain soon passes and the sun comes out. Now that I've got used to my new sandals, I'd like to take a stroll around the yard. I'd like to march up and down its length amid the hens and the ducks. I might even make a rush towards the big fat pig and show him who is the new king of the farmyard, this little man of Grannie's strutting around like a peacock in his posh sandals.

Yesterday afternoon, after the wretched rain had finished showing me its anger, Jack left a space at the front table. He took the pack of playing cards from the press cupboard and spread them out on the oil-cloth. He counted out fifty of them. He took two of the cards and made a tent with his fingers. Then he made a second tent, followed by a third.

He handed me two cards so that I could make myself a tent. He was the soul of patience as he took hold of my fingers and, just as he'd recently done when teaching me to walk, he helped me make my very first tent of cards, only to see it come tumbling down. He smiled and then laughed. I laughed too. What else could I do?

He spent the next half hour using up all fifty cards. He made two tents side-by-side and placed another card across the top of them like a bridge. I marvelled at this – even more so when he made three tents and a bridge of two cards on top of them. He hadn't yet finished and by now, the two of us had forgotten the earlier rain. He placed two more tents on top of the three tents before capping everything off with a single tent on top.

'See, Ned,' he said (using my name instead of the words 'young fella'), 'I have made you a brand new castle like the castles you see in Grannie's books.' I wanted him to make it all over again. And so (the little devil that I am), as soon as he made it, I promptly knocked it over, thereby destroying his beautiful handiwork. Jack wasn't cross. He merely laughed and started building his castle all over again.

Today is another day of pouring rain. With Jack and Grannie again trapped in the cow shed and the ducks still prattling away, I am bored to death with staring out the window. I see the playing cards lying idle on the window sill. I take them up and count a few of them onto the table. I'm determined to build at least one tent like Jack's. It's not only the ducks that can show off. What great news I will have to tell him when he comes in. 'See the fine castle I have made for you, Jack.' But my efforts are still in vain and my fingers are not yet steady enough.

Rose, our sheepdog, has just hurried in to escape from the rain. She throws herself across the fireplace, something she is not allowed to do. I will spend time with her instead of with my cards.

As soon as she spots me approaching, she wags her tail. She twists her head from side to side to snap at a beetle who has carelessly made its way out from the pile of turf. Without a thought, she swallows it. She and I have become fast friends of late and I spend a while stroking her fur till she demands a change and rolls over on her back. I tickle her belly. Both of us have no thought other than our present playfulness.

I am not allowed to go out on rainy days like today and though I'm on my own while Grannie and Jack are milking, I know that the two of them are close by and that I am safe and snug in here. I spend a good deal of time gazing into the fire, listening to the crackling of the logs and watching the redness of the turf and the shadows that the flames make on the back wall. I watch the smoke flying up the chimney. I poke my head up to see can I spot the blue sky overhead.

No sun has yet appeared and it goes on raining heavily with the accompanying wind howling across the thatch. Grannie and Jack have been in the cow shed much longer than usual and I begin to get worried. When are they coming back? I hurry across the floor to the half-door, mindless of the rain that continues to splash off of the yard's cobblestones. I haven't time to pay attention to the ducks and their quacking or to think about the quaking hens. The wind goes on whistling and I hear the doors rattling. The mice in the rafters are quiet for once in their life. They are a little bit afraid of the rain. It's a bit like how I feel. But, a minute later, I hear Grannie and Jack returning with the buckets.

Today is Thursday and I am up and dressed. I could not be happier. While she was putting on my britches, Grannie started humming a new verse in my ear:

Johnnie when you die will you leave me the fiddle-o?
Johnnie when you die will you leave me the bow?

I am not sitting on her knees this time. I am far too big for that sort of thing at this stage of my life.

It's time for me to say my morning prayers. Grannie has taught me how to join my hands while I'm praying and how to turn my pointed fingers up to God, how to turn my eyes towards the Sacred Heart picture the way she does. My list of blessing prayers is a long one but we finally get to the end. I haven't said a single prayer for the Boodeeman or that other rascal, Ned Needles.

Jack takes down the last three eggs from the press cupboard shelf. Grannie puts them into the tin saucepan and covers them with just enough water. She fixes the saucepan on top of the fire among a nest of burning twigs and logs. In no time, I smell the burnt tin smell of the saucepan from the fire's fierce heat.

She knows from her years of experience how long the eggs take to boil. Jack likes his egg to be soft and runny. So does Grannie and so do I.

He smiles to himself. He loves the way his mother reaches in to take the saucepan out of the fire – the way she challenges the intense heat of the flames and how she hasn't an ounce of fear in her. Her gnarled old fingers are well past getting scorched. She grabs the hot handle of the saucepan in the folds of her apron and races to the half-door with it. She empties the water onto the flagstones in the yard.

Jack cuts thick slices of soda bread and puts layers of butter on each slice. That's the way he likes to butter his bread. Grannie likes it that way, too. On each of our slices, he sprinkles a little salt to make the butter taste better. He cracks my egg open for me. He dips a teaspoon of butter into the yoke and adds more salt. For what seems like ages, he stirs the mixture round and round with his knife until he's satisfied.

Grannie pours the three of us a mug of milk. We are ready for our breakfast. We eat in silence. I can't stop looking at Jack with all that butter on his bread – all that butter in his egg as well. Some of it has run out from the side of his mouth and I am about to break out laughing, for his face looks unusually strange and his lips are streaked with yellow yolk. Grannie doesn't seem to notice it.

I wonder what today will bring. While Jack goes off with Rose to unchain the cows and take them back to the Bull Paddock, Grannie busies herself clearing the table. She wipes clean the oil-cloth with her dishcloth. As always, she is humming to herself. Shafts of sunlight fall in through the window onto the table and on her face. A thousand particles of dust dance around her.

She washes her crockery and cutlery in the grey enamel pan. She arranges the plates and saucers on the press cupboard shelves and puts the cups on the hooks. I am given the job of putting away the apostle spoons, for these are objects that I cannot break. She swirls the water round in the pan and throws it out onto the backs of the inquisitive hens who have come flocking round the half-door and demanding her attention. They flap their wings and scatter. But they'll be back soon, for she cannot keep them away for long. They know she'll be bringing their mash to them soon.

She has yet another small task ahead of her. She uses a large spoon to clean out the ash-hole under the wobbly stool. Unlike me, she has no time to stand gazing at the blackness of the hob or the smoke spiralling up the chimney. I am amazed at how busy she is.

When I was fast asleep last night, Martin, the creamery manager, cycled up with a parcel. His sister, Moira, had come home from England and had brought with her this parcel from my mother. Inside it was attached a letter, telling Grannie how sick and tired Patsy and she are from the terrible bombing raids of the Germans.

Grannie and Jack pray for her and Patsy every night and when they are chatting in the evening after I've gone to bed, they spend time wondering how anyone can possibly stand the noise of the bombs. They worry about the terrible danger my mother and father are in and I always end my blessing prayers with, 'God, please stop the war,' though I don't know what it means.

Martin watches Grannie unravel the parcel. Inside, it is a fresh set of clothes for me. For now that I can walk a bit, my mother would like me to step out in some kind of style opposite the neighbours. There's a woollen hat to keep the cold from my head on those mornings when the frost lies heavy round the yard. There's corduroy britches and a jacket and two blue shirts.

Grannie holds them up towards the light of the half-door and inspects them to see are they the right size and will they look good on me. Jack watches her closely. It's not every day that such finery as this comes in the door of our little thatched house.

Today is Friday and it's already nine o'clock. We haven't had our breakfast yet. Jack and Rose are busy marshalling the cows back down the lane towards the Bull Paddock after they've been milked. Grannie is by the fire, far too busy dressing me up in my new clothes to give a thought to anything else.

'Let's go check on the ducks and the hens, Ned. Let's see if Mr Fox or Mr Weasel came calling on them during the night. The geese are already out in the field, so we can count them later,' she says.

She fussily fixes my woolly hat round my ears. She puts on her own woolly hat. She does not forget to tend to the two skillet pots near the fire. She has made sure that the lids are fixed on tightly so that the hens and Rusty the cockerel don't come in foraging round them when we are off searching for eggs.

Jack shot a fine buck rabbit last night above in Mucklin. This morning, it's been boiling nicely with its juices in the smaller pot. Grannie has a pile of pink spuds in the bigger pot. They are already boiled in time for our dinner when the morning's work is done.

She closes the half-door behind us. She takes me by the hand and we head off down the yard. She unhasps the hen house door and, with her stooped back, peers inside. She lifts her stick to count her fowl. They start muttering all together. I wonder what they are telling her. *'It's high time you let us out and into the fresh air. What kept you so long?'* She holds the hens back with her stick and lets the ducks out first. They are bigger and bolder than the hens and make deafening quacks once they're free of the hen house door. They waddle off in a long line towards the stream. On the way, they drink the swill behind Moll's cart. The big, yellow sun shines on the drakes' feathers, bringing out their peacock colours of blue and green.

The hens are soon out – all except one. This little hen has not yet come out. She's inside in her tea chest in the far corner, hatching out the clutch of eggs that Molly Hughes brought down to Grannie the other day. Grannie peeks in the tea chest at her.

Her little hen has been sitting on her eggs for a while now. But a few days from now, her chicks will struggle out of their eggshells and then their chirping will fill the hen house. Grannie can't wait to see half a dozen palpitating lives struggling around in the tea chest and a proud mother hen peering up at her. From now on, she will call her the Little Red Hen. For days to come, I will hear nothing but the music of these pretty chicks. The yard will be full of it. I will spend my mornings watching them wobbling across the yard after their mother. When she gets tired of their persistent squabbling, she will gather them under her wing and squat down behind Moll's cart. For the next half hour, she will have a bit of peace and quiet with just the odd croak of satisfaction out of her.

A week later, Grannie's favourite young goose (Grey Legs) is sitting on her own eggs among the twinkling dock leaves. It's been raining but she pays no heed to it. Her nest lies behind the cow shed where Jack has made preparations for her privacy by surrounding her with the briars that he cut from Old Tim's ditch.

They will keep her hidden from the rest of the farmyard. Her eggs are most precious and they should arrive any day soon. Jack wants to show me the fluffy newborn goslings and their colours – a mixture of green, yellow and brown.

Apart from the pigs, I am mostly afraid of Grannie's geese – above all, the fierce gander and his red ferret eyes – especially now when he is firmly standing guard in front of Grey Leg's nest. Today is no different and I hold firmly onto Grannie's hand. Cautiously, we peep round the back wall of the cow shed where we hope to find out if Grey Legs has laid any of her eggs this morning.

'Stay here, Ned!' says Grannie while she approaches her goose to inspect her nest. The watchful eye of the gander follows her. He knows that it's best not to stand in her way. Were he to do so, she would frighten him to death with her waspish tongue and a belt of her sound stick.

She gives one more look back to see that her little man is not trotting after her. She moves back the briars and lifts the protective wings of Grey Legs. The young goose has been composed and madam-like up till this moment but now she has her eyes firmly riveted on Grannie and her stick. They seem to recognise each other. I can see Grannie is not one bit afraid of getting pecked by her favourite goose and for the next day or two, she will regularly take me out with her to inspect the nest and count the eggs.

I see her stoop low and stretch herself out on the wet ground to get in beneath Grey Legs. She moves her to one side gently so that she can count the eggs and see if any of them are broken

By this time, Jack has finished his morning's work. He tiptoes out to the edge of the cow shed. Maybe (like me) he feels afraid of the gander. He watches his mother as she lies half-hidden underneath Grey Legs. This is a sight he loves to behold: his mother and the goose both locked closely together. He quietly chuckles to himself when he sees how his aged mother has skilfully counted all twelve eggs without once disturbing her goose. Even the gander seems to acknowledge the good work that Grannie has done.

In a week or two, the fluffy goslings will make themselves known to Grey Legs and from that moment on, they will keep her busy. She will take a matronly stroll up along the Blue Button Field and they will follow behind her in a dutiful line. She will lead them out safely under the gate towards the second field.

Grannie and I will spend our mornings watching this little scene as Grey Legs confidently strolls round the nearby fields – all the time looking back at her little flock to see are they keeping up with her. There are more smiles yet to come from Grannie and myself when we see the goslings tumbling into the cattle's hoof holes and the wheel ruts left by Moll's cart when Jack was taking out the dung to spread on his potato field.

Another morning and Grannie and I are out early. The wind today is alive and well, banishing the rain clouds. Neither the ducks nor the geese seem to mind the wind but it blows the hens down the length of the yard as they struggle to keep on their feet and get away from it. I grab Grannie's stick and run ahead of her. I chase the hens out into the haggart and she smiles at me. It was just a month ago that I took my first wobbly steps in an effort to walk like Jack and her and now she sees me running down the yard.

As soon as the hens reach the haggart dung heap, they start scratching for worms. They have one thing on their mind: to lay the little brown egg each day for our breakfast.

I run back triumphantly to Grannie and now I chase after the ducks with her stick. They waddle off ahead of me – in and out round the two carts of Moll and Lightning. It's as though we are playing a game of hide and seek. I am bigger than both the ducks and the hens, something I'm beginning to realise. A day or two later, I find out that the geese are not one bit afraid of me. They hiss and poke out their necks when I look at them and they threaten me with their beaks. Grannie laughs out loud when she sees me running back to her like a little chick to its mother hen and whimpering. I am still only two and she takes me in under the protective folds of her apron.

Each morning, I continue to collect the hens' eggs for her – these days on my own. I haven't yet found all the hens' hiding places. They have a habit of hiding their eggs in the most inaccessible places, deep among the nettles and dock leaves or out near the nest of briars that kept our young goose Grey Legs safe.

Grannie sometimes decides to go out searching with me. On these days, we walk in the most unexpected places. 'We'll find the eggs, Ned. Never you fear, just be patient, child.' That's what she says and she keeps a firm hold of my hand in case I fall among the nettles and get stung. It doesn't take long for her to improve my egg searching ability and in the following week, I go out searching on my own again. I am allowed to search everywhere apart from Grey Legs' nest. But I am also forbidden to go near the stinking pool of dung and cattle piss outside the cow shed door, a place that Jack calls the Perilous Sink, though I don't know what this means. The words 'perilous' and 'sink' are like new words out of a book.

In less than half an hour, I track down a hen or two – no matter where they're hiding. For as soon as I hear one of them cackling, I know where to find her and armed with Grannie's stick, I race off in that direction.

Today, I have found two eggs behind the hay reek. One of them is in a hen's nest in the long grass, the other egg looks a different colour. It might have been lying there for a week but I will take it to Grannie and she will let me know if it's a good one.

Before I reach the yard, I find one more egg at the foot of the rose bush. I call Grannie out to let her know where I have found the latest eggs.

'See the eggs I brang you today,' I cry, still using the odd incorrect word from my babyhood days whenever I'm over-excited. She takes the eggs from me and again she smiles. She puts the eggs in her apron and ruffles my hair. The two of us walk in the half-door and I feel like a conquering hero returning home from battle in one of her storybooks. I haven't yet noticed that I have a few red stinging nettle marks on my shins. I've been far too busy looking out for a hen and her latest egg.

Grannie administers dock leaf juice to these burning stings, humming to herself as usual. 'There, there, my child,' she smiles. 'You're now as good as new. You're not going to die.' Then she has another thought. 'Go off and make friends with the gander.' She doesn't mean a bit of it. She is simply teasing me like Jack does sometimes when he has a fit of good humour. She knows only too well that the fierce gander is able to make me wet my new britches.

There is plenty of housework for Grannie to do while Jack is down in the Bull Paddock letting loose the cows. But first of all, it's time to feed her family of ducks and hens. The geese can look after themselves and are long gone to the fields, foraging among the weeds. Grannie gets out her tin tray from behind the gramophone and ladles onto it a mess of potato skins and scraps of bread from the skillet pot until the tray is half-full. She will have a busy time feeding her fowl for the next half hour.

They see her racing towards them armed with the tray and her little trowel from the flour bin in Jack's bedroom. The ducks have jumped out of the stream in record time and are seen waddling at speed towards Lightning's cart where Grannie has her galvanised sheeting on which she'll feed them. Some of the hens are already ahead of the ducks and Rusty, the cockerel, is sitting on the lace of the cart and supervising the proceedings.

'Shoo! Shoo!' cries Grannie as she hunts away some of the more adventurous hens who have come flying in around her skirts. I am closely following behind her. The disorderly hens almost knock me off my feet, so anxious are they to get at the food.

The rest of the hens come flying in from the haggart and wait for Grannie to throw more food onto the galvanised sheeting. She is well used to calling her little kingdom of fowl and, without a thought, she bawls out, 'Chuk-chuk-chuk! Chuk-chuk-chuk!' Three quick calls followed by three even quicker ones, her voice rolling down the scale in a loud sing-song. There's no need to call any of them to the tray, as the older hens are already pushing the younger ones out of the way. She shovels the mash onto the tray, spreading it out as far as she can so that even the smallest hen has no bother getting some of it. The ducks are fiercer than ever in their attempts to swallow as much food as they can and leave as little as possible for the hens.

Grannie crossly scatters them with the toe of her boot so her precious egg layers can get enough to eat and lay tomorrow's eggs.

'See if you can count them, Ned,' she says half-heartedly. She has already counted them herself. By this time, they are all quietly pecking against the galvanised sheeting and it's easy for me to count them.

While they are eating, the morning sunshine hovers all around them. There's such a variety of colour in their sunlit feathers, especially in Rusty, the cockerel's, tail feathers. Admiring their colours is one of my favourite pastimes. There is always an invisible intimacy between the ducks, the hens, Grannie and me.

Grannie hands me a few bits of bread out of her bib pocket to throw at the angry ducks. 'Quack-quack-quack!' they mutter by way of thanks.

The day has already been full of activity for the two of us but now it's time for Jack to get busy with me as well. As soon as he has driven his cows into the Bull Paddock, he saunters back up the lane. Even before he reaches the flagstones, he hears his mother's shrill voice chastising her ducks and encouraging the hens.

It's time for him to fetch the two buckets from behind the half-door and give me my little sweet-gallon to bring back water from Brindley's well. He'd love a mug of well-water but there's none left. He bumps into Grannie and myself as we go back inside with our empty tin tray.

'Come with me, Ned. Let two-men-of-us go fetch your grannie the water for today's cooking.'

I like the way he says 'two-men-of-us' instead of 'my little man'. It shows that I am getting to be a big fellow these days.

Grannie studies me. She reaches for my woolly hat on the nail above the holy water font. With more fussiness than usual, she covers my head and ears to keep out the chill that lurks round the well. She gives me an enamel mug, which I place inside my sweet-gallon. 'That's for getting yourself a drink of water when you are down at the well,' she says and she hurries both of us out the door before going back in to heap more logs on the fire.

Jack and I walk on as far as the stile. The rocky steps down into Old Pat's Avenue are exceedingly steep – far too difficult to climb down for a child as young as me. For, though I've come a long way since I first stumbled onto my feet and staggered across the floor, I have yet to learn how to climb up and down steps as difficult as these. Instead, Jack leads me round the low ditch and in through Old Pat's gateway. It's green like Grannie's geranium boxes. We stroll on down the avenue. We turn right and make our way through the nettles and briars to get to the well.

I stand beside it and watch Jack swirling the dead flies from the well's dusty surface with his bucket. Around me are some giant spider webs with rows of gossamer threads linking their webs to the nearby bushes. This is a fairy place like those places in Grannie's books. Inside one of the webs is a dead fly, trapped there forever. Jack stops swirling the bucket. He looks at me. He sees me staring at the web. He sees the trapped fly. If only (he thinks) we three could stay trapped together for years to come, so happily have we lived our lives since this little chap came here – especially on mornings like this one.

But the thought quickly disappears. He hates to think of the damn war going on, of the Germans, of the killings going on and he heaves a sigh. What has all this nonsensical war got to do with the three of us? He returns to his task of filling the buckets and my sweet-gallon with water. From one of the buckets, he hands me a mug of the frosty water to drink.

As he works on, I stop and listen. I hear footsteps approaching. It's someone in a pair of heavy boots. Then I hear the sound of a tapping walking stick. It draws nearer and nearer. It's coming from the far end of the avenue. An old lady appears round the bend that leads to Old Pat's farmhouse. The farm was once owned by Sam Brindley but, thereafter, belonged to Old Pat's father and his wife, Mary Endless. She spent years making her fortune in the cornfields of Minnesota before returning to her beloved Pat. Poor Pat died many years ago, leaving her a widow. It is said she's as old as Methuselah (whoever that might be) but Grannie says she was once a beautiful girl in neighbouring Curryquinn, full of sap and with rosy cheeks.

The tapping of the old lady's stick stops. I lift my eyes from the well and peep out through the briars to take a good look at her. She staggers round the bend of the avenue and moves forward, one step at a time, till she's no more than a yard or two away from me. She edges her stick out from under the folds of her black skirt. The skirt reaches down to her boots.

Young as I am, I can see that she's even older than Grannie – indeed, old enough to be Grannie's mother. On her head, she wears a little bonnet. It is tied under her chin with a piece of string. Her fingers are long and skinny, much longer than Jack's.

For one moment, I feel drawn towards a lady who lived her youth in the distant past. There's just a yard or two between herself and myself as we stand looking at each other. Pale sunlight shimmers across at us from the laurels. The laurels are very still, as though holding the two of us together in their green arms. Jack doesn't seem to notice, so busy is he filling the buckets and my sweet-gallon.

The old lady doesn't say a word, simply looks across the space at me: an old lady from America and a child that not so long ago was rushed away from the ruins of the bombed-out streets of London. Time seems endless just for these few seconds.

The old lady wraps her shawl tightly round her shoulders to prevent the chill creeping into her bones. She smiles at me and I smile back. Up until now, she looked like a witch from a fairytale. But with her lovely smile, that is no longer the case. She wheels away from me and edges her boots and her tapping stick slowly back round the bend before vanishing like a dream.

The lark is singing high in the heavens and the pink of the dawn has melted into a limpid blue. Jack is out early and is off to the hills around Mucklin, his rifle slung over his shoulder. He's in search of a rabbit or two for our Sunday dinner. It's not only Jack who is busy. I, too, am feeling the strength in my feet and legs now that I'm able to walk all the way down the lane to Brindley's well and then walk all the way back to Grannie with my sweet-gallon full of water.

I must have heard the lark. It's time to get out of bed. Beyond the rosebushes, I can hear the little wrens – a whole family of them – chirping away to one another in the hawthorn tree next to the hen house. I can hear Grannie's sharp voice as she pelts the tongs at Rusty, the cheeky cockerel, who has dared to fly in from the yard and perch on the half-door. He has never done this before. But he has an eye on the skillet pot of mash – that is, he did have until he saw Grannie's tongs flying towards him. He shrieks like blazes when the tongs strike his lovely tail feathers, knocking the merriment out of him.

I stretch my arms over my head and wipe the sleep out of my eyes. The smell of Grannie's fire, the turf and the logs all welcome me out from the bedroom towards her. We have the usual smiles for one another. I carry my work-britches towards the fire to air before I put them on. Like Jack, I sleep in my shirt, so there's no need to air that. I don't need Grannie to dress me as she once did. A chap of my age is able not only to put on my own clothes but to buckle my sandals as well.

Grannie stops from scraping the dirt off of the spuds before washing them in the skillet pot for our dinner. Together, we have a moment or two of silence. Then, I begin my list of blessing prayers, starting with my prayer for our ass, Lightning, and our mare, Moll, as well as all Grannie's fowl – even the fat pigs as well as the newborn chicks and goslings. I make sure to pray for Jack and Grannie. They are the soul of my life, something I cannot put into words.

I tiptoe towards the half-door. I head for the ass's cart at the end of the yard where a comfortable bag of straw is waiting for me to climb onto. I now have the farmyard to myself: me and my quiet thoughts, me and my eyes and my ears. No more praying today – no more counting the logs or the hen's eggs – no time to be listening to Grannie reading to me from her storybooks.

The little family of wrens is silent in the hawthorn tree. But other birds are chirping in the honeysuckle next to the fuchsia bush outside the pig house. Maybe it's the same little family of wrens. Perhaps they have changed their dwelling place. From where I am sitting, I can smell the perfume of the pink rosebushes on the front wall of our house. I can smell the conflicting smell of the rich dung on the heap outside the pig house door. I like both smells.

We've had no rain for the last few days and the sun is predominant in our yard and on the rosebushes round the front windows. Our stream is four feet wide and, at present, it is full of rainwater that came down from the hills. I never get tired of looking at its long, liquid muscles. They remind me of the flesh of Grannie's skinned rabbits. The ducks and their ducklings waddle down the yard and stand in a line, balancing on the rocks edging the stream. They quack excitedly. Though the stream is full, it is not roaring along angrily as on stormy days. On those sorts of days, they wouldn't dream of taking their ducklings to such a dangerous place. The little dears would soon end up below in the haggart with their legs cocked up in the air.

73

From my perch on the ass's cart, I see the hens parading round the jambs of the cart, looking for the crumbs left over after their recent feast of Grannie's mash. Some of them are balancing on one leg, others pecking under their wings to keep themselves clean in case Rusty the cockerel casts his eye in their direction. An older hen finds she has trouble breaking open a snail's shell. It won't budge. The other hens are disinterested in her attempts. I see two younger hens in a heap of flying feathers further up the yard as they attempt to outmatch one another and see which of them is superior to the other.

Meanwhile, the older ducks shake theirs tails excitedly. It's the signal that the stream is safe enough for their little ones to follow them into the water. The ducks look up and down the stream to see where the best spot is for jumping in. They plunge in with a hearty splash. The ducklings follow them. They turn round and round like twigs, their heads aloft and their beaks skywards. Oh, the little show-offs and the noisy excitement of their first swim! Their mothers continue to quack encouragement to them.

Jack is busy feeding his calves at the far end of the haggart. He carries his stick and, from time to time, strikes the biggest calf on its bony back to stop it from poking its head into the bucket of skimmed milk being drunk by the smaller calf next to it.

Grannie is busy, too. I see her at the half-door, shaking the dust from the sacks which keep our feet warm when we're kneeling on the floor beside our bed to say prayers. My list of blessing prayers is not nearly as long as hers or Jack's.

Now that I'm older, I'm forever jumping from one scene to another and my interest in the hens and ducks proves to be a short one. I wander across the yard and gaze in over the hedge at the blooming flowers in Grannie's garden. I look out past it into Sam's Grove across the lane. The trees over there are so high, much higher than our thatched house. The gentle breeze causes the top of the trees to sway and hiss their own kind of song.

The ducks and ducklings come out from the stream and shake their tail feathers dry. They toddle off across the sunny yard.

The hens hide beneath Lightning's cart to escape from the blinding heat of the sun.

At times like this, when I'm on my own without Grannie or Jack, I am not always sure what to do with myself even though I've every reason to feel self-assured, dressed as I am in my new britches, my blue shirt, my brown sandals and white socks.

I constantly remind myself that I'm much bigger than any of these farmyard fowl. Can't they see how big I am? But they continue to take no notice of me. I know it's wrong to frighten them with my stick or chase them into the haggart, no matter how much I'd like to at times. The sun is getting higher in the sky. It's shining directly into the stream. I walk over to the rocks around it. I balance on a rock and look down. The stream is calm again and I see my reflection and that of the blue sky and the sun. I am small and the sky's reflection is big. My hair is the colour of wheat. I gaze at my smart clothes and my face. I have never taken a close look at my face before. It looks shiny after the way Grannie washed it with her face flannel earlier today.

Absentmindedly, I throw a pebble into the stream, breaking my reflection into fragments as well as that of the sky and the sun. Seconds later, the water is again untroubled. A shadowy figure tiptoes up behind me. It is Jack, returning with his empty milk buckets from the time he spent feeding the calves. He peers over my shoulder and I see his reflection in the stream alongside my own. We stand there motionless, just the two of us and not a sign of the stream's visiting ducks or their playful young charges. It makes a lovely picture, a serious-looking child and a smiling Jack with his hands on my shoulders. The renewed reflection of the sky and the sun make a halo around our heads.

Grannie's voice rings out loud and clear, breaking the moment's silence. She is standing at the half-door. 'Come in for yeer eggs,' she cries, using the old way of speaking.

Jack plops a pebble into the water. The dreamy picture vanishes and the stream has turned murky. My uncle is laughing but I am not. He has ruined the loveliness of it all and I feel upset.

However, my morning feed of eggs together with my mug of milk is waiting for me. It'll soon change my mood and I'll be getting my smile back. I also know that I'll be taking my first really long walk with Grannie today. We will walk across the Blue Button Field and on to the field beyond it. We will fill her bed bolster with a dozen cabbages for this week's dinner table. We will put aside a few odd bits for our pigs as well.

Up till now, I have always stayed close to the yard and the haggart where I've been as happy as a lark, each day following Grannie's footsteps and helping her as best I can.

'You little nuisance,' she sighs whenever she sees me staying too close to her skirts and tripping over her boots – be she cleaning the creamery tanks with the scrub brush, sweeping the goose droppings from the rainy yard, collecting her eggs in the nettles around the haggart or tending to the flowers in her little garden.

But now there are other things on her mind. The two of us head out the door to go cut our cabbages. She strides on ahead of me. She's a tough old lady and on most days hastens over the fields on her own. She does so in all kinds of weather: on frosty days, hurrying to keep herself warm or on rainy days with a potato-sack across her back to keep out the rain. She doesn't seem to worry when it comes to foul weather, but attacks the fields like her mother, Ellen, did before her. But today, now that I'm big enough to walk long distances, she's only too glad of my company and there's no need for her to be on her own.

We step across the haggart, Grannie carrying her sharp, black-handled knife, the one that Jack uses for killing the pig. I carry the bed bolster. It is light enough for me, for I am used to carrying much heavier loads like armfuls of logs from behind the pig house. We reach the Blue Button Field. The buzzing of bees fills the air around the purple clover and amidst the nodding heads of the wildflowers. The horseflies are also busy among the thistles. They flit from one circle of cow dung to another.

It's not that easy for me and my new sandals to get across the field, for it is full of wheel ruts and hoof holes. They've been

76

left there by Moll's cart when Jack was taking out dung to throw on the field for next year's spuds and cabbages. He and Moll have spent weeks taking cartloads of it out and spreading it on the field. When he stares at his new crops, he'll be the happiest man in Tipperary. It's the time he loves best – admiring the results of his handiwork.

Grannie and I walk on in silence, her big boots thumping the daisies out of the way. The sky is full of white clouds.

We reach the second field, where she takes off her apron and lays it on the headland. We sit there a moment, admiring the hills around us and listening to the re-echoing voices of Gret's children across the valley as they hurry their cattle into one of their father's fields further up the hill, the field known as the Heights.

Grannie can't sit here long with me. She rolls up her sleeves and gets on her feet to do her work, leaving me by myself on her apron. It's a moment of peace for me and I sit here contentedly.

Her energetic fingers get busy with the knife. She selects which cabbages are best for the dinner table. I watch the white butterflies. They seem to love the rows of cabbages and they dance in pairs around Grannie's head. She is well used to them. She has soon cut several heads of cabbage. She lays them out for me to count and inspect. It's easy work, for I have recently learnt to count to well over 100. After all, I'll be 3 years old next summer. I have the job of bringing the cabbage heads up to the mouth of the bolster.

'Grannie,' I shout, 'you have twelve cabbage heads cut already.' She leaves off her work and is satisfied that she's cut enough to last the week. She presses the cabbages down inside the bolster and ties its mouth with a few twists of twine. She places it in the hedge near the gate leading into Bill Corcoran's land. Jack will come back in the afternoon and carry it home. The bolster is too heavy for an old lady like Grannie to carry on her back.

While we were away cutting our cabbages, Jack was driving Moll over to the Silvermines creamery to get his milk taken in by Martin, the creamery manager. In return, Martin will give him back our two tanks filled with skimmed milk as well as a slab of butter.

Like most of the farmers, Jack will have little time for dawdling at the gates or exchanging news about the war that's going on in England. Such conversation is left for Sundays after Mass when the men rush out the church door to light up their fags and have their chat. There's nothing else to do on Sundays. It's a day of rest or for trotting off to a hurling match.

It's one o'clock and it's dinnertime. The three of us sit at the front table and eat platefuls of mashed spuds mixed with milk, butter and onions – what Grannie calls 'champ'. We drink our mugs of milk and take a mug of spring water from the bucket behind the half-door.

Jack takes a potato-sack and waves it round his head. 'Come now, Ned, let two-men-of-us take a walk across the fields and bring Grannie back the spuds for the week's dinners. I'll bring back her bolster of cabbages on the way back. We'll be home before your grannie has cleared the table and put away the plates.'

With scarcely a wave of goodbye to Grannie, I hurry out the half-door and run after Jack. Lots of steam is rising up out of the dung outside the cow shed. The white clouds of this morning have almost gone, just a few strips caressing the hills mixed with one or two pink lines that were made by the early sun.

I am getting good at racing my legs off. I have to be if I'm to keep up with my uncle. He sees me stumbling my way round the ruts in the field. He throws me up on his shoulders and we make our way to the gate leading to the second field. By this time, the sun is blazing over the fields and nearby hills – glistening and almost white in its brilliant light. The green tops of the pine trees above Bill Corcoran's land are puffed out in the breeze. I'm as happy as a foal in a field of long grass.

We reach the headland where Jack takes off his waistcoat and turns it inside-out, leaving the shiny side for me to sit on and warm my bum while he's working. He winds up his pocket watch. He stretches his arms over his head and soon I hear the smack of his potato-spade against the soft earth. His nose is almost down in the clay. It's as though he is a part of the earth. He digs up a good few clods of earth mixed with potato stalks and he shakes the earth off of them. He spends the next half hour hard at work among the drills, pulling out batches of chickweed that he'll burn later on once it's dried. I am given the job of counting the spuds that he's dug. They are far more in number than Grannie's twelve heads of cabbage. There's also far more dirt and clay to deal with, as well as a few shiny worms for me to shrink away from.

Wheeling down from the trees on the ditch, half a dozen rooks come visiting us. They follow behind Jack, their inquisitive beaks forever searching for the worms in the freshly dug soil.

I hate the sight of worms and Jack knows this well. While I'm busy at my counting, he throws a long worm at me. It hits me on the jaw before wriggling down my shirt.

'Shite! Shite!' I scream, using the filthy word that Grannie used the time she pelted the tongs at Ned Needles when he came to steal our pig. I am too young to appreciate the rascally devilment that lies behind Jack. Nor do I understand why he is lying on his back, laughing uncontrollably at the sight of me shouting out the rude word 'shite!'

The rooks aren't our only visitors this afternoon. While Jack's been occupied digging his spuds, his neighbour, Bill Corcoran, is also busy. Bill has recently proposed marriage to a young damsel from out near Glown and it's a well-known fact that no man can marry his ladylove unless he has a house into which to bring her. He has been clearing a site for the house he intends to build for his wife-to-be.

Sadly, there's an obstacle to his plans – a few acres of furze bushes at the top end of his land. That's where the corncrakes live – a species of bird found nowhere else around here. But it's also the best place to build his house, right in the centre of the furze bushes. That's because from this spot, he and his future wife will have the most wonderful view of the River Shannon ten miles away. The corncrakes will have to find a new home somewhere else and the furze bushes will have to be burnt. They are dry enough and thorny enough in this hot weather to make a quick blaze and leave the grass bare for him to lay the foundations next week.

While I am counting the spuds, Jack and Bill exchange a few words at the gate between our land and Bill's. They seem as happy as a pair of larks. Jack returns to me, shaking his head and smiling broadly. He has no more spuds to dig and he starts helping me put into the sack the ones that we've dug, making sure I have counted them correctly.

Meanwhile, Bill is seen racing through his furze bushes, sprinkling them with paraffin and setting light to them with his box of matches. The gentle afternoon breeze turns suddenly fierce as though alarmed at the new smoke and the tinderbox heat from Bill's burnt bushes. It's not long before the field is a blaze of fiery colour with the black smoke rising up in thick clouds and sailing away towards me and Jack. In a few minutes, the two of us are coughing like blazes, so full are our eyes and lungs with Bill's smoke.

'How do ye like the smoke from mee bushes?' laughs Bill. 'Ye are more than welcome to it and the heat from the flames,' he shouts. Isn't he the rascal to be taunting Jack and me like this?

'Well now,' said Jack in between coughing (and without the trace of a smile), 'aren't you the son-of-a-devil to be blinding with smoke a poor man like meeself and this young chap from England!'

So angry am I that I forget about the worm that Jack pelted at me and I run to the gate and shout as loudly as the smoke will allow me to, 'Shite! Shite! Shite! The devil shite on you, Bill. You've nearly blinded us.'

I can't understand what happens next. Bill and Jack are bent double in fits of laughter after hearing me curse Bill so savagely – and to think that a mere child like me could have learnt such language and have gotten himself into a rage such as this. That isn't all. When I see the way the smoke has affected them and the way they are laughing instead of crying, I grow angrier still and make even greater use of the 'shite' word.

This provokes another fit of laughter. So hard does Jack laugh that the tears roll down his cheeks, leaving dirty streaks on his face from all the black smoke. It's a miracle (thinks Jack to himself) that the furze bushes don't stop their burning from the sheer shock of witnessing a young lad like his nephew cursing as profusely as a grown man.

For my part, I am left wondering how long the flames will go on burning and how far the smoke will travel. I wonder if the cows in the Bull Paddock will start coughing like me and Jack or if we'll get a drop of milk for our tea this evening.

Jack wipes my dirty black cheeks with a bit of his spit and dries them with his jersey. He walks across to Bill's gate and (with as a stern a look as his laughing eyes can muster) he points a finger at him and warns him never dare to upset again the fine young English gentleman standing in front of him.

Patting me on the shoulder, he lifts the heavy sack of spuds onto his back as though it were a feather and the two of us head off home. We walk in silence but my mind is elsewhere. We reach the Blue Button Field and I have forgotten all about the hoof holes and wheel ruts. All I can think of is how Bill almost drowned us in smoke.

As soon as I get in the half-door, I will make sure to let Grannie know about the smoke and the fierce flames – and how it almost set fire to the ditch and the trees. I know she'll be angry. But, unlike me, she won't use the filthy 'shite' word that she used against Ned Needles. She is far too polite a lady to use that word more than once in her lifetime.

Later on, when I'm kneeling down and saying my night prayers, I ask God to forgive me for my rude word. However, when I have finally raced through my list of blessing prayers, I do not say a single prayer for Bill Corcoran. He's just as big a rascal as Ned Needles.

When I'm in bed (and still angry), Jack tries to calm me down. 'Isn't Bill the living devil,' he whispers, 'to be setting fire to his furze bushes while we were digging our spuds.' He finally tucks the blankets close around me and goes on stroking my head until I'm fast asleep. I do not have a single bad dream throughout the night.

Though young, I have come to realise that Grannie never has time to sit down and rest by the fire.

Gret brought down two new goose quills last week. Molly Hughes dropped in some more on her way to the creamery. Grannie keeps them next to her own quills on the ledge at the side of the leathern tapestry. She now moves the two long tables out from the walls onto the middle of the floor and gives those areas a good sweeping. She puts the tables back in place and tends to the rest of the floor. With her new goose quills, she scrapes out lots of cobwebs that are lurking in the corners of the living room. Next week, she'll dust each of the bedrooms in turn.

Now for the main task. The spuds have to be prepared for our dinner and the cabbages have to be washed and cut into small pieces for me, suitable for holding on my fork at the table. These days, she spends dinnertime teaching me how to hold my knife and fork like herself and Jack. It will take a good while yet before I am able to copy her successfully. My fingers aren't ready.

Last night, Jack heaped up a bucket of spuds the minute we arrived home with our sack load. This morning, he pours a gallon of water into the bucket and, with his upturned broom handle, spends half an hour pulping the major dirt off of them before handing each of the spuds to Grannie. After that, I watch her with her scrub brush as she washes the spuds thoroughly clean before boiling them. The fire is soon blazing away under the skillet of spuds. It'll be the turn of the cabbages next.

An hour later, she strains both skillet pots – the one for the spuds and the one for the cabbages – holding the handles with the corner of her apron. She is surrounded in a cloud of steam and is invisible for a second or two.

With her apron, she next lifts the kettle of boiling water from the crook on the crane to make Jack his tea. He'll drink several mugs of it before the day is out – just as he does every day – and he'll ask his mother for more.

She has almost finished this part of her housework. She is bent down low between the two skillets and the kettle and I catch a glimpse of her red calico petticoat. I am bemused. I have never seen it before. I can see that she has forgotten to take off her woolly hat. It is full of holes and she hasn't time to darn it. Jack's socks are more in need of her darning needle than her hat.

She gropes behind the front door for her hens' feeding bucket and fills it with oatmeal for her visit to the hen house. Finally, she does the same with the pigs' feeding bucket. After our dinner, she will mix the leftover spuds with the oatmeal and the few cabbages ruined by the slugs – as well as the slops from the teapot together with a saucepan of milk.

I am turning over the pages in one of Grannie's daughters' school prize books. It's the Cinderella story which Grannie has just handed me from the apple box under the tapestry. That's to keep me quiet and stop pestering her. There are lots of glossy pictures in this book and each of them is trying to tell me Cinderella's story. Grannie looks across at my bent head and smiles admiringly, for she likes to see me with a book in my hands. Then she gets back to the task she started earlier: dusting away the cobwebs.

Jack will be back soon from Brindley's well with the two buckets of water. I was too tired to go with him today after taking my long walk to the second field yesterday for the spuds and cabbages. And another thing – following the fright I got from Bill's burnt bushes, I have slept not just the whole night long but half the morning as well.

Tomorrow is the day for going to Mass in the Silvermines village. Everybody will be there, old and young alike. The road from Dolla to the village is more than two miles long. It'll be filled with asses and carts, horses and carts, as well as a few ponies and traps owned by those who have a few more shillings in their pocket than the rest of us.

Jack will make sure that all is in order. He'll be up before dawn. The cows will be chained into their usual places in the cow shed. He will fork loads of hay into the troughs in front of them. That will keep them busy till the three of us get home from Mass.

Then Jack and Grannie will each grab their stools and get busy milking.

From under the blankets in my cosy bed, I'll have time to listen to Jack singing one or two of his rebel songs as the milk hisses into his bucket till it's full. Grannie knows the words of all his songs. Her memory is formidable but she still hasn't learned to sing.

Meanwhile, this Saturday evening, her work has to go on. She has a small pile of Jack's socks beside her on the front table. In addition to the glow from the oil lamp, she has lit a fresh candle to make sure she doesn't prick her finger while she's darning. Once more, she is humming to herself.

Half an hour later, she heaves a sigh. She holds up the sock. She is finished. She hangs both of Jack's socks on the crane over the fire to air in preparation for Mass.

Jack is also busy. He gets down to his shaving, filling the enamel pan with boiling water and testing it with his fingers. He lays it on a chair in front of the fire. Grannie holds up the broken bit of looking glass for him to study his face while he shaves. He always leaves a few cat-hairs beneath his eyes the way his father, Will, did.

The yard stream is full and running along smoothly. Next step is also a Saturday evening task for him. He takes the bar of carbolic soap out to the stream. He strips off his shirt and throws it on the hedge. He stands in his wellingtons in the heart of the stream. He washes his chest, shoulders, neck and arm sockets and rubs himself dry with the hard towel. From time to time, Grannie peers out over the geraniums, admiring his manly chest. 'Just like my beloved Will,' she sighs.

She gets back to her work. She takes the clothes iron from the fireplace where it has been resting on a bed of hot coals. She grips the brown paper bag that's wrapped round its handle and hurries back to the front table. She stretches out her pillowcases on top of a towel and begins to iron them smooth and warm. This is an easy job and takes but a few minutes of her time. Saturday is the only time that she does her ironing. She doesn't iron the sheets. Last of all (but most importantly), she irons Jack's Sunday shirt.

They have finished their Saturday evening chores. The sun has almost quenched. There's a half-moon hanging proudly across the lane above Sam's Grove. Grannie takes her chair outside in front of the half-door to absorb the cool shades of the evening. She listens. All the birds have gone to roost, just like her hens, ducks and geese. Even the rooks in the pine trees are all quiet, their little feathers bristling in the cold wind that's streaming through their nests. Not another sound – only the murmuring stream.

The silence is interrupted by a small group of young men stopping outside our flagstones to play pitch 'n' toss with their pocket of pennies. Some are more skilful than others. They know how to curve each penny in the air at exactly the right distance so as to touch the mott. The two coins that land closest to it are placed on a flat stick and fired into the air. The crowd of onlookers sitting on the singletree at the entrance to the grove shout out 'a wren or a harp!' (the images of the face on the pennies). The winner is the one who has chosen the correct coin-face, a wren or maybe a harp, whichever has landed face up when the coins land.

Grannie hears their shouts of laughter. She loves the way these lads seem to be swallowing up life and her mind travels back to the time when Victoria was the queen – when herself and her brothers pelted their iron horseshoes at a mott in a similar way while her younger sisters played skittles on the flagstones during those Saturday evenings of old.

It's now Sunday and everyone is ready for the road to church. No one will be late. It's the one day when we all have a moment to reflect on our lives and ask God's help in everything we do. It's not just Jack who's up at dawn. All the farmers have their cows to think of – their milk to think of and their creamery cheque each month as well.

Jack tackles Moll. He makes sure that his mother is warm enough to face the cold morning wind. She is wearing her blue basket hat and her mother's wedding brooch. She has her gloves wrapped up to her elbows. She leans on her best walking cane – the one with the silver handle. Jack has polished her boots till she can see her face in them.

I am wearing my Mass clothes. Last night, Grannie washed me from head to toe. 'You look like a prince,' she said as she again ruffled my hair.

Off we go. The rhythm of cart wheels is heard coming down from the hillslopes above Curryquinn, Logg and Mucklin – all the way down as far as Dolla and out onto the creamery road that leads to the Silvermines village.

A cataract of people soon enter the church. The women are always up at the front and as close as they can get to the statues of the saints. The men shuffle into the back of the church. They place their better knee on their caps and twiddle their fingers through their rosary beads with thoughts of their ancestors. Their departed mothers (in some cases) are foremost in their minds today.

The Mass is said in Latin. We call Father Woods 'Speed the Plough' for he can say his Mass in less than twenty-five minutes. I have come to Mass since as far back as I can remember. I am always astonished at the beauty of the altar compared to our own little thatched cabin, the twinkling candles all in a row, the altar boys in their red and white cassocks and soutanes, Father Speed the Plough in his shamrock green chasuble with the golden trimmings and his long, white, dress-like robe which reaches down to his toes but which never trips him up.

His sermon is the high point of the Mass. All our eyes are on him when he delivers his words. He's as good as a stage actor. This time, it's the tale of the ten lepers who were healed by Jesus and how only one of them came back to say thank you to Jesus and how Jesus was so sad at the ungratefulness of the rest of them that tears filled up his eyes.

Our priest knows when to pause and he knows how to hang his head low and to let his message sink home. He suddenly looks very sad indeed, as if he's really about to cry. We know that it's because of the lepers' base ingratitude. He doesn't have to say another word. Yes, Father Speed the Plough is a wise man. He knows that none of us is a bit like those lepers and that we're all grateful souls at heart. He turns back onto the altar to continue saying his Mass and takes one last look back at us. His sorrowful look would melt a stone. He is sure we'll bring more than our usual miserable few coppers next week to put on the table outside the church door.

When Mass is finished, the men are the first to burst out through the church door. They head over to the conifer tree wall and light up their fags. A few minutes ago, there was plenty of smoke inside in the church from the incessant incense when the leading altar boy filled the first few rows of the congregation with its plumes and had the women coughing like blazes. But there's as much smoke now out here at the wall from all the fags being puffed. It's a blessing for the men to get out in the fresh air. Unlike the women, they feel trapped when they're inside the church, fearing that Father Speed the Plough might point his finger of shame at them and ask them to account for their hidden sins.

The men start chatting. Their main talk is about the war. Are the Germans winning? Have the Americans yet come into the fight? It goes on and on. It's the only chance they get to talk to each other. Jack grips me by the hand. His grip is hard. One day (he knows), I'll have to go back to England to Nell and Patsy. He drives this aching thought out of his mind. It'll break his heart when that day comes.

The women are in a huddle, gossiping like the men. Grannie is talking to May Ryan from Barnagore. She's her younger sister, Winnie's, daughter. She is a schoolteacher here in the village and well-loved by her pupils. Grannie is proud of her. Maybe (she thinks) one day I will have the privilege to grow up and become a teacher like May.

The Silvermines village is soon deserted, not a soul in sight, just a ghostly silence and a few old women sitting on their chairs outside their front doors.

Like the rest of the households, this is the one morning for a feast. We sit at the table and devour two rings of black puddings, two rings of white puddings, two fried eggs and two sausages made by the monks in Roscrea. The three of us eat quickly and in silence. We have plenty of leftovers to give to Rose the sheepdog. There's no sound of children's voices playing in the nearby fields. Like us, all of them are too full of food and they will rest for the remainder of the morning, then lie asleep on the ditch this afternoon and just snore.

Evening comes along. The fire crackles merrily. Grannie is washing the dishes. She puts them away on the press cupboard shelf. We say our prayers by the fire. She takes me by the hand and, moments later, tucks me into bed. As always, she brushes my cheek with her lips. 'There now, my fine young fellow,' she whispers, 'sleep well with the angels until the big yellow sun comes up again.'

I hear her boots tramping across the cement floor as she makes her way back to Jack. At the front table, with the light of her candle, she will continue reading her Messenger book with all its stories of the black children out in Africa. At the back table, next to the gramophone and the box of records, Jack will read the next few chapters of his cowboy novel. There'll be no music played this Sunday evening. It's a time for respectful silence, just the ticking of the clock on the press cupboard shelf.

Some Sunday evenings, Grannie takes out her post-office copybook and fills up half a dozen pages, writing a long-winded letter to my mother and giving her all the latest news. She writes fluently, her pen scratching. She writes about Bill's burnt bushes – about me and my work in the cabbage field and so on. She is a tremendous letters writer. 'As good as a solicitor,' says Jack.

It's difficult for her to know when to stop writing and give her pen a rest, so full of news is she. She usually ends her letter with these words: 'Well, Nell, I have scribbled enough for this evening.' Scribbled? She never scribbles but always takes great pains to write in a perfectly copper-plated script. For she knows that her letter will be travelling on a long journey – all the way to London and to Nell – to bring comfort to her daughter in these dark days of the war. She knows that Nell will read it to Patsy.

Then she will read it to the two Tipperary nuns who come calling to her basement flat for a slice of cake and tea every Sunday when the 11 o'clock Mass is finished.

It's a new week. Jack likes to get up early. Silently, he creeps out from the side of my warm body in the bed. He loves this precious time of the day when he has the world to himself and when not even Rusty our colourful cockerel has lifted his feathers from his roosting stick.

As much as Jack loves to take me out with him, this is one time when it's far too early for me to get up. There will be other times for the two of us to take our walks and for him to tell me his stories as we amble to Brindley's well or go off picking spuds for the dinner.

He takes a look out the back window. The sky is just beginning to lighten and the pale sunlight is breaking in over the trees surrounding the haggart. It will soon reach Sam's Grove in front of our house. He takes a mug of water from the bucket and closes the door behind him. There's still silence and an air of desolation round the yard. Not a soul but himself. Not even the singing wrens, who are still dreaming their little lives away. He wanders down the lane. Though there is no breeze, he notices the aspen trees shivering on the ditch across from Sam's Grove. They always shiver.

When we were going to the well last week, he told me a story about other aspen trees – ones in the garden of Gethsemane where Jesus was saying His last prayers. It was a long time ago and I'm not sure I'm old enough to have understood all that Jack told me. There are times when he forgets how young I am. However, he will repeat his wealth of stories several times in the coming years until I have taken each of them to heart.

While we were filling our buckets at the well, he told me how the aspen trees that surrounded Jesus in the garden bore witness to His anguish as He thought of his cruel death the next day and how they kept shivering like our own aspen trees in their efforts to support him during his sorrow.

89

This morning, he walks on past Brindley's stile and heads towards the Dolla River. Thick puffs of fog reach up the lane to meet him. He throws back his shoulders and steps spritely on till he comes to John's Gate. He expects to see his cows pushing against it, eager to be milked and their udders painfully fraught with milk after the long night. But they are nowhere to be seen.

He takes off his socks and wellingtons. He rolls his trousers halfway up his legs and walks across the Bull Paddock. His feet are soon drenched in the spay of the morning dew. Like his father before him, he always walks in his bare feet when it's early like this. The dew is a cure for any ache or pain in his feet. That's what his father told him.

He rambles over the Bull Paddock and edges his way through the bulrushes, then on towards the crab-apple tree in search of his cows. During the night, they must have wandered out the gap leading to the Danes' Hill. He once told me there's a crock of gold buried there. A family of leprechauns keeps watch over it. However, I'm beginning to know when he's lying.

He sees his cows at the far side of the Danes' Hill, strolling along the side of the ditch and eating the briars. Our young sheepdog, Rose, has hurried down the lane to catch up with him. But there's no need for her to help. Jack is already leading the cows out through the gap and meets his little dog halfway across the Bull Paddock.

The cows traipse out through John's Gate and up the lane. They lead him home when he should be leading them. They are eager to get milked and he has no need to hurry them on. Nor has Rose, who is padding along at his side. She looks up at him and wags her tail. The cows spray the lane with showers of their watery shite. Jack steps nimbly out of the way to avoid getting drenched with the spatters. So does Rose.

They reach Old Tim's lane behind Grannie's garden. It leads into our cow shed. Our stream runs across it. Anxious as they are to get milked, the cows stop to quench their thirst with gulps of the stream's cold water. It takes a while for them to drink enough of it. This gives Jack time to fill his pipe with tobacco and enjoy a few well-earned puffs of smoke for himself. There's nothing but the sound of him puffing on his pipe and the murmur of the stream and the slurping tongues of the cows. I am wide awake by now. I can hear the sound of the cows' hooves coming in along Old Tim's lane. One of them starts bawling as soon as she sees the cow shed inviting her to step inside and get milked.

It's time to get out of bed, for Grannie to light her fire and for me to wash my face in the enamel pan. We have lots of work to do this Monday morning. Grannie will be washing the clothes as usual. She will be busy as a gnat and I will help her wherever I can. I know what I have to do first of all: go with her to search for eggs where the two of us have recently heard a hen cackling. That's where we'll find the eggs.

I never seem to get a moment's rest. I will have a great deal of news to tell Jack when I set eyes on him later: how I didn't get scalded by any nettles on either my hands or legs, not even once, and how I saw Rusty the cockerel jumping onto a hen's back and how he started singing like blazes the minute he leapt down off of her. There are times when I am unable to stop spouting out my news, like Grannie with her long-winded letter writing.

Later on, when the bedsheets are aired and dried, I have a new task to come to grips with: learning how to 'draw a sheet'. That's what Grannie calls it when she tries to teach me how to do this complex job even though I am still quite young and in no way ready for performing it to her satisfaction.

'You're never too young to learn, Ned,' she says. She holds the corners of her end of the sheet in her fingertips. She shows me how to hold mine in a similar way by the two corners. I stay where I am while she draws her boots slowly backwards. Then, I draw my sandals backwards too, until the sheet is drawn out to its full length. She starts to edge her way slowly towards me until she can fold her half of the sheet onto my half. She repeats the gesture, fold after fold. Only then can she carry it indoors and lay it on the bed. From now on, this formidable task of drawing out a sheet is something I will get better at – like my other tasks.

91

The three of us have eaten our eggs and drank our mug of milk and the living room is a blaze of heat from Grannie's fire. It's time for the milking to begin. Milking time in the cow shed is the one time when Jack and Grannie are at one with each other, when both of them are settled down on their milking stools with their heads tucked into their cow's belly.

Jack walks out behind his mother and her walking stick and I walk out behind him in my sandals. I follow them through the pig house gap and out past the woodpile. We reach the stinking heap of dung outside the cow shed. To get past it, Jack hoists me up on his shoulders in case I slip and fall in the dung. From my perch on his shoulders, I see my own blue reflection in the watery dung and Jack's too, as well as that of the sun's smoky light.

Grannie put the fear of God in me a long time ago about this huge mass of dung. Like Jack, she calls it the Perilous Sink. I don't know what this means. But it seems as important as some of the lofty words that Father Speed the Plough uses at Mass. If ever I am tempted to go near this sink pool or to climb up on it (she says), I'll get sucked straight down through it and into the bottom of the earth and get myself drowned. 'Keep far away from the Perilous Sink, Ned!' That's what she says. She won't have to tell me a second time!

Later, Jack has to change the cows' bedding, at present a mixture of straw, ferns, cow dung and piss. He has to slop it out the doorway onto the dung heap with his shovel. He regularly replenishes the bedding with a few cartloads of ferns that he brings home from the wood, mixing it with fresh bundles of straw. During the first few days of this freshly tidied bedding, the cows are in their absolute heaven and none of them want to leave and go back to the Bull Paddock.

The two tiger-barred cats belonging to our neighbour, Gret, are always looking for adventure and searching for mice and rats. Jack doesn't mind them coming down the lane to visit us when it's milking time. Each day, he fills two old sardine tins with milk for them when he's halfway through his milking.

This day, I can hear the two cats happily purring inside the cow shed doorway as their bellies get filled with milk. One of them, however, walks with a limp. She once caught her foot in a rabbit trap. As soon as they've been attended to, they dance their feet nimbly round the wet spots of the sink pool, avoiding the thick mucky spots before chasing off down Old Tim's lane in search of a few stray magpies.

Last week, when Jack and I were reaching for our buckets and sweet-gallon to go fetch the water from the well, we saw an unusual sight outside the half-door: a row of rats lying on their backs, their white bellies turned up to the sun. Each one had a little pool of blood seeping from its throat. Gret's cats had killed them and dragged them up in front of our half-door, making a neat and tidy line of them. Perhaps it was their way of saying thank you to Jack for their daily sardine cans of milk.

Jack caught each rat's tail and threw all of them into the briars inside the ditch in Sam's Grove. He wouldn't mind a bit if Gret's cats repeated this exercise every day of the week, for rats are a terrible nuisance, especially in winter when they have the cheek to come into our yard up as far as the feeding tray and frighten the lives out of Grannie's hens and ducks and even her geese.

Now that the two wild cats have gone, I'm left standing inside the doorway of the cow shed. I've time to look around me and up at the wagtails' nests in the rafters. I watch the cows munching their hay from the trough in front of them. I listen to them coughing. Their breath quickly warms the cowshed as it pours out of their mouths like smoke and into the air.

Jack and Grannie continue to milk. Now and then, the cows look back at them, their eyes glistening in the duskiness of the cow shed. Jack milks the awkward cows – Grannie, the easier ones. He squirts milk towards me in the hope of landing it on my face like he did when he pelted worms at me while picking spuds. He laughs at my surprise. I cry out but in the presence of Grannie, I don't dare use the 'shite' word.

Jack is happy and he keeps up his singing. It's always at milking time that he sings his rebel songs. His favourite song is the *Old Fenian Gun*. He's a fine singer, though a bit too nasally, says Grannie.

I hear a sudden cry from her. Her cow has lashed its shitty tail against her jaw and made it red. She gets up off her stool, cursing her cow into hell. She belts it viciously across the back with her stool. She knows how to humble a cow. Then the milking continues as normal.

If Jack sings in order to make his cow give him more milk, perhaps Grannie's cruel punishment of her cow will make the cow's milk dry up altogether. It's a thought that crosses his mind. And yet he laughs to himself. For he admires the angry spirit of his mother, a woman of stern mettle and not to be meddled with, not even by her cow. The rest of the cows seem as surprised as I am at Grannie's sudden outburst. I turn my eyes up to the wagtails' nests but they have flown away.

My mood soon changes and I go back to watching the cows chewing their hay from the manger in front of them. Their eyes have a vacant and disinterested look about them. How different from the way they looked last springtime! How tender was the look in their eyes on those days when they gazed down at their newly-dropped calves! How gently did they lick the blood away from them! How pleasant it was for me to behold the new chestnut colour of a shiny calf when it had been cleaned by its mother!

The cows continue to nod their heads while the milk flows out of them. They swish their ropey tails from time to time – almost like a happy dog. I see that their tails are matted with shite and there are several midges round their gable end and many flies flitting round their udders, the smell of the milk enticing them to come in from the dung heap. A few ticks have clung to the cows' udders. Jack and Grannie pick them off and squash them before they are able to draw the cows' blood. One or two flies adorn the frothy surface of the milk bucket. When Jack and Grannie are finished milking, they will carry the buckets back into the yard and strain the flies away through the muslin cloth.

94

Last year, Jack and Grannie did not take me out to witness them milking. I was too young to withstand the dirt of the dung heap and I was left alone inside the house to keep warm by the fire and listen to the crackling of the logs on the fire. Sometimes, I was afraid of the wind rattling the doors or the rain spattering down the chimney.

I told neither Grannie nor Jack. But my britches were sometimes wet. I was a nervous child. Maybe the bombing of the Germans back in London had made me this way. Even the cawing of the crows or the flapping of their wings caused me to shiver when I least expected it. This morning, it's all a distant memory as I watch Jack's fag burning its way down to a stub while he's milking. The smoke from the fag wreathes its way in faint plumes across his face and makes him squint. It helps to banish the midges and flies from around the cow's udder.

Each day is new and this morning, when the buckets are full of this morning's milk, Jack hands me a mug – the one with the blue and gold hoops on it. I dip the mug into the warm milk in the bucket. I drink it down fast and pay no heed to one or two flies floating on top of the milk. Jack smiles when he sees the white moustache on my top lip. I acknowledge his happiness with a loud belch and he smiles even more. Peering round her cow's backside, Grannie sees the funny side of this. From now on, I will drink a mug of fresh, warm milk this way. At bedtime, I will drink more milk, this time from my mug with the words '*made in China*' written on the bottom of it. 'The milk will make you big and strong, Ned,' says Grannie.

Fiddler Joe, the husband of our good neighbour, Gret, was looking at his barn. He had plenty of turf stacked in there. It would last him at least till after the harvest, but not so his woodpile, which was now much depleted. He'd have to cut down a tree from the woods on the hills.

Farmers here in Dolla have always worked with their nearest neighbour. 'Help and be helped' men called it, be it at the haymaking or the thrashing of their oats – be it saving the turf or bringing it home from the bog out in Glown.

So, when Jack was called upon by Fiddler Joe, he took his bowsaw from on top of the pig house. He took his sharpened axe from behind the half-door. He forgot to take the long reins meant for pulling down the final branches of the tree once it was almost cut through. Grannie pelted it out the door after him and she gave him a dash of holy water so that himself and Fiddler Joe would have a successful day. With a full bottle of milk and a few thick cuts of soda bread smeared with jam – as well as two hot roasted spuds in his pocket – he headed up the lane to meet Fiddler Joe.

During the past week, the two of them have been out on the hills above Mucklin, looking after their rabbit snares. That was when they spotted a fine row of whitethorn trees – the best trees for lighting our fires. The two men were bent on sawing down one of them – possibly even a second one. It would be a great day's outing for them – a day that men like best of all – when they are far away from the rest of the world and deep in the wood's mysteries.

Fiddler Joe is the best singer round the lanes and there are many other fine singers nearby, each with their own unique style and with a rake of songs handed down to them from their forebears. His voice is not a bit nasally like Jack's and he is able to add the odd little tremor in a verse so as to do justice to his song.

Unlike other men, who tend to their rosary beads only when they are at Mass, he starts each morning the same way by saying a decade of the Rosary just as his mother did before him. He prays for the soul of his grandfather, who died in the river abroad in Glown. He prays for his saintly mother and father, both of whom died happily in their bed.

Jack and Fiddler Joe spend the rest of the morning and half the afternoon working with their bowsaw and axes. Fiddler Joe has a second pair of reins which he needs for shaking the branches and pulling at the tree when it's about to fall, so that it'll topple out of its roots. After they've finished sawing down the tree, that's when they'll get down to the serious task that they've come for: sawing the branches into suitable lengths for their axes to split into quarters. They will leave most of the tree's main trunk intact and come back in a day or two to saw it in half, one part for Jack and the other for Fiddler Joe, before carrying it home in Fiddler Joe's cart.

When Christmas arrives, Jack will drag his half of the trunk into the centre of our fireplace and leave it burning as a yule log throughout the twelve days of Christmas. Sawing the tree trunk in half will have been a hard enough job but dragging it into the middle of the fireplace will be back-breaking. Jack will need the help of Fiddler Joe and his two older sons, Dan and Shawnee. They are both big strapping fellows.

It's half-past ten. The cows have munched their way through all the hay in their manger and, with Jack away sawing timber with Fiddler Joe, Grannie has removed the chains from their necks. She and I have already supped our tea, eaten our boiled eggs and drank down our mug of milk. Grannie is armed with her stick and I am ready to go with her and take the cows down to the Bull Paddock and as far as the Danes' Hill.

It's a special day for me, as today is the first time that I'm going with her on a long journey – three times further than my previous trips with Jack to Brindley's well or across the fields with Grannie for the cabbages. I can't tell her how much I am looking forward to it as I haven't the appropriate words yet.

With her help and for speed's sake, I quickly put on my socks and sandals. I have my own little stick (like Grannie), ready to prod any cow that might be walking too slowly. I feel ready to act the part of a real farmer like Jack today.

Grannie puts a few more logs on the fire. I wonder what time Jack will be back from the woodcutting with Fiddler Joe. She closes the front door and puts the key under the geranium box. She holds my hand as we go to fetch the cows from the cowshed, carefully ensuring that I do not get my sandals wet when we are tiptoeing past the Perilous Sink. We tiptoe just like Gret's wild cats do, winding our way in and out like them. I have watched them doing it before.

The cows need no advice from Grannie as to what they should do next. Nor do they need to feel the strength of my prodding stick. They don't even stop for a drink at the stream but lead Grannie and myself down past Brindley's stile.

Grannie has changed her bib, casting off the dirty one that she was wearing while she was milking. She doesn't want to be seen by anyone when she is dressed shabbily like that. This bib is a bit different from the old one. It has a pink rim round the edge and it has two large pockets. She tests the depths of these with her fists. She parades proudly on behind her cows with me until we reach John's Gate. The cows look in eagerly at the long grass waiting for them inside the Bull Paddock.

Grannie stretches her finger upwards onto the string crossover rope that hangs round the gatepost and we follow the cows in. She peers round, looking for a few mushrooms for Jack but finds none. Apart from a rabbit, her son's favourite meal is a few trout from the Dolla River, coupled with a handful of mushrooms. Maybe she'll take a second look before we get back to the gate.

There are two trees in the Bull Paddock. There's an old oak tree in the centre of the field and a tall pine tree just outside the edge of the wood next to a rabbit run used by carefree young rabbits, who like to come out in the evening when it's safe and they can eat as much as they like and run around the field to their hearts' content. Poor dears! They don't know that the rabbit run is where Jack will place his snares, having recently seen their droppings.

Grannie stops beneath the shadow of the pine tree. The ground is full of fir cones.

'How many horses have we, Ned?' she whispers.

'We have our mare, Moll, and sometimes Fatty Matty's Fandango when we are ploughing,' I reply.

She gathers two of the best fir cones she can find and puts them in her bib pocket. 'These will make fine horses when we make you a berry farm,' she says and I'm left wondering what a berry farm is. I've never seen one before.

We reach the crab-apple tree. It's a tree that Gret's children love to raid when they're coming from school. They take home loads of crab apples to roast in their mother's fire. The cows love them too.

'How many cows have we, Ned?'

'Six,' I reply.

Once again, she selects the better crab apples and puts them in her pocket alongside the acorns.

We stroll over to the rose-hip bush. 'How many calves have we, tell me?' she asks.

'Four,' I reply.

She collects four ruddy rose hips from the wild rose-bush and puts them into her bib pocket too.

We head on towards the gap leading to the Danes' Hill. The cows move past it and on towards Bill Corcoran's ditch. We leave them there and they get busy with the tasty briars.

On our way back towards the lane, we reach the oak tree where Grannie has another question. By now, I am beginning to tire of all her questioning.

'How many asses have we, Ned?'

'You know very well,' I say. My voice is no more than a sigh. 'Just our ass, Lightning.'

She takes a handful of acorns and selects the biggest one – the one that is rounder and with a greener cap than the others. Lightning would be pleased with its shiny covering – that's if he could talk to it or if it could talk to him.

By now, the sun has come to life and is gleaming high in the sky, which is blue as far as our eyes can see. The grass has no dew left on it and my sandals are dry.

Outside the gate, there's a bush on Old Pat's ditch. I don't know the name of it. Grannie chooses a dozen small white berries from it and puts them in her second pocket – gently, because they can easily burst.

'These will make fine geese for your farm,' she says, 'and I know where we can find other berries that'll make red hens for the farm: from the hawthorn tree next to the hen house. It has a load of berries on it and if we don't collect some of them today, the rats will gobble them up when winter comes on.' I can't help thinking of our ducks. We haven't any berries for them yet. Perhaps we will later on.

We walk up the lane and arrive at the flagstones. We head into the haggart where there are several trees under which Grannie has decided to place my new berry farm. The grass is dark under there and the earth is soft. She points to the far corner. 'This is the spot where Jack used to play with his berry farm when he was a child like you. Come, Ned, let's go and collect some twigs.'

I like doing jobs that please her and, at once, I run round the haggart, picking up the twigs which the wind has knocked down. By now, I'm beginning to guess what a berry farm might look like and I'm glad that Grannie is helping me make one – especially since Jack once had one. She will show me what to do with my collection of berries as soon as we've arranged the twigs to form the ditches.

I am now getting on for three years of age. Up till now, it was natural for me to follow the lead of my two guardians. Grannie knows that I have finally reached an age when I'm able to make a few choices of my own as to how I want to spend my time rather than follow her round like a lost lamb.

Once my berry farm is complete, I can choose to play with my horses (Moll and Fandango) or I can choose to play with my calves, whichever of my berry animals I want to play with. Not only am I the right age to start making these choices, but (in Grannie's eyes) it is time for a child my age to spend an hour or two in child's play – just like Gret's children, who always seem to spend a great deal of time out playing. I know this is true, for I hear their merry laughter at all hours of the day.

One of the few things I've been engaged in so far has been my attempt to build a house of cards with Jack. But, whereas he built his house – what he called a castle – as high as three storeys, I have never managed to make anything other than a miserly little tent of two cards. However, I have recently learnt to put a flat card on top of them to form a bridge.

This needed a lot of patience and has often been my pastime while Jack and Grannie are busy reading their books of an evening. 'Well done, Ned,' Jack says as he runs to the bucket for yet another mug of water, ruffling my hair on the way like Grannie does.

Grannie and I are so busy that we haven't stopped to look for a single egg – precious though they are. She has forgotten that she's wearing her best bib and we sit down on the soft earth beneath the haggart trees. It's a deep shady spot and never spattered with rain or bothered with the wind. I realise I'm going to be completely hidden from the rest of the world whenever I'm in here – just me and my berry farm of animals. It'll become my own small universe.

Grannie and I hunt round the haggart for suitably small twigs. 'Find ones that are the same length as the twigs the crows use when they're building their nests,' she says. She is much quicker on her feet than I am and far more discerning than me. She has been collecting twigs all her life to build her fires.

At last, we have enough twigs. She helps me lay them out and turn them into ditches around a number of square fields. Each field has a gap in the side of its ditch so that I can make my berries parade from one field to the next. The branches of the trees seem to watch over us from above, just me and Grannie in this quiet corner of the world. It is dark in here and the blue of the sky is nowhere to be seen.

We finish making our twig ditches and admire the new fields we've been making. There's no sound, neither the cackling of the hens nor the quacking of the ducks, neither the braying of Lightning nor the snorting of the pigs. All we are thinking of is my new farm and what we can do to make our berry animals feel comfortable once we've sorted them into groups.

The hens and the ducks know we are busy in our hideaway. They don't come in to disturb us but stay at the far end of the haggart, sitting on the dung heap, staring at us. The ducks have their heads buried under their wings as if asleep. The breeze from beyond Corcoran's well has turned stronger. It's fierce enough to tumble over ducks and hens alike if they don't look out.

At last, our berry farm is ready for use. The ditches are all in place and the fields are covered with laurel leaves for grass. But my farm is still empty.

Grannie removes all the berries from her bib pockets. 'Choose, Ned,' she says.

It's a strange and new experience, asking me to choose which berry animals I'd like to place in each field. I choose one of the fir cones. I am fascinated by its size and by its roundness and its chain-mail covering. I turn it around in my fingers. It's bigger than the other berries and only a fir cone can be used to represent our mare, Moll. I place it in the centre of the nearest field.

Something is missing. Perhaps Moll is pining for Fandango, her ploughing companion. I pick out another fir cone and place it next to her. This one is Fandango. He'll be just the right company for Moll and they will be happy together. I stand back and take a look at my first bit of handiwork. My two horses look cosy and content, standing side by side in their new field. If I try hard enough, I can almost hear them talking to one another.

Grannie is a wise woman and she knows when to disappear. She tiptoes away and leaves me alone to play with my berry animals. It's time for her to tend to her fire. It's my first time playing on my own and a moment of uncertainty fills me. I can feel the coldness of the morning. I can hear the voice of the wind. I huddle down on my knees to get a better view of my new fields. I select more groups of berries, this time the little white berries, the nameless ones, for my geese. I place them in the second of my twig fields. I select several red haw berries for my hens. I bounce them along through one of the gaps and position them in the third field. From now on, my berries are my private treasure, with only the waving branches of the trees above to keep me company.

Jack will give me his old shoebox from the bottom of the press cupboard. It has a lid on it. I will keep my berries tucked inside it once I have played with them.

Now that Grannie has disappeared, I go round the haggart on my own and find more twigs. I add a few more fields to my farm until I have eight fields in all. There will be a lot of choosing for me to do from now on.

Finally, all my farm animals are positioned inside the twig ditches of the farm: the ducks, the hens, the geese, the two pigs, the horses, the ass, the cows. I stand up and inspect my morning's labour. Grannie has not seen the result of my choosing, though she was the one who selected which berries to pick for my farm. Perhaps these are the very same sort of berries that Jack played with when he was as young as I am.

Now that I've finished my work, I will go and get Jack's shoebox and put the berries away – field by field. I will treat them carefully, the way Grannie and Jack treat their animals. I will go back into our house and give my farm and its animals a bit of peace, ready for the next time I come to visit them. I might even put the pigs in the field next to Lightning instead of in their present field. I have so many choices to make from now on.

Another Saturday morning and it's time for a few of Gret's children to make one of their Saturday visits to Grannie. It's Sweeney and Bucko as usual. But this time, they are accompanied by their little sisters, Rosie and Daisy. Their ages from top to bottom range from Sweeney (10) to Bucko (8), then Rosie (6) and Daisy (5). The two bigger brothers (Dan and Shawnee) are far too old to be seen wasting time on a visit such as this one.

As soon as they've finished doing Grannie's jobs, the four children will get some of her humbug sweets. They can't spend too long with her, as she has to help Jack milking the cows when he brings them back from the Bull Paddock.

While Gret's children are busy, I'll have a chance to slope off to my berry farm and play with my animals. Meanwhile, I am still in bed, rubbing the sleep from my eyes and scarcely awake from my dreams.

'What news have ye brought me today?' says Grannie, reverting to her old Irish way of saying 'ye' instead of 'you.'

Sweeney offers her his latest news. 'The war in England is going better by the day,' says he. 'Mother got a letter yesterday from her sister, Bridie, and she says it's true. The Germans are getting more than they wished for.'

This is great news, thinks Grannie. It's high time they got a taste of their own medicine. And yet, this news is also sad to hear. She knows that when the war comes to an end, I will have to take my suitcase back to England, back to Nell and Patsy. This thought makes her shudder all over again. She dreads to think what her life will be like, and for Jack, after my departure. But, most of all, she can't imagine what life would be like for a small child like me, who has never known any kind of parent other than herself and Jack. She gives herself a good shake and forces her mind onto other things.

The children get busy with her chores: sweeping the yard, cleaning out the dung from the hen house and arranging new straw bedding on Moll's and Lightning's carts. She disappears into her bedroom and rummages round in the drawer of her altar table to search for her humbug sweets. She picks out a handful and returns to the eager children. With a few mumbled words of thanks, they skedaddle across the stream and head for Sam's Grove. They sit on the fallen tree trunk and a delightful few moments of silence follow as they savour their sweets. They have never seen other children chewing sweets and that makes them enjoy them all the more, even though their mother will not be pleased at them taking sweets from Grannie in case they rot their teeth.

They'd be far better off breaking open a few hazelnuts. All they've ever been used to up until now, at least her older children, are the few raw turnips that they steal from farmers on their 3-mile trek to school each day.

Jack is heading down to Happy Grove to visit Tom Maher, the hurley stick maker, and have a word also with his brother, Jim, the carpenter. The three of them will make themselves scarce for an hour or two this morning. They are going on a trip to the slopes beyond Mucklin, just behind Molly Hughes's place at the bend of the river to saw down an ash tree.

Though Mucklin is the kingdom of all the rabbits (as Jack never get tired of telling me), there won't be a single rabbit in sight today. They'll be scared to death of the three men with their noisy axes and will hide in their burrows.

This ash tree is the tree Jack spotted when he and Fiddler Joe were sawing down their whitethorn tree a few days back. Some ash trees (like this one) have just the right shape to them, with a curved half-hoop at the base of the trunk. It'll make a fine hurley for any child and Jack knows who the lucky chap is who'll be having his own brand new hurley – me, Grannie's little man.

Tom will cut the hurley into shape and plane it down in his workshop. He will smooth it to a perfect finish and coat it with a few drops of paraffin. His brother, Jim, will put two metal hoops across the boss of it – the same way some of Tipperary's fine hurlers do in the belief that their hooped hurley will puck the ball even further up the field.

Jack will give Tom and Jim a sack of his best spuds (the Kerr's Pinks) in exchange for my new hurley. As soon as he gets the hurley, he will wrap it in tissue-paper and hide it on the ledge next to the hob behind the goose wings that Grannie uses for dusting. It will stay there till the day comes (ah, the thought!) for me to head over the sea to my new world – far away from all that I've known and loved here in Dolla.

Though Tom Maher is renowned for his skill in making hurleys, his brother, Jim, is no slouch either when it comes to woodwork. Inside his barn, he keeps lots of odds and ends and among this untidy mess is the old Victorian pram in which Tom and he spent their babyhood days. Their mother, Peg, was often seen wheeling the two of them down to Gerry's shop, her shopping bag resting in Jim's lap.

Jim has an idea. Not even Tom is aware of it. He scouts round the barn till he finds what he's looking for: the wheels and the undercarriage of his old pram. Over the years, both of them have come away from the pram's frame and are lying forlorn under a heap of turf in the corner of the barn.

Jim also knows that when this war ends, I'll be going back to my parents in London. Thanks to Tom, my new hurley will be strapped to the side of my suitcase – something to keep me company on the journey across the sea. It will remind me of the good times spent with Grannie and Jack and with Rose the sheepdog and all the animals on the farm.

But what about today, thinks Jim? Why keep dreaming about the end of the war or about the day when I might have to go away? It's today that truly matters. A child needs a toy to play with. When he saw his brother, Tom, making me my hurley, he made up his mind to make me a penny go-cart.

It'll not be my first toy. Grannie made me a sock-ball last year. She made it out of Jack's old socks and half a dozen bottle corks from Gerry's pub. She rolled the socks into a ball and made the whole thing tight and firm. I remember how I bounced it round the yard as she looked on. She had to laugh. It was just like the times she and her brothers and sisters once played with their own sock-balls.

Me and my sock-ball frightened the ducks and the hens for a day or two and we gave the gander something else to set his mind to instead of his constant battles with the pig. For days on end, I played with it while Grannie and Jack were in the cow shed milking. In the end, I grew tired of bouncing it round the yard. I ran round to the back of the house where the wall of the house was only 5 foot-high and threw it up against the thatch and tried to catch it when it bounced back to me.

This went on for a week or two until the day came when I threw it too high and it landed on the thatch and wouldn't come down. I stood and stared, only to see it eventually roll slowly down and land in my arms. This was a moment of pure joy and I threw it up a second time. This time, it remained lodged in a hollow of the thatch, refusing to roll down like last time. My joy had turned to despair. I thought it would stay buried in the thatch forever. It

106

would have done, if Jack and his fishing rod hadn't come to my rescue and brought my precious plaything down safely.

This year, much has changed and especially during the milking hour, I spend a good deal of time with my playing cards and my attempts to erect a second storey to my building. I also find myself spending more and more time with my berry farm animals. I even have the odd conversation with some of the berries when I find them in the wrong field. That's when I let myself get cross like Grannie does when her cow hits her on the jaw with its shitty tail and I raise my voice at them for straying away from the other animals.

Jim Maher knows nothing about these variations to my day. He gets busy, planning his design for my penny go-cart. It doesn't take him long. He cleans the wheels of the pram in no time at all, removing the bits of dirty turf from them. He gives them a furious polishing to make them shine. Finally, he brings out the tin of axle grease that he uses on his cartwheels the days he's driving to the bog for turf. He makes sure the axle and wheels are firmly fixed together before sawing the go-cart's frame. He gives the wheels a spin to make sure they won't screech when the go-cart is pulled along.

Now comes the easy part of the job. He selects a number of old floor boards that are lying up against the side of the turf. He saws them into equal lengths, each 2 foot long and 6 inches wide. He nails three of the boards together so that they make a bottom for the go-cart. He nails two more boards together to make one side. He does the same with the other sides. Now he is ready to nail the four sides together and assemble the go-cart completely.

He finds a tin of blue paint left over from the day Tom and he painted the gates leading into their yard. He finds some red paint left over from the time when he dipped some horseshoes into the tin the way Shy Denis does when stamping them round the base of the wall outside his barn. He spends the rest of the morning painting the floor and sides of the go-cart – the outside walls blue and the inside walls red, the floor, a mixture of red and blue. It's sure to have a splendid effect.

Tom comes into the barn to see Jim at his work. He casts his eyes over the finished go-cart. 'Magical!' says he. Tom is a man of few words at the best of times.

Jim cuts off a length of rope from his roll of fencing twine and makes a delicate pulley with a handle for me to put my hand through and drag my go-cart along on my travels each day. He imagines me taking it along the yard and out into the haggart. I might even drag it out into the Blue Button Field to amuse Jack's calves, or down the lane when I'm strolling with Jack to bring back water from Brindley's well. As with my berry farm, the choices I will make will be endless. And Jim is a happy man when he puts his paint tins away.

Nothing of this is known to me until the following week when Jack and myself are taking back the cows after milking. There, in front of us, whom should we meet standing at John's Gate but Jim himself. He is carrying a potato-sack on his back. There is something bulky inside it. What could it be? Might it be a stray wildcat?

When Jim is ready, he catches me by the shoulders and looks me in the eye. 'Close your eyes, Ned, and keep them shut tight till I tell you to open them.' He smiles at Jack.

I keep my eyes shut tight but my heart is bumping with excitement. I can hear him fidgeting with the mouth of the sack. I know I'm in for a surprise. I can feel it.

Jim opens the sack, still winking at Jack. He takes out the newly painted penny go-cart. He spins the wheels with his thumb to make sure they spin noiselessly. He checks the rope in case it might break away from the cart if pulled too severely.

'You can open your eyes now, Ned,' says he.

To this day, I can see the three of us – Jack, Jim and myself – standing solemnly outside John's Gate and the restless cows waiting patiently for Jack to open the gate and take them up the lane to be milked.

108

END OF PART TWO

MORNING

Between 1942 and 1943

I will be getting on for four next spring. But that's a long way off. I am still only three and not too old or too young to be seen strolling around with the go-cart that Jim Maher made for me, or to do the very opposite: sit on Grannie's straw bag that lies idle on the cart, the one that she sits on when she is driving her ass and cart to Gerry's shop. Both moments – me and my go-cart – me and my growing thoughts whilst sitting on the bag on the ass's cart – are precious times.

It also gives Jack and Grannie a bit of peace and quiet from me always following one of them: either Grannie when she's feeding her hens or looking for eggs, or else strolling with Jack down to Brindley's well for the day's water.

This week, the centre of my attention is my go-cart. We are old friends by now and seem to be tied together as though we were twins. I stroll with my new toy amongst the ducks and the hens. They are no longer afraid of this strange contraption. Some of them even follow behind the two of us to see where we are leading them, the same way they follow Grannie when she comes out to greet them and feed them with her bucket of mash.

I am braver these days than I once was. I'm a bit more adventurous too. I take my go-cart out to the Blue Button Field and pull it along on a lengthy walk down as far as the Rotten Tree.

My collection of berries is still fast asleep in my new farm. Not a stir out of any of them, not even from the fir cones.

I hasten back to the haggart and, one-by-one, I carefully take them out and place them in my go-cart. It's a hefty load from the two fir cones (Moll and Fandango) down to the family of haw berries (Grannie's hens).

I return to the field with my berry load of farm animals. It's time I gave them a proper outing away from their twig-fields under the tree. I parade them up as far as the gate leading to the second field. I am tempted to take them even further – out as far as the field of cabbages and spuds – but I am afraid of getting lost. I am not yet that brave as to think I no longer need to run back to the protection of Grannie's skirts if I have to.

111

The regularity of each day, the security of knowing where I am going with my new go-cart, is sometimes replaced not only with my time spent sitting on Grannie's straw bag on the ass's cart but in wandering off on my own without a single thought about my new go-cart or my berries.

I stand on the flagstones and look up and down the lane, the place Jack calls the Open Road. But I don't wander any further and for good reason. From my earliest days, Grannie has worried the life out of me with her tales of a monstrous ogre lurking inside the ditch in Sam's Grove and of a wicked witch inside the ditch above Old Tim's lane. I am smart enough to heed the tone of her voice and to obey her warnings.

Today is Wednesday. Grannie has taken some duck eggs up the lane to Gret. She'll be back in an hour after their long exchange of news – mostly about the war and the Germans. She'll bring back a pile of cooking apples in her shopping bag and make Jack and me a big apple tart with cloves in it for our Sunday pudding.

Now is the moment for me to do something I don't usually do. I don't even hesitate. I creep into the Big Cave room where I sleep with Jack. I know where I'm going this morning: to Old Harpy, the dusty piano. A new bag of icing sugar is inside its lid. I saw Grannie hiding it there yesterday after she drove home from Gerry's shop.

I take out a handful of icing sugar and stuff it into the pockets of my britches. Grannie thought she had successfully hidden it by covering it with a tea towel inside the lid. She will never think I had the nerve to steal some of it. This is the second time.

It seems my recent amusement of throwing my sock-ball up onto the thatch and trying to catch it as it rolled down – and my rambles with my go-cart and its berry farm animals – has turned me into a young adventurer, a child looking for something new to occupy my growing mind each day, even paying Old Harpy a visit.

With my icing sugar tucked safely away in my pockets, I skedaddle out the yard and in among the haggart dock leaves, scattering Rusty the cockerel and his flock of hens. I climb over the stick where Jack feeds his calves each morning and run into the Blue Button Field. I have the place to myself. I am giving my sandals a right good airing today, racing all over the field. The calves join in the fun. They race down towards the Rotten Tree and look back at me.

I hear Grannie's big boots in the distance as she strides back home from Gret's place. She stamps into the yard, leaning on her stick, her back stooped lower than ever. She never complains but Jack says she has the sciatica in her back. I don't know what he means.

'Where is that young limb of mischief?' laughs Grannie, throwing her arms in the air. 'What's he up to now?' These days, she is used to me wandering off on my own.

Meanwhile, I continue running after the calves. I scatter a family of rooks looking for worms under the heaps of dried cow dung. They storm away angrily over the ditch. I have frightened them. What a brave little man I am!

I see a few feathers nearby and I start to search round the field to see if there are more of them to collect. I'll see how many I can muster. I will also pick a bunch of wildflowers – the tall ragwort and the yellow dandelions. Flowers and feathers. I will give them to Grannie as a present. They will make up for my bad behaviour in stealing the icing sugar from under the lid of Old Harpy. But I am getting tired. My legs are not used to such stringent racing round my extensive new world.

Within the next few weeks, I make journeys with my go-cart all around the Blue Button Field and across the field with the cabbages and spuds. I get to know each of the new ditches and hedgerows. I learn to avoid the thorny briars even though I see new and exciting things among them like the thrush's nest in the briars by Bill Corcoran's gate. When Grannie and Jack come next to pick spuds and cabbages, I will show them this nest. Maybe there are baby eggs in it.

I trudge back to the haggart. The ducks are waddling proudly back from there and into the yard. They have heard Grannie calling them with her bucket of mash. The hens are already in the yard, lined up round the galvanised sheeting under the cart. Once more, they have to be quick in reaching the mash in case the ducks beat them to it and gobble it all up before they get a chance to dip their own beaks into it. Grannie's hens are scared of the selfish ducks. I have watched the way the bigger ducks scatter them. I chase after them and they fly out over the cart. The ducks are stronger than the hens. I am stronger than the ducks.

Well fed, Rusty and his family of hens return to the haggart and lie down on the dung heap. He keeps a watchful eye on each of them. He is always on guard in case Mr Fox or Mr Weasel come calling. He is the hens' best friend and they know it.

The dung heap catches my eye. It shimmers with the sunlight, as do the hens' feathers, especially Rusty's tail feathers. He is a proper dazzler. It seems as though the whole farmyard is asleep after their fine feed of mash. The place is silent as the grave. Grannie has fed her fowl far too well.

The silence is soon broken. One little hen, young Speckles, gets up and shakes the dust from her feathers. She lays down again. Rusty moves around her. He makes a clucking noise, serenading her, and Speckles gets up, almost indifferently. She supports him on her wings for a second or two. Afterwards, our fine cockerel starts crowing loudly. Can no one get a bit of peace and quiet this morning?

Speckles lies down again. Rusty continues to crow. All the other cockerels around the lane answer him back. What an infernal racket!

Today is Thursday and the sun never seems to stop shining. I'm sitting on the flagstones over the stream. It's like a little bridge and I like listening to the murmuring water beneath it.

The flagstones are hot, almost too hot on the seat of my britches. The bridge is not nearly as big as the metal bridge across the Dolla River. I watch a dozen flies dancing over the water. They show no sign of flying away.

Yes, I am a child often alone these mornings, just me and my thoughts. I am unable to express myself in words. I'm looking forward to being four.

Way over yonder on the back streets of London, there are other children the same age as me. They are suffering the cruel highlights of this wretched war with the Germans. Aren't I the lucky child to be sitting here aimlessly on the flagstones with the sunlight on my back and the flies dancing over the stream?

There's so much to take in: the gurgling stream, the brilliant flowers in Grannie's box-trimmed garden, the shadows of the rooks as they fly above me on their journey from Sam's Grove to Bill Corcoran's cornfield, the newborn chicks who cheep out their infant cries of alarm and run back under the soft belly of their mother, the Little Red Hen.

I have had my dinner – the usual big feed of spuds mixed with butter, milk and onions accompanied by my mug of milk.

Grannie is busy writing yet another one of her long letters (it's the second one this week) to my mother, Nell, in Paddington, telling her of the recent changes in me and my behaviour. She's a wise old lady and she knows about the icing sugar that I stole from inside the piano lid, but she says nothing. She tells my mother how much I am enjoying this newfound freedom with my go-cart and the adventures I'm having with it. She tells her about my growing confidence now that I'm no longer a frail toddler.

It's still Thursday and it's the afternoon. I have returned to my favourite space: the Blue Button Field. Once more, I watch Jack's calves racing each other from Old Tim's ditch down to the Rotten Tree. It seems to be their favourite pastime.

Last week, Jack taught me how to bend down and touch the ground with my fingers and tell him what I could see when I looked back underneath my legs. It almost threw me off balance.

'What can you see, Ned?' says he.

'I can see beyond the Rotten Tree.'

I could see the hills in the distance. I could see the clouds floating over the hills. I could see the blue sky. But I could tell him none of this for I hadn't the words yet.

Next day, Jack tried to teach me how to roll over in a somersault but, just as when I tried to build a house with his playing cards, it was far too difficult for me and I gave up trying.

Jack can somersault. I have watched him doing it. I wonder what Matt Burke on his way to the forge thought of him and his play-acting. I wonder if the other farmers can somersault like Jack. I wonder if Father Speed the Plough can somersault.

There are so many thistles in the Blue Button Field. Lightning would love them if he were here and not below in the Bull Paddock. Some of them are almost as tall as me. I try to count them. I am well able to count these days. It's many months since Grannie was teaching me how to count the few eggs in her morning's search and when Jack was helping me count the logs. I have long been able to count up to 100 and will soon be counting as far as 1000. But I know I will never see a thousand eggs or a thousand logs.

I begin counting the thistles. There are so many of them that I soon get confused. I can't count all of them. I have to start again. Many of them have a blue and purple flower on top of their head. It's the colour that has given the field its name, for these round flowers are like blue buttons.

I am beginning to lose patience with myself. I race my sandals in through the long grass to show the bewildered calves what I can do. I knock off the heads of a few blue button thistles with a small stick to show them what else I can do. There are many other wild flowers at the lower end of the field. I dip my nose into some of them to catch their smell. They have no smell. I would like to make a new bunch out of them for Grannie as a present but I have given her a present already this week out of feathers and the ragwort and dandelion flowers.

The goose and the gander have ambled back from the gate that leads to the second field. The gate has a row of potato sacks nailed across it to stop them straying out there and getting themselves lost.

They are leading their goslings in a straight line down the field. The goslings are bigger now and, just like me, are no longer babies. It is their first big adventure, all the way from the hen house, out through the haggart, on through the Blue Button Field and as far as the potato sacks on the gate.

They pass by me on their way to the haggart. They march back into the yard where the ducks waddle away from them contemptuously. For the ducks have far more colours on their bodies – especially the drakes – than the plain white colour of the geese. However, they are not nearly as lovely as the goslings.

I spot two white butterflies. They are very close together as they dance amid the wildflowers. I cannot tell which butterfly is following which one. They dance on and on and never separate. They have landed on a tall-stemmed buttercup. The buttercup bends down its head towards them. It sparkles in the sunlight.

It is now the evening. It's been an eventful day in an eventful week. It's time for me to say my prayers. It will soon be time for me to throw off my britches and get into bed. The logs are still blazing away on the fire. The face of Jesus in the Sacred Heart picture looks down on the three of us. There are no shutters on our front window. A huge moon looks in at us from above the black trees in Sam's Grove. It is surrounded by a million creamy stars. It is a great mystery to me how it manages to stay up there and never falls down.

When Grannie's husband, Will, died in '28, Jack decided that his duty lay with his widowed mother, my grannie. After all, he was the oldest of the fifteen children and wanted to help her run the little farm rather than run away to Australia with his intended bride, the lovely Moira Slattery.

After that, he and Grannie worked tirelessly to make a success out of the land. That's when some of the neighbours started giving them the name of the *Old Pair*. There were twenty three years in age between them both, yet their everyday presence with one another bound them closer and closer together as the years passed by and the name of *Old Pair* grew to be more acceptable and was used with a smile, especially by the women.

In other households, there might be as many as a dozen children. If a woman had less than three or four to her name, then the merry drinkers in Gerry's pub could be heard whispering unkindly about her husband's supposed lack of bodily equipment. 'There must be something wrong with Mikey and his private machinery,' they'd snigger.

Cruel though these jibes were, in the days after my arrival, a much kinder side to the sniggerers was seen. They could see the unique situation with Grannie, Jack and myself. Was there ever so rare a family as ours? No one else had only one child and neighbours began to talk about the little child from England who escaped from the German Blitz to come and live here instead. It seemed like a fairytale – one with a happy ending – and they kept their affectionate eyes on the three of us from the moment I arrived in Dolla.

Unlike other children in nearby households, I know I have no brothers or sisters to keep me company. Passersby see me strolling aimlessly round the yard. They take note of my unusual position and that of my guardians.

Long before I could walk, Jack was in the habit of parading me up and down the lane on his shoulders. You'd think he had nothing better to do with his life when he'd stop to chat with a neighbour like Mrs Fidget as she drove her ass and cart home after shopping in town. How proud he was to have this chance of showing her his little nephew from over the sea!

As the first two years fled by, I found I had oceans of time to look around me whilst in the yard: listen to the call of the birds, watch the changing scenery or cast my eye over the behaviour of Grannie's farm animals, like the battles that went on every day between the pig and the gander. But time creeps up on a child and it has grown natural for me to develop a number of other interests: my go-cart, my berry farm and my sock-ball.

More than that, I have grown used to hearing the voices of other children further up the lane and while the three of us are sitting by the fire in the evening, I start asking Grannie about them. I'm intrigued by their shouting and merrymaking. It goes on from

Saturday till Sunday afternoon and again during their holidays from school. I can't help wondering what they are up to, what's making them as happy as they are.

These thoughts don't occupy me all the time and most mornings, Jack and myself continue our strolls to the well and further afield to John's Gate to fetch back the cows. Jack places my feet on the middle bar of the gate and grips my hands around the top bar. I am safe and secure when he is standing behind me. He points out all that lies before me, like the mad hare bounding along through the bulrushes or the several rabbits (more counting to be done) at the edge of the wood. He guides my eyes to their hind legs and the way they stretch them back before getting down to the serious matter of nibbling the juicy grass.

'Look up! Look up, Ned!' he cries. And I see a crowd of black rooks swooping their way through the oak tree's branches before soaring high into the topmost greenery of the nearby pine tree.

Each day is different with Jack and with Grannie, too. She increasingly spends time helping me to memorise the prayers her mother taught her. Their meaning is far beyond my understanding but I soon learn half a dozen prayers, some of which are very long-winded.

Other mornings, she spends time reading to me one of several stories from her past children's school books. I feel the warmth of the fire, the music of her voice and the charm of the stories. I am still unable to read but Grannie directs my eyes to the glossy pictures which explain much of the story. The temptation to understand the words is getting stronger by the day.

Today is Friday. It's morning and I'm sitting on the flagstones again. The weather is very warm. The big yellow sun has already risen high in the sky and the cold chill of the earlier morning has gone away.

Jack has brought back a pocketful of coloured stones from the Dolla River. He was down there this morning, spying on the trout and planning a fishing raid on them soon. He tips out his pocketful of stones onto the edge of the flagstones. There are sandy-coloured ones – purple, brown, pink, yellow and lavender. He has chosen them carefully. There are even one or two chalky white ones and a jet black one.

As soon as his morning's work is done, he kneels down beside me and starts to make shapes with one of the sharp stones. He draws his lines straight and patiently. He draws a square. It is rusty-coloured. On top of it, he draws a roof to what looks like a house. He picks out a lavender stone and adds a chimney to the roof. He colours the inside of the lavender roof with the rusty stone. He proceeds to draw two windows and a doorway with the black stone. He fills in the rusty square with the lavender stone. I have never before seen such a colourful house as this.

'I know a young chap who lives here,' he adds. He points to his drawing and smiles at me. I know he means me and, if he had more time to spare, he would probably make up a story round my new house. For his house is more real than his house of playing cards.

He gets up off of his knees. 'That's enough for today,' he says. 'Tomorrow, or maybe next week, the two of us will draw on the other flagstones if the weather holds tough and I will hold onto your fingers and guide you as you draw.'

A few passers-by, young lads from further up the hill, stop and stare at us. They are shy fellows – almost afraid of life itself and especially of adults. They edge towards the flagstones and look down at Jack's house of many colours. They say nothing but perhaps they will find some stones from the river and make a coloured house of river-stones for themselves.

Each morning, my uncle brings back more stones. One day, I hope to draw a house of many colours by myself without Jack holding onto my fingers. But that won't be soon.

It rained last night. Jack's drawings on the flagstones have vanished along with the rain. The sun is out now. Grannie is busy in her garden. This time, she is getting rid of the weeds. With her little trowel, she has turned over the soil in a good few places. A few worms raise their heads. A blackbird sits on top of the bushes across from the stream, watching. So does a little robin. The worms might be in for a short life.

I have just drunk a mug of warm milk fresh from the cow. Jack has given me a thick slice of soda bread, well buttered the way he likes it. He has layered it with sugar, the way I like it, too.

I am winding my way in and out among the hens. I have Grannie's stick in my hand – her best walking stick with the silver handle. I wave it half-heartedly at Rusty the cockerel. But he doesn't shift himself out of the way. Grannie peers out over the box hedge round her garden. She laughs at me and my threatening stick. Even the hens are not afraid of me today.

I pelt a stone into the stream, breaking its surface into smithereens. The ducks jump into the stream. They have no fear of me and my stone either.

Inside her garden, Grannie has caught sight of a frog. It is a yellow one – a sign of good weather. She brings it over to me and shows me. The small frog is scared out of its life. Its throat is bubbling in and out.

Grannie carefully places it in some mud at the edge of the stream. It skips away. I am thinking about this. Unlike the worms in her upturned soil, it will live another day. Then, next to me, on the hedge beside the two creamery tanks, I see a spider's web. The spider is inside it, waiting for a fly to come inside her sticky web.

The flagstones are again white and clean. I stretch across them, full length on my belly. At the foot of the nearby tree, I spy an ants' nest. The ants are very busy. They are red ants. It is a colour I have never seen before, more orange than red. There seem to be thousands of them, more than I can count. They march out from the base of the elm tree's bark.

Now that I am halfway to being four, there is much more for me to look at and listen to, more to contemplate. Yesterday, it was the sight of three small ladybirds on the leaves of the bushes across the stream, colourful as the haw berries on my berry farm and very waxy-looking.

The red ants are still busy. I have sometimes seen Grannie stamping her boots on the beetles inside our house when they race out from the turf under the stool and try to escape towards the half-door. Maybe I should kill the red ants too. It's a cruel thought. It passes me by quickly.

I see a few snails left over after the night's rain. They are slowly crawling through the mud that was left behind after the rain. The mud has furrows in it from the wheels of a cart that passed by recently. There's a heap of horse-dung too. I think of the twig ditches round my berry farm. If I mix with my fingers the mud and the horse-dung, I might make a better set of ditches for my berry farm. It's another new thought. I will talk to Grannie about it.

My thoughts are interrupted again. A black and yellow caterpillar is crossing the lane. It is making very slow progress, like the snails in the mud. I am on my hands and knees, following its path with my eyes.

I smell a new smell – machine oil from Rowanberry's big red tractor as it comes hurrying down the lane. Maybe it's the smell of the blue exhaust which it leaves behind in the air after coming out of the back of Rowanberry's tractor. It's an enticing smell and I love breathing it in. It's a rare treat for me.

The caterpillar has reached the safety of Sam's Grove. It is slowly climbing up the ditch. It is busy like the red ants but not nearly as lively as them.

Grannie looks on. She listens to me humming to myself and she knows I am happy. She chuckles to herself. I have caught the habit of humming from her, for she is always humming when she's busy at her work, whether it is baking her soda bread, darning Jack's socks or skinning a rabbit.

Jack likes listening to her when she's humming. 'She's like a well-worn gramophone record,' he says. I don't know what on earth he's talking about. I am not yet clever enough with words.

Grannie has forbidden me to venture out past the flagstones but I am tempted to do so. I know there's a big world waiting to welcome me in the lane, now more than ever and that it's full of other children just like me. Grannie, just like Jack, calls the lane the Open Road and (she says) it can lead me to God-knows-where. What does she mean? Perhaps she's trying to warn me of

122

something unknown when she sees the eager look in my eye, especially the times when I'm standing on the flagstones and peering up and down the lane.

She has no need to worry. I am afraid to venture that far, even though I'm never afraid to take a stroll to the Blue Button Field on my own and even as far as the second field. I can always run back to Grannie and Jack from those places if I feel unsure of myself. The lane is a different matter. I've never been let go there on my own.

And yet... I am tempted to go meet Gret's children, tempted as never before. Not even the icing sugar inside the lid of Old Harpy has been as enticing as this. My racing sandals tell me to get a move on and pay them a visit. I know what I'll do: I'll take my new go-cart up to show them. I'll ask Grannie if she'll go with me.

Rosie and Daisy are Gret's two youngest children. They are not much older than me. I have seen them recently on a Saturday morning when they came down with Sweeney and Bucko to help Grannie do her chores and keep the house and yard in good order, I have watched them scurrying over the lane and into Sam's Grove, tightly gripping their reward of Grannie's humbug sweets once they've finished their jobs for her.

When they were here last Saturday, they never said a word to me. For, like all small children, they are far too shy. But on other days, when they are out in Fiddler Joe's thistle field, I hear them running madcap with their big brothers and bawling like animals.

They have given me something to think about, especially Daisy, who is small, like me. What sort of house do they live in? Have they a Sacred Heart picture looking down on them? Do they say their prayers like me? Do they count eggs and logs like me? Have they toys like my sock-ball, my berry farm and my go-cart? Have they learnt how to use the swear word 'shite' like me when I'm angry or when I fall over? I have much to think about and I have plenty of time to do so. Do they go to the school in Killeen along with their big brothers, Sweeney and Bucko? Can they read big books like Grannie's books in the apple box? If they can read, will they teach me how to read some of their books too?

Jack and Grannie are nowhere to be seen. Jack is repairing some of his fencing over near Bill Corcoran's gate. Grannie is busy baking an apple-batter out of yet more of Gret's cooking apples.

I am standing on the flagstones, staring at nothing. I see a bicycle. It is speeding down the hill from the cross of Mountisland. It is ridden by a bigger boy who's no longer going to school. It is Shawnee, one of Gret's older lads. When he sees me, he starts showing off like blazes, stretching his bum high in the air and wobbling his bike from side to side across the lane as though he's about to fall off and get killed. He is soon gone from view and all that remains is the echo of his singing voice piercing my ear. To this day, I hold onto the picture of him and his bike, his sandy head of hair rising high on his pole and the smart way he's been entertaining me. By this time, he has probably reached Gerry's shop to collect his mother's messages.

As far back as the cross of Mountisland, I hear the sound of a horse's cart – then another horse and cart. Men are driving into Nenagh for the weekend leg of mutton. I hear other sounds too – carts coming up towards us from below John's Gate. The drivers are bringing home the skimmed milk and pound of butter from the creamery. It'll be Jack's turn to go next week. This week, it's Old Tim's turn. They take turns from one week to the next. The carts coming down the lane are faster than those coming up the lane. Old Tim's mare, Sally, plods along drearily. But she is almost home. I can hear his creamery tanks rattling against one another.

I run in to Grannie and interrupt her baking. I tell her that Old Tim is here. He'll have lots of news to tell her, especially about the latest action in the war. He'll have our skimmed milk for Jack's calves. He'll have the bit of butter for us as well. Jack will quickly devour most of it. He will spread it in thick layers on his bread. He may as well eat it with a spoon, so much does he love butter.

Old Tim drops off our two tanks onto the cement slab. Though I am often afraid of strangers, I am never afraid of Old Tim. Why should I be? I am standing close beside Grannie. She is holding my hand. The two of us step back inside the half-door. Grannie wipes the stains of her baking flour from her hands. She sits down by the fire with me. She asks me to tell her my latest news and what I've been doing with myself all morning.

END OF PART THREE

HIGH NOON

Between 1943 and 1944

Another new day comes dribbling in and the stars have been snuffed out. Pink light leaks up from the horizon above Fiddler Joe's hillside farm. The big yellow sun will soon follow. I can hear the branches of the hawthorn tree beating against the hen house roof. It is time for me and Jack to rise from our bed and go out and greet the world.

These mornings (more than ever), the wanderlust is on me. I go with Jack to fetch the water from Brindley's well. I don't take my sweet-gallon with me this time; I take my go-cart instead and pull it along behind me down the lane. Jack can see how much I cherish my new toy and how much happiness it brings me. I love the sound that the wheels make. I love the way the red and blue colours of the cart's paint sparkle in the sunlight. I have filled it with the berries from my berry farm. It will give them a change of scenery today. Sometimes, Grannie allows me and my go-cart to go up the lane for a stroll on my own – but only as far as Gret's gateway – while she stands on our flagstones and keeps her eyes on me. She's like a mother hen, ever ready to protect her young chick.

Now and then, a farmer like Matty Simons from the Look-out will drive out past me. He is on his way to town to buy a few cattle and settle them in one of his outfields. I feel like a bit of a farmer myself, pulling along my cartload of berries behind me as I stroll on my way to Gret's gateway. I can't help throwing an eye at Matty, for I'm anxious to show him what an important fellow I am – me and my go-cart and it loaded with berries from my berry farm – me and my newly found freedom out here in the lane and acting the part of a young farmer.

Today is Tuesday. Yesterday, Grannie did all the washing and drying of her bedsheets, pillowcases and towels. Now that I'm used to travelling up the lane, she is going to take me on a visit to Mrs Fidget, the lady who lives a little bit further up the hill, out past Gret and Fiddler Joe's farm.

Mrs Fidget is a great letter-writer like Grannie and she gets lots of news from England where her son, Tom, works. He is not a navvy like so many of the other Irish lads who took the boat over the sea. He works for Day's Leather Shop on Kilburn High Road, selling ladies' handbags. He knows a great deal about the war in England and elsewhere: which side is winning – whether it's the Germans or the rest of the world. Like his mother, Tom likes to write long-winded letters home. In this way, he is unlike other men from the lane. They never seem to bother with a pen and ink. They're too busy farming.

Grannie may be old but she is a good deal faster than me and she races on ahead of me to get to Mrs Fidget's. She can't wait to hear Tom's latest war news. She depends on it. The war will come to an end one day and she'll be losing me forever. Shudders the thought. She stops at Mrs Fidget's half-door. She has half a dozen duck eggs in her shopping bag wrapped in newspaper. But the reason for her visit in addition to catching up on the war news, is to show off her little grandson from England. She keeps looking down proudly at me.

I am wearing my best clothes and am every bit as excited as she is. For, apart from going to Mass on Sundays, this is by far the longest journey I have ever been taken on. And this time, I am not sitting comfortably on Moll the mare's cart next to Grannie and Jack; I am making use of my own two legs. I will be on my best behaviour and (as Grannie has reminded me) I will speak only when I am spoken to by Mrs Fidget. Even if I get angry or upset during our visit, I will not use the 'shite' word. I wouldn't dare.

Mrs Fidget has another child apart from Tom. Her name is Ellie. She is eight – the same age as Bucko, one of Gret's sons. I shake hands with her. I don't know it yet, but Ellie is about to bring me much happiness to add to the wonderful times I already spend with Grannie and Jack. Though I am much younger than she is, I am anxious to make friends with her and I quickly learn that she feels the same way as I do. For (without her big brother Tom) she is a single child like me with no one to play with.

Her mother hunts us out the half-door so that she and Grannie can have a proper chat. Ellie has something special to show me. It's her recent birthday gift. No other child ever gets a birthday gift. No child has even heard tell of the word 'birthday'. If I dared mention Ellie's birthday gift, Grannie would remind me that every day in the year is a birthday – a gift from God.

The previous Monday, Shy Denis rose up early from his bed. He has no children of his own and although he is very shy in the company of men (and to a lesser extent with women), he is not shy with children and he has always had a soft spot for Ellie.

Denis is a rare one. The whole neighbourhood knows that to be true. When the time comes for ploughing, he is the only farmer who takes his horse, Billy, to plough throughout the night – often as early as three in the morning, especially when it's a night of the full moon. He swears that this is the best time to plough – the time when the horse bee is not yet awake. He'll tell you that the horse bee loves the rich smell that comes out of a horse's bum – what he calls 'the smell of the ammonia'. He gets himself agitated when he tells this bit of clinical news to others and for a moment or two forgets how shy a fellow he is. These little critters (he says) can drive a horse mad with fury when they settle under its tail and dig their stings into that most delicate of spots.

In the far-off days when he used to plough by day, there came a morning when the horse bees stung poor Billy so badly that the misfortunate animal dragged Denis and his plough the length of the field and damn near ruined his plough and almost killed him. The other farmers nod their heads as if in agreement. But all they want is to calm him down a bit. They prefer his natural shyness rather than listen to him gabbling on about why he ploughs at such an ungodly hour of the night. Jack, however, understands him and is inclined to agree with his unusual reasoning. Yet, neither himself nor Fiddler Joe, or any other farmer for that matter, has ever thought fit to follow the example of Denis and go out ploughing at night, especially at three o'clock in the morning.

Ellie had her birthday last Friday and Denis arrived at her mother's door. He was looking a bit more flustered than usual. He took off his cap as he entered the half-door. 'God save all here. God bless the work,' he murmured. Ellie and her mother could see he was hiding something large behind his back. In a flurry, he lifted it out of his sack and showed it to Ellie. In his other hand, he was carrying his dead mother's walking stick.

'This is the rusty rim of mee poor dead father's creamery tank. It's been lying around the yard doing nothing since the day I was born.' This was rather a lengthy speech from Denis and Mrs Fidget hurriedly gave him her best chair to sit down on.

'As ye can see, it's still in one piece – a miracle,' he stammered. And he led Ellie and her mother out onto the lane and up as far as the cross of Mountisland, a little way up the hill. He gave the rim of the creamery tank a few spins before letting it roll away from him and, with his mother's walking stick, he proceeded to belt it down the lane.

Oh the joy of it! To see the way the bowlee wheel went speeding round and round. It was a moment of pure magic when Denis stretched out his hand and offered it to Ellie. 'This'll make a fine gift for you on yer birthday,' he whispered and without another word, he turned on his heel and went rushing up the hill before Ellie or her mother could say thank you or realise he had vanished.

Ellie takes me by the hand and we amble down to her mother's hen house where she keeps this precious new bowlee wheel. It's the moment when our friendship truly starts: a little boy and an older girl already well established in school.

Ellie is not like any of the other hillside children. Jack says she is a bit posh like Lady Dunally. For she is always dressed in clothes that are fresh and new-looking and just as expensive as her dress for Mass. No one has ever seen her dirty or with a stain on her clothes. She wears sandals just like me and doesn't go round in her bare feet like other children, who are only too glad to cast off their shoes as soon as they get home from school. They spend the rest of the day barefooted while they race round everywhere, even through the stony shallows of the river. Their feet are as hard as leather and their legs are often splashed with dung from the lane. Jack was the very same when he was young – preferring to be in his bare feet rather than wear boots. This pleased his father, Will, no end as it spared him having to repair his shoes too often with pieces of leather.

Ellie has flax-coloured hair pinned back with a hair clip. She has a smiling round face. However, her childish beauty is somewhat marred, for she's got one black tooth. The rest of her teeth are as white as pearls. Her black tooth (I get to learn) has become blacker by the day – the result of eating the sweets her soft-hearted father, Rody, gives her when he comes home after his day's work. If she is not careful, she'll soon have a second black tooth to keep the first one company.

She leads me out onto the lane. She lets me carry her stick. She holds the bowlee wheel against her chest. We walk up as far as the crossroad. I have never been this far before. We are much higher up than Grannie's farm. If I stand on my tiptoes, I can see the River Shannon from here. I wonder what Ellie is thinking of as she peers off in that direction. That's where Nenagh Railways Station is and she has often heard the whistle of the Limerick train from up here.

She balances her stick and her bowlee wheel and after a short pause, belts it down the hillside as far as her mother's gate. To hear the metal sound of it ringing off of the roadway, to hear the way my new friend shrieks with laughter in her effort to control her new toy – were the likes of it ever heard tell of before?

Time and again we head back to the top of the slope, me stumbling along behind her. It is far too difficult for me to try bowling Ellie's bowlee wheel but I can't take my eyes off of its speed as she continues to command it to do her bidding. I am entranced by it all.

'Run, Bowlee, run! Run, Bowlee, run,' she screams and any old lady who might be enjoying a few winks of sleep this afternoon is surely wide awake by now.

Grannie and Mrs Fidget are standing at the gate, shaking their heads in delight and laughing at the sight of me and Ellie and the antics of Shy Denis's bowlee wheel.

It's time at last for us to go home. I don't think I'll sleep a wink for the rest of the week. I can't stop thinking of Ellie and her black tooth, of Ellie and her bowlee wheel, of Ellie and her merry shrieks. My dreams will be full of it and will stay that way at least until Sunday when it's Mass-time with Father Speed the Plough. He'll be distracting me all over again with his fancy talk and his posh altar clothes.

In the meantime, I forget to play with my go-cart, my sock-ball or my berry farm. They lie idle where I last played with them, lonely and forlorn – at least for now.

The days and weeks speed quickly by. I am rapidly approaching the time when I'll be four. Grannie sees how much I am ripening into childhood and moving away from my earlier days when I was forever hanging round her skirts. I can scarcely remember the events of those days, so busy am I with my constant urges to reach out towards Gret's children. But I haven't forgotten Grannie or Jack altogether and no matter where I go rambling, I carry them with me in my thoughts and in my heart. They are a part of me.

Grannie is her usual busy self – be it inside the house, out in the yard or the haggart, scurrying down the lane or up the lane on her visits to one neighbour or another. Of late, these are the times when she takes me with her, always a chance to show off her little grandson.

Today we are visiting Mrs Collins, the mother of Old Pat. She is the ancient lady that I once saw – just for a moment – when I was fetching back water from the well with Jack. I took a good look at her and she took a good look at me. She is a tall and stately lady with jet black hair and long, bony fingers.

On that day, she was standing at the corner of the laurel hedge and leaning on her walking stick. It was a once-in-a-lifetime meeting between a child fresh over from the German Blitz and an old lady fresh back from the cornfields of Minnesota where she'd spent the previous thirty years tending to an old Irish priest who left her his fortune when he died. Sad as she was at his passing, she wasn't long making up her mind what to do with his money. She came home to the green hills of Curragharneen, half-a-mile above Dolla and the home of her oft-remembered childhood.

Grannie and Mrs Collins stand in the old lady's yard. There is no conversation between her and myself for, at my age, I am not too good at exchanging words with anyone other than Jack and Grannie. To everybody else, I mutter only the few words that Grannie has taught me to say ('I am very well, thank you') when anyone asks me how I am when someone shake hands with Grannie after Mass. And when old Mrs Collins asks me how old I am, I slowly raise my head (the way Grannie has told me to do whenever I'm addressed and required to speak) and I proudly reply, 'I am three and I will soon be four.'

Grannie gives me a nudge as if to say, 'That'll do for now, Ned.' All that I hear from then on are the voices of herself and Mrs Collins. Grannie can speak as fast as a train, says Jack. So can Mrs Collins. It's a battle to see which of them can speak quicker.

They talk on and on of many events, but they raise their voices higher than ever when talking about the cruelty of the Germans ('the savage Huns', Mrs Collins calls them) and the way they are leaving London devastated and in ruins. Their faces are a picture of sorrow over this war, a war which has claimed the lives of a number of young Irish lads.

Grannie gets herself into a terrible state – angrier than I've ever seen her before. She raises her stick and tells Mrs Collins what she'd like to do to those dreadful Germans if given half a chance. Her words are far from ladylike and she pokes her stick up into the air again and again. The stately Mrs Collins can't help smiling – though she is far too ladylike to burst out laughing at the crude courage of Grannie and her lethal stick.

Jack has his own thoughts these days. He knows he can't be keeping his eye on me every hour of the day. At present, he is busily cleaning and polishing his gun, the unlicensed one that belongs to his cousin, Tom Hayes. Everybody shares everything, whether it's a butter churn or a recipe for cooking – whether it's a gun like Tom Hayes's or a recent novel by Zane Grey.

I happily spend these few moments with Jack before seeking new adventures on the lane. I watch him cleaning out the barrel of the gun with a length of cotton attached to a wire. He spends ages doing this until he feels that he's made the barrel good as new. He blows through the length of it and screws up his eyes as he examines the result of his handiwork. He wipes the gun with a few drops of paraffin. From the drawer in the press cupboard, he takes out a box of cartridges. They are blue with a shiny golden tip. He counts a few of these precious items into the palm of his hand before wrapping them in brown paper. He leaves them behind the bacon box where Grannie stacks her gramophone records.

I have seen him doing this before. I have also seen him preparing snares for the rabbits below in the Bull Paddock. I know he'll be heading for the hills around Mucklin to shoot a rabbit or two for the pot. Perhaps he'll take me with him now that I'm bigger and can walk a good bit further than I used to walk. He might have a few rabbits left over for Grannie to sell. If so, she'll be scurrying down to Gerry's shop and coming home with a pocketful of shiny money and a smile on her face.

It's very quiet up at my new friend, Ellie's, house. She must be tired from the hours she spends racing alongside her bowlee wheel. I think she is giving her toy a bit of a rest today. I miss her and hearing her joyful shrieks.

In the meantime, Grannie has given me permission to walk down as far as Brindley's stile on my own, even down as far as John's Gate. She tells me I have to be back home for my egg and mug of milk as soon as I hear her banging her tin tray on the flagstones. She also allows me to walk up the road on my own past Gret's gateway and as far as Ellie's place. The banging of her tin tray will again tell me when it's time to return home. It won't be long before I can race my sandals past John's Gate and down as far as the metal bridge that overhangs the Dolla River. Then I'll be a real man of the world. I'll be able to frighten the little larks in the dyke and the sparrows in the bushes beside the bridge. Nor will it

134

be long before I can test my legs on the steep slopes leading up to the crossroads at Mountisland and that's twice as far away as Gret's gateway.

Gret's children have been on holiday from school for the last month or two. So it's not just Saturdays and Sundays that I hear their joyful laughter all over their thistle field. Some of them have gone down the lane to paddle in the river. Other children are also visiting the river. Some bigger girls from the far side of Dolla have travelled a mile up the river to the sally hole where they can strip off their clothes and give themselves a good wash with the carbolic soap. After that, they can play to their hearts' content for the rest of the afternoon, splashing one another to high heaven like a pack of wild asses.

Some Sundays, the bigger boys go off rambling with the men out along the Bog Road and on to the river in Glown. They, too, have the most pleasant of afternoons, the men bouncing around in the huge sally hole. They smile when they see the boys pretending that they're swimming. However, they keep one of their feet firmly on the riverbed. They hold their chin well out of the water and their arms out in front of them, making out they're doing the breast stroke like the frogs in the wet meadow.

The grown men and boys love these days out in Glown every bit as much as the girls love swimming below in the sally hole. They spend a great deal of time leaping from the high surrounding rocks and into the middle of the deep pool. Their bravery is a sight to behold, for, like the boys, none of them can swim a stroke. It's all sheer pretence on their part.

When the light begins to fade and the twilight draws in, they will come home tired and jaded in mind and body from the sheer joy of this afternoon. A day of swimming is one of many joyful Sundays in summer when they can throw off the cares of saving the hay and tending to the turf.

The hot summer goes on unbroken. Nature is lavish and children everywhere enjoy the wonders of life, be it raging over the fields, paddling in the rivers or climbing up the woodland trees.

Everything is a song. Everything is laughter unlike the wintry days of December and January when a man might feel he was in the grip of the hangman.

It's time to step out and meet the children of Gret and Fiddler Joe. The eldest lad, Dan, has chosen to become a carpenter and has spent the past two winters attending the town's evening institute and improving his knowledge of various woods, from making tables and chairs to angling timber planks together for the roof of a new house. He is sixteen and, if luck prevails, he will soon be on his way to Dublin for a steady job, maybe further afield than that. Then he'll be able to send money home to his father to buy a few more cattle. He'll be able to buy his mother a posh fur coat against the coming winter; something she has often dreamed about. She'll be cock-of-the-walk when she takes her place in the front pew at Mass on Sundays.

He can see it all, his future as a carpenter and his newfound wealth when he establishes himself in Dublin. From his first month's wages, he will buy himself a brown gabardine suit. For the first time in his life, he will wear a stiff white collar and a blue silk tie. It's all in his head – the world that awaits him in that great big city yonder. He will come home for Christmas dressed as a fine young gentleman and every bit as well-turned out as Lord Dunally. He'll get himself a taxi-ride from Nenagh and step out of it when he reaches Gerry's pub for his first pint of stout before turning up the lane to see his beloved parents. And yes, he'll have the price in his pocket of that fur coat for his mother and a few more cattle for his father. But for now, he stands dreamily in the yard, his feet itching to be off.

The second son, Shawnee, is fourteen and has just left school. He admires his older brother enormously and – if luck prevails – it won't be long before he will follow in Dan's footsteps and take the road to Dublin. For now, however, he is often at work with neighbouring farmers, learning the skills that have kept Fiddler Joe a busy man all these years, keeping a roof over the heads of his children since the day he arrived from the Round Hill and married his beloved Gret. The younger children – Sweeney, Bucko, Rosie and Daisy – look up to Dan and Shawnee.

Jack has gone down with the cows. Grannie has topped up the fire. It'll last for another hour before she tops it up again. She grabs her walking stick and takes me by the hand.

'Where are we going, Grannie?' I ask her.

'It's high time you met up with some new friends and gave your go-cart and your other toys a bit of a rest,' she replies and off we go.

I keep tripping over my sandals, so fast does Grannie and her stooped back speed up the lane. Today's a good day for getting out of the house and travelling even for this short distance. There's nothing but a few frothy clouds in the sky and Old Tim's ditch is glistening with summertime flowers. I see the smile on Grannie's face. There is something of the child still left inside her after all her years of hardship and she loves to get out and about.

It has never entered my head that I am in any way different from other children. Yet, everyone knows that I'm an English child and that I came here to my mother's birthplace, a victim of the German Blitz.

Just before we reach Gret's gate, Grannie stops and cocks an ear. She listens to the cheerful voices of Rosie and Daisy. It's a good start. They are kneeling on the flagstones over the stream with their coloured bits of rock from the river just like Jack and I were doing the previous week. The sun is baking hot but they don't seem to notice it. Rosie is guiding the fingers of Daisy and helping her draw a hay shed and a much larger church with a gate in front of it and a steeple on top of the church.

The two of them look very serious and are colouring in their buildings with a variety of colours. I look down at them and can't help staring. I have never seen a hay shed coloured yellow and brown. I have never seen a church that is orange and lavender. But the flagstones now look much prettier than they did before and the church, especially, seems to twinkle. The rain tonight will wash both the hay shed and the church away.

137

Grannie kneels down beside the little girls. I kneel down too. I draw them my own version of a house. I draw a door, two windows and a chimney. Rosie and Daisy smile at me. I smile back at them. It's as if I have been playing with them all my life.

Grannie spots an opportunity. She hurries past and goes into Gret's house with her holy Messenger book for Fiddler Joe. He loves reading holy books. She stays there for the next hour, gossiping with Gret. Her tongue is never short of words. Herself and Gret are soon cursing the Germans into the four corners of hell. They look up at the Sacred Heart picture next to the portrait of Michael Collins, the Republican hero, and they ask God to forgive them for their hatred. They finally run out of words to say about the war and the Germans. Then Grannie hurries me back home.

Next morning, I am awakened by the shouts of Sweeney and Bucko from across the valley stream. They are racing round their father's thistle field and trying to catch their ass, Slowcoach, by the tail. They are maddening the life out of the poor creature in their attempt to get up on his back.

Until now, Slowcoach had been the most contented of asses. For all asses love nothing better than a field of thistles and Slowcoach is an ass that can stay eating them all day. Sweeney has assured Bucko that today is the day when he'll get up on the back of this precious animal and hammer the laziness out of him by riding him round the field. 'I'll soon chastise the devilment in him,' he shouts. 'Before I'm finished with him, he'll be the fastest ass in Tipperary, but don't let Father hear a word of what I'm up to.'

He needn't worry his head, for Fiddler Joe is a long way from home. He went to Nenagh at an early hour today to bring home half a dozen unwanted tar barrels from the railway station. In the next day or two, he intends to divert the water from his yard stream with the help of these barrels. For, as soon as September brings the heavy rains down from the hills, the stream will make its way up along his yard. In recent times, it has even been known to flow in through Gret's half-door.

138

With Jack and a few more hardy fellows, he plans to cement the barrels into the earth and force the stream to channel its way through them and out into the dyke bordering the thistle field. Since last September, Gret has been praying for this to happen and, in her mind, she sees the stream flowing majestically through the barrels. The yard and house will be safe forever.

After spending the morning with Rosie and Daisy and drawing on their flagstones, all my instincts are dragging me back to them today. However, on hearing the shouts of Sweeney and Bucko, I am anxious to know what they're up to and, sadly, I have no time to play with the two girls. I reach Gret's gate, the one that leads to the thistle field. I spot their big brother, Shawnee, coming up out of the dyke. He is carrying a bucket of water from his father's well. He rarely uses Brindley's well. It's too far away. He leaves down the bucket and spends a moment or two watching the antics of Sweeney trying to catch Slowcoach and get up on his back. He has to smile when he sees his young brother failing miserably to do so.

'Let me help you,' says he. 'I'll show you how to quieten Slowcoach and get up on his back.'

He waits until Slowcoach has stopped racing round the field. When the ass finally stops, he walks quietly to his side and starts whispering words of endearment ('You're the best little ass in Ireland') into his ear. This takes time. It takes patience. He continues to whisper until Slowcoach is almost friendly with him. Sweeney and Bucko can see that he's in no hurry to mount Slowcoach. They are full of admiration at the way he is dealing with him.

Eventually, Shawnee leads Slowcoach over to Old Pat's ditch, all the time whispering the same loving words of friendship into his ear. He gets up on the ditch and then (quietly and stealthily) throws his leg out over his back.

He gives him time to get used to him sitting on him before attempting to walk him round the field and getting him ready to trot. Maybe it will teach his young brothers a lesson – that an act of kindness is far better than an act of cruelty. Throughout this little exercise, I have been standing halfway between Rosie and Daisy and their big brothers. I haven't realised that I've been watching Gret's lads this length of time. I wonder what will happen next. I can see no movement out of Slowcoach. *Will this creature ever move*? thinks Shawnee. But it looks like Slowcoach has made up his mind to stay perfectly still for the rest of the day. The lad's gentle whispering has made no impression on him whatsoever.

Slowcoach is a wise old ass but also a stubborn one. He knows that Shawnee will get tired of making these efforts to move him, that he'll gets off his back and go back to his bucket of water. Then there'll be plenty of the day left for him to go back to doing what he loves best: nibbling thistles.

I suddenly hear the banging of Grannie's tin tray off of the flagstones, summoning me home and I race back to her. I can't wait to tell her my news. Never before have I seen an ass as stubborn as Slowcoach. He's not a bit like our ass, Lightning.

When I reach home, I drink another mug of milk and rush through Grannie's plate of spuds, butter and onions before galloping up the lane for another bout of entertainment.

'You'll get a knot in your stomach from eating so fast!' yells Grannie as she hurries out to the flagstones after me. By this time, I'm already halfway up to Gret's gate. It's early afternoon and young Dan has just finished completing today's carpentry homework. This is the week that he concludes the coursework he must pass for the Dublin job. He feels confident enough that he'll succeed, to such an extent that he has already bought his ticket for the train.

However, he hasn't yet had courage enough to tell his mother, only his father. His departure is going to be a big blow to them, especially to Gret. He knows full-well what will happen after he's gone. She will spend a week in bed, sobbing her heart out. But she'll get back her cheery self in no time at all once he sends her the money for the extra few cattle and the lovely fur coat that he promised her.

There's something playing on Dan's mind. He takes a look up the yard at the barn and the pony's trap resting inside the

140

doorway. It's the trap that his father borrowed from Johnnie Sherlock. No other vehicle is good enough for him to drive his precious son to the railway station opposite the neighbours. His precious Dan must leave for Dublin in some sort of style and Johnnie's trap is the one everyone keeps talking about, the one with the gold trim round the door and the frame and handle rail.

Dan keeps studying the trap. He has an idea in his head. It's a good one. He claps his hands and summons his brothers and sisters to form a line at the haggart gate. He hurries back to the barn and lifts Johnny's trap by its shafts. He's astonished at the weight of it. But without even wincing, he makes his way down the yard, pulling the trap along behind him. He stops at the haggart gate and puts down the trap. He looks at Rosie and Daisy and myself. Without a word, he lifts the three of us into the trap and places us on top of the straw bag. We stay quiet as mice. We don't know what he is going to do next.

Gret is standing at the half-door, looking just as lost and confused as everybody else. Her inquisitiveness and that of us all is about to be satisfied when we see Dan bending down between the shafts. He spits on his fists – the way he has seen the tug o' war lads doing at the show fair before starting to pull on the long beribboned rope. Then he slowly raises the trap.

Sweeney and Bucko have their eyes glued on him. Maybe the trap is not as heavy as it looks. Maybe Dan is playacting. Maybe he was born to be an actor. But they aren't sure. They are half in dread he'll hurt himself.

After a few hearty grunts, Dan shouts, 'Clear the way, lads! I'm on my way.' He gives the trap a rattle, swerving it side to side to see if the wheels are ready for him to move the trap along the yard with the weight of us three inside it. The rattling and the swerving make Rosie and Daisy shriek. Me too. We peer out over the side. We'd like to get out of the trap but its door is shut tight and there's no escape.

Now is the time (I think) for me to act like a brave little man. After all, Grannie has always referred to me as her own little man. But I'm unable to be brave. I'd much prefer to be back home, tending to my berry farm or contemplating a brisk trip down to the metal bridge with my go-cart.

Dan bends forward in the direction of the lane and begins pulling on the shafts. There are no more shrieks out of us. He's doing a first rate job and steering the trap along at a steady pace so as not to frighten us again.

Everybody can see that the trap is a tremendous weight and they hold their breath. The suspense is hard to withstand. There's not a sound out of anyone.

Why is Dan doing this? Only he knows: no one except Fiddler Joe knows that he'll be leaving us soon. He'll be sad as well as excited. He can't go away without leaving us a lasting memorial of himself. His bravery with the trap will make sure of that. Dan and the trap have reached the stream where he comes across a new difficulty, one he hadn't thought of till now: to turn the trap round and head back towards the barn. It's another tremendous task but he's determined not to be beaten.

'Here, Shawnee, give me a hand,' he whispers. Shawnee is only too glad to step in and oblige.

Without another word, the two of them turn the trap round towards the barn. Then Dan begins his struggle towards the barn. This is the toughest part of all and it'll greatly test his muscles. For the yard slopes up from the stream and as far as the barn door. It's not much of a slope but enough to put an additional weight on both his arms. They already ache.

But today is going to be Dan's day, the day when he finds his true vocation in life. Maybe Sweeney and Bucko were right. Maybe their big brother should be acting on the Abbey stage above in Dublin?

'No need for you to push the trap behind me any further, Shawnee. I can reach the barn by myself,' says he. 'At least I think I can,' he murmurs to himself.

He has no time to rattle the wheels and frighten his passengers. His eyes are on the barn door ahead of him. But there's a rascally twinkle in his eye. Look at the way he starts moaning. See the way he aches and groans and the painful slowness of him

142

as he edges the shafts along – inch by inch – out past his mother's doorstep and on towards the barn itself. Even the little wagtails who have their nest in the barn's rafters are in awe of him. They stop flitting in and out with morsels for their chicks.

He lowers the shafts and gently lifts the three of us out, handing down me first (since I am the youngest) and then Daisy and Rosie last of all. It has been a wonderful ride, better by far than any ride had a pony been pulling the trap. We can see the mighty effort Dan has made. His face is covered in sweat.

The previous smirks of Sweeney and Bucko at Shawnee's expense when he was dealing with Slowcoach are now replaced by something else: a look of admiration – a look of kindness. For when Dan points to the trap ('It's yeer turn for a trip in the trap, lads') they shake their heads and refuse to step up on the trap. They have no wish to tire his muscles further. They can see that his arms have been stretched to the limit. Their refusal is such a relief to Dan that he almost runs over and hugs them. They turn away and trudge into the haggart to take another look at Slowcoach, who is happily munching his way through the thistles.

Dan strolls into the living room along with his mother. She pours him out a mug of water from the bucket. She takes a few roasted spuds from the hot ashes of the fire and plants them in front of him. She fills him up a mug of milk and sits down opposite him. This is the time for silence. Neither of them knows what to say. It's as if she understands (but doesn't realise how to put it into words) that things have been playing on her son's mind, that he'll soon be leaving her.

Meanwhile, Rosie and Daisy have been trying to lift the shafts of the empty trap but their arms won't let them. I try to help them. But even with all our efforts, the three of us are unable to lift the trap an inch. However, Rosie and Daisy seem happy enough that I have done my best to help. I feel I've become one of them.

I stroll back home just in time to see Gret's two wild cats dancing down the lane. They race towards our cow shed and place themselves next to Jack's sardine tin for their daily drink of milk. They are the best of time-keepers and need no alarm clock – just like Jack's cows when he goes to fetch them for milking and sees them waiting for him inside John's Gate. It's a mystery how their swollen udders tell them the time.

The days speed by rapidly. The lane's children, especially the younger ones like myself and Daisy and Rosie, are ripening into a new and more adventurous age of childhood, bursting our lungs out in daily bouts of energy, often accompanied by gales of laughter.

I am unavoidably drawn away from our yard. I have little time for sitting on Grannie's straw bag on the ass's cart or dreaming my life away gazing at Grannie's latest flowers in her garden or watching the antics of the ducks and hens or the regular fights between the pig and the gander.

The attempt to ride on the back of Slowcoach and the bravery of Dan in pulling myself, Rosie and Daisy down the yard in the trap have swept me off my feet. Whereas previously I was happy on my own, these days the yard and the house seem to pen me in. As soon as I've had my egg and mug of milk, I'm off out the door and ready for the latest adventure with my friends.

Mrs Fidget has a fine bicycle. It looks shiny and new. This morning, she has hopped down off of it just outside our flagstones. A minute later, I hear Ellie racing down the lane to catch up with her. She is belting her bowlee wheel more skilfully than ever and stops at the flagstones behind her mother. This is the first time she has come down the lane to play with me. She is wearing posh clothes with white socks and sandals. I am wearing socks and sandals too. Maybe I am a bit posh like her.

Mrs Fidget is cycling to town for the Sunday dinner of mutton. It's her turn this week. At other times, it's her husband, Rody's, turn to cycle in on his own bike. Hardly anyone else has a bike, let alone two bikes. Others get to town in the ass's cart like Grannie does or else they walk the five mile journey there and again back home.

After a brief exchange of words, Mrs Fidget hops up on her bike and whizzes off down the lane. She's as lively as a young

144

foal, says Grannie. Maybe that's how she got the name Mrs Fidget, since she's always in the utmost haste and hasn't a second to spare. Once she gets to Nenagh, it takes her the whole day to sort out the messages, for there's lot of gossiping to be done when a fidgety lady like herself goes into town. She'll have a pile of news to tell Grannie when she gets home – most of it about the war. It'll take the rest of the week for her to tell it all.

Ellie doesn't mind being left on her own. She will play with me for the rest of the day, herself and her black tooth, her large shiny eyes, her dimpled cheeks and freckled nose. She is already like a sister to me, like Rosie and Daisy, and I am only too glad to see her bringing her bowlee wheel with her this morning. She is wearing a pink hairclip this time instead of the green one.

She lays her bowlee wheel safely inside the box hedge round Grannie's garden and I lead her out through the haggart gap to introduce her to my berry farm. The berries look a bit tired and worn from all the moving about I've been making them do this past week. 'They haven't woken up yet,' I tell her. 'It's time I made them change over from their present field into their new field.' I spend a few minutes fussing over each of my berry animals.

After telling her where Grannie and I collected the berries, we leave them behind us. We return to Grannie, for we've heard her banging her tin tray. We eat our eggs and we drink our milk in silence. It's all done in a terrible rush. We wipe our lips clean with our sleeves and leave the table. Grannie stamps our foreheads with holy water from the font at the door. Ellie takes me by the hand and out across the stream. We head up the lane towards the crossroads above her house.

She and her bowlee wheel have travelled this part of the lane many times recently. She knows all the ditches and all the bushes, knows where the shy wild strawberries are and where they are hiding themselves – and under which leaves too. She knows where the blackberries are and among which thorny briars.

We eat a few strawberries. They are sour. We eat a few blackberries. They have little white worms in them but we don't mind. I watch Ellie eat a handful. She gives some to me. I have

145

never eaten blackberries or strawberries before. She laughs when she sees me frown. She wipes the juice of the blackberries on her hands. She wipes her face with the juice and then wipes mine.

'We look like red Indians now,' she laughs. Her laugh makes me very happy and I can't help laughing along with her. I don't know who the 'red Indians' are but I know that Ellie is clever. She goes to school. She must have read about them in a book.

We are near the crossroads and she tiptoes ahead of me. This is where her father, Rody, showed her the robin's nest one Sunday afternoon when they took their stroll after Mass. There were two eggs in the little bird's nest.

'It's forbidden for anyone to touch a little bird's nest,' her father warned her. 'It would break the little creature's heart if her eggs got broken,' he said.

We walk in through Ellie's half-door. She has something to show me. We enter her mother's bedroom where the family altar is covered with flowers. On the chair beside it is a large necklace made out of flowers. But the flowers are faded now.

'This is what I wanted to show you,' she says. 'Let's go collect some more flowers and make a new necklace, Ned.'

We come back down the lane and at last find ourselves in the Blue Button Field where we stroll amidst the clover and dandelions. There are so many other flowers here as well. They stretch all the way from Old Tim's end of the field down to the Rotten Tree.

'Pick only those flowers with long stems,' she says and she plucks a tall buttercup and twines it round her fingers. We spend the next half hour collecting wild flowers till Ellie says we have enough. With our arms full of flowers, we return to the yard. Ellie takes down Grannie's straw bag from the ass's cart and lays it out on the flagstones. We count the wild flowers onto it. Ellie didn't know I could count. It's easy as pie for me.

'We have enough to make up a lovely necklace for your Grannie,' she whispers. She doesn't want her to know what we're up to. But Grannie is on tiptoe, peering out the front window and she smiles to herself.

Ellie and I seem to be miles away from anyone else. If a horse and cart or someone like Jack Scissors on his mare, Betty, were to sail past us for his pint of stout and package of biscuits, we wouldn't even notice them – not even a tractor with its lovely exhaust smell, so busy are we.

The making of our necklace is going to be a delicate and serious operation. Each stem is slowly twisted round another stem. Ellie does most of the work. I merely hand her the next flower. We both work hard until the necklace is at last complete. It is very fragile. It is good to be here.

We must not break what we've done. With my help, Ellie lifts the necklace from the straw bag and we carry it gently towards the half-door. It's a wonderful sight – all that shimmering colour in the flowers. We tiptoe in and leave it on the front table.

Grannie (wise woman) is nowhere to be seen. She is hiding herself in Jack's room behind Old Harpy, the piano.

Suddenly, I hear her big boots coming back towards us, 'Goodness gracious, children, what's this we have?' she cries.

'It's a necklace for you,' I tell her.

'You can wear it round your neck at teatime when Jack gets home from his fishing trip,' says Ellie, shyly hanging down her head.

Grannie wipes her eyes. 'I've a cold in mee head,' she stammers. She seems overcome with joy and she dashes into her bedroom. She brings back a handful of humbug sweets for Ellie and me to share.

We spend no time thanking her but rush out into the yard. We scoop up the straw bag and sit down together on it in the ass's cart. We are silent for the next half hour, gobbling down sweet after sweet. Ellie will soon get another black tooth. Maybe I'll get one too. I'd like to have a black tooth. I would like to be able to show it off to Rosie and Daisy. It'd also be a sign of the new friendship between myself and Ellie, though I am far too young to put this into words.

The daylight begins to merge with the early evening. Mrs Fidget cycled back from town a good while back. Ellie stands for a moment on our flagstones. Her eyes are shining like before. It has been a hard day's work for both of us but she has shown me how to make my first necklace of flowers. I'll be able to make a second one for Grannie if I'm ever tempted to take more icing sugar from inside the piano lid. It would be a fine gift for her and would ease my shame for stealing from her in the first place.

Jack came home with three fine trout from his fishing trip on the Dolla River. He was just in time to milk his early evening cows. He brought home a good few mushrooms from the Bull Paddock. His pockets were full of them as he emptied them out onto the front table. 'We will have a fine feed tomorrow,' he said. 'There's nothing better than mushrooms with trout.'

It seems ages since he last played with me – the time he tried teaching me how to somersault abroad in the Blue Button Field. I was younger then and all he succeeded in doing was frightening his calves to death. They fled down the field and hid behind the Rotten Tree, peering back up the field at him.

Grannie will be her usual busy self this evening, gutting the trout and cutting off their heads. She will borrow some onions from Gret, who has a few extra rows of them in her vegetable plot. They are as big as Jack's fist. She grows a few carrots there as well. If she gave them to Slowcoach, her lazy ass, he might shift his legs a bit quicker on the journey to Sunday Mass. The onions will add to our feast. I have never eaten trout, let alone mushrooms, before.

This morning, as soon as Jack finishes milking, I will ask him to help me put more life into my farm and find new animals for its fields.

Last night, before I said my prayers and prepared for bed, Grannie spent time reading to me. She showed me one or two of her past children's storybooks – the prizes from their schooldays. There were loads of animals strewn among the pages, all shiny and new-looking. There were kangaroos and lions and tigers, even monkeys.

This has given me an idea. I think I'll make a second farm and get enough mud and horse-dung from the lane to make firmer

148

ditches than those made of twigs round the edges of my fields. Tomorrow, I will ask Jack to help me find fresh berries for the additional animals. He knows (if anyone does) where to find them and we will take a ramble up to the crossroad. On the way up there, I might see Ellie and thank her for helping me present Grannie with a necklace of flowers. I wonder if the robin redbreast's nest is still easy to find amid the briars. I'd like to point it out to Jack if he'll go looking for berries with me.

It's now Friday and as soon as Jack gets back from the creamery, the two of us are going up the lane to find the new berries for extending my farm. I have told him about the kangaroos, the lions, tigers and monkeys. I have told him about the new ditches and fields I'm planning to make. I might even make a new farm altogether, completely separate from the old one. I haven't yet decided what I'll do. I have so many choices to make.

On our way, we pass Gret's gateway. I haven't seen or heard any of her children out playing this morning. But I think I know where Rosie and Daisy are. They spend most of their time down in the dyke surrounding the valley stream. They have made themselves a cubby house down there.

On the day when Dan arranged our ride in the trap, they invited me to come and visit them as soon as I'd get a chance. Like me and my berry farm, their cubby house allows them to escape from the rest of the world. It's also their chance to get away from the mischief of their big brothers. They can be a nuisance at times.

Jack and I carry on our way towards the crossroads. All of a sudden, Ellie shoots past us, belting her bowlee wheel all the way down towards Brindley's stile. She hasn't a moment to stop or even wave at us in case her bowlee wheel runs away on her.

Jack and myself keep searching the ditches. He has brought Grannie's shopping bag with him. Like Ellie, he knows every bush and flower among the briars. At this hour of the day, the ditches are still full of dew, shining like diamonds, thanks to the many cobwebs and the sunlit patterns made on them. Jack and myself are

149

as happy as a pair of tinkers. A little breeze comes down from the crossroads and refreshes our nostrils.

Jack Scissors rides past us on Betty. He is driving her at full speed, bouncing up and down on his bum. My heart gives a jump, seeing how a young pheasant narrowly escaped Betty's flying hooves. Jack lifts me up on his shoulders to search through the briars. I grab a handful of purple elderberry sprays. He places them carefully in the shopping bag. I find some sloe berries a step or two past Ellie's house. 'Don't eat any of them, Ned, they are sour and will sicken your stomach,' he warns me. These he also puts in the shopping bag.

Across the road and opposite Shy Denis's cabin, we find a crab apple tree. Unlike the crab apple tree in the corner of the Bull Paddock with its scarlet crab apples, this one has white crab apples on it. I count half a dozen of them into my hand. All that is left for us to do is look around the sycamore tree in front of Mick the Smith's forge. Though autumn hasn't arrived, I find a few of last year's sycamore 'helicopter' berries, those whirly ones that spin round in the air when Jack drops them down from shoulder height.

Our search is complete and we return to Grannie and the yard. We are hungry. It's time for yet another mug of milk.

Like Ellie, Jack brings out the straw bag from the ass's cart. He stretches it over the flagstones. Together, we arrange our new collection of berries. Below the hawthorn tree, there's a rusty old egg saucepan. It lies there, useless, but Jack knows what to do with it. He scrapes as much mud off of the ditch as he can to fill up the saucepan.

We take ourselves into the haggart and stop under my tree. With a stick, Jack marks out the boundaries of my new fields. I return to the stream and bring back water in my sweet-gallon. Both of us are working in earnest. Hasn't Jack got anything better to do than this, the big child that he is?

We make four ditches for the new fields. I want to mix the watery mud with some fresh horse dung that Jack Scissors' mare, Betty, just dropped in the lane. Sweeney and Bucko said it would make firmer ditches than the mud on its own and that it would last forever. Oh, the liars! I am still not old enough to recognise when I'm being teased.

Jack is no fool and he forbids me to dirty my hands with Betty's dung. We soon finish making the ditches. We spend a while selecting which berries to put into each field and what names to give them. The new fields look splendid and now I have two farms instead of one. That means more choices for me to make. I can play with the old animals like the haw berries and fir cones from the Bull Paddock or I can spend time with my new animals like the kangaroos from the crossroads.

Bucko is always following his big brother, Sweeney, round the fields or down by the river where they look for unknown crab apples to take home and roast in the hot ashes or to see if the hazelnuts are sufficiently ripe. All Gret's children love hazelnuts and use their bare teeth to crack open the outer casing and devour the sweet nut inside. Their teeth are as hard as shovels.

This time, Sweeney has run away from Bucko. He's not usually that unkind but he has gone with Dan and Shawnee in search of the corncrakes' eggs at the far side of Old Tim's fields, a place known as Fort Dangerous. That's where the corncrakes build their nests and have done so since bygone days. It's hard to find them, for they hide deep amid the furze bushes.

Bucko would have been disheartened at this betrayal by Sweeney had he not found something else to amuse himself with – an old bicycle lamp that belonged to Fiddler Joe. It seems it's no longer of use to anyone. But Bucko has a use for it. He intends to make drawings with the black graphite inside its casing.

This morning, Grannie and Jack are busy as usual – Grannie with her clothes-washing and Jack with his sharp knife. He is cutting hazel wands and spars for the thatching he plans to do over the rafters of his bedroom. It's my bedroom, too, as I share the bed with him. Neither of us wants to feel the rain spattering down on us when the September rain comes pouring through the thatch.

Like Bucko and Jack, I also have things to do. I am on my way to visit the cubby house of Rosie and Daisy, but whom should I spy coming down the lane towards me and carrying his father's old bicycle lamp but Bucko. He hasn't spotted me yet, so deep is his concentration on his lamp. Now that his father's tar barrel tunnel is directing the stream away from the yard, he has no flagstones on which to draw. He turns me around and, to my puzzlement, we walk back down the lane till we reach my own yard. I wonder what he has in mind.

We stop at Grannie's flagstones. They have been left as clean as a whistle from last night's rain as well as this morning's bout of hot sunshine. Anyway, I haven't been drawing on them for the last month, so busy am I with my new friends. Bucko gets down on his knees and spends ages trying to open the lamp with a sharp stone so as to extract the lump of graphite from inside it.

He finally frees it and twists it round with his fingers until he has made a long rope of it the same way his mother rolls her dough when baking her apple tarts. He puts the rope of graphite back inside the outer casing of the lamp and leaves the end exposed. It's as if he's making a giant pencil out of the graphite. I see what he's up to. He intends to draw with it and use the metal of the lamp as its handle.

I kneel down beside him and watch him as he starts to draw with his graphite. He has a much better way of drawing than Jack or myself had when we were drawing with our coloured stones and the faint lines those stones made. I can see how steady his hand is. Murmuring happily to himself, he draws a series of long, wavy lines. He tells me that he's making a river. He draws six of these wavy lines until they look like a river on the move. It stretches from one end of the flagstones across to the other side.

I tell him about Jack and his recent fishing trip and the trout he caught. Bucko proceeds to draw three giant trout. They are drawn above the river as there's no room for them in the water. Their mouths are wide open as if they are gasping for air. There's only one drawback to Bucko's artistic display: the river and the trout are both coloured black. It's the only colour available from the graphite. I wouldn't dare criticise him and his lack of colours. My own skimpy drawings with my coloured stones are no match for his artistry. Yet the trout seem more like birds than trout to me. It's as if they are about to fly off into the sky.

To complete Bucko's morning's artwork, he draws the sun above the river and trout. It's the big yellow sun that we children love so well. But it too is black. He gets up and hides his new graphite pencil inside the box hedge round Grannie's garden until next time. Both of us look down at the flagstones and smile at one another.

He takes me by the hand. I don't mind. He can do that, for he is eight years of age like Ellie and he's a big boy. We head off towards Rosie and Daisy's cubby house but take a different route from usual – down through the briars in Sam's Grove and down lower still along the slippery slope above the valley stream. We can see Rosie and Daisy in the distance. They wave across the stream at us. They were not expecting Bucko, as I was the only one invited. They welcome him just the same. I take off my socks and sandals and we step across the stream to meet them.

The valley stream is usually sluggish but that's not so today. For the recent rains, coupled with the work that Fiddler Joe did in re-directing his yard stream, have given it a new lease on life and it runs along smoothly. Its water is as clear as crystal as it sings its way down towards Old Pat's fence before tumbling into the Dolla River. We shudder as we feel the icy chill of its rippling wavelets round our ankles.

I don't remember Bucko ever coming to play with his little sisters until now. Maybe it's his first time. Usually he spends his mornings racing round the thistle field with Sweeney and trying to get up on the ass's back like I saw him doing the other day – or else he is playing leapfrog with his older brothers. This often ends with them wrestling him to the ground and tickling him to death. How often have I heard their screams of laughter from my perch on our ass's cart!

Their oldest brother, Dan, never plays with them – he's far too busy with his carpentry books. But when he does venture out into the field, he's at a loss what to do but stand back and scrutinise their playacting. Much as he'd like to, he cannot join in like he once did; he's now almost a man and has to act the part sensibly.

Rosie and Daisy wonder why Bucko has come to visit them. We tiptoe out of the stream and climb up on the far bank to reach the little girls. For a long time, Rosie and Daisy had begged Fiddler Joe to make them a cubby house, so much so that he got tired of hearing them prattling on about it. In recent weeks, he cut up the old barn door that was destroyed in the heavy storm last winter. He made two boards, each 4 foot long and a foot wide. He smoothed them with his wood-plane and gave them a shine with sandpaper. He had some logs left over from his trip with Jack out the hills to fetch home timber for the fire. He made these logs the same length. There were six logs in all.

That evening with Rosie and Daisy dancing down the thistle field alongside him, he scooped out the side of the dyke overlooking the stream. He fixed the two boards firmly into the dyke and planted three of the logs along the length of the first board at even distances. He placed the second board across the top of the logs and nailed it down with a few of the nails he was holding in his teeth.

When they saw the new shelves that their kind old father had made for them, the little girls could see how their new cubby house was taking shape. All they'd have to do was fill the shelves with bits and pieces to make a pretend tea for themselves now and then. Perhaps their father would come and join them from time to time. But that, they thought, might be asking too much of him.

Unknown to any of us, Rosie and Daisy have been as busy as bees ever since Fiddler Joe made them their shelves. They asked their mother to give them some coloured buttons from her button box. They picked out lovely pink and blue ones – yellow ones too. They raided her ash pit and dug around the edge with their father's spade. They found a number of coloured bottles that had been thrown out over the years: little gin bottles and holy water bottles. These were the best ones to put on their shelves as vessels for pretending to drink lemonade. They found a few broken willow-patterned plates and broke them into smaller pieces to make plates for their imaginary cakes. They found an old jam jar to bring back water from the stream to pour into a rusty old kettle and make their visitors a cup of tea.

Bit by bit, their shelves began to fill up with an overload of items until they began to look untidy, no matter how neatly they tried to arrange their utensils. If they weren't careful (like me and my second berry farm), they would have to ask Fiddler Joe to sand down a few more shelves so they could space things out better. In the meantime, they remembered the tin mugs that the tinkers left behind at the metal bridge after they'd left for Kerry. They would use these as cups the next time they invited guests to tea.

Bucko and I now take our places round the boards. The little girls give us mugs of water and we have a happy time pretending to drink our lovely tea. Rosie pours us pretend milk from the jam jar. I smack my lips together like Jack does after sipping his strong tea first thing each morning.

Daisy has spent the previous week tearing up brown paper bags out in the barn, ones that her mother keeps for lighting the fire. Rosie had selected some small, coloured pebbles from the valley stream. The two of them then wrapped the paper round the pebbles and turned them into sweets like the ones Grannie keeps in her altar drawer.

Bucko and I thank them profusely when they hand us our sweets. We have a wonderful time unwrapping the paper and admiring their lovely colours. We make appropriate sheep's eyes and keep rubbing our bellies as we eat our feast of pretend sweets and we ask our little hosts for more.

They hand us their special willow-patterned plates. Their fingers are very delicate about it. The plates are filled with mud cakes which have previously hardened in the sun. They beg us to eat a few coloured buttons as a special treat – their new biscuits. No one, only Father Speed the Plough, has ever been given biscuits as far as we know. We are being honoured, indeed, and we hold the cakes and biscuits in our hands politely and cock our little fingers aloft like posh ladies do, while Rosie and Daisy look on inquiringly to see are we enjoying our cakes and biscuits. We make mincing noises and we sigh to show them how happy we are.

'Heavenly!' cries Bucko, who seems to be enjoying himself more than he was a day or two ago when I saw him chasing Slowcoach the ass.

Rosie turns aside and smiles at Daisy. She can be a bit fussy at times like Mrs Fidget. She notices that the shelves are still untidy and that she is in danger of losing a few of her coloured buttons and that the jam jar of water is about to spill over. With Daisy's help, she begins to tidy up and clear away the plates and tea cups, making their cubby house neat and tidy the way it was before her guests arrived. She spreads everything out meticulously and thanks us for coming on our visit. She and Daisy say, 'Call soon again,' because that's what their mother always says when guests come calling at her door.

Bucko, rather shyly – the way boys can be at times like this – thanks his little sisters for the splendid tea and we leave them to get on with their exciting day beside the stream.

As we struggle up the bank, I hear Rosie singing her Tables Song: 'one and one make two-ah – two and two make four-ah.' She will go on singing this song till 'ten and ten make twenty-ah' like the children do when marching to school. Daisy tries to join in. On the day when she sets out for Mr Flanagan's school, she'll be able to recite the Tables Song as good as any of the others. She'll have even learnt a few of the longer tables – at least the 2s, the 5s and 10s. Rosie already knows the 3s and 4s and can hold her head up high opposite her brothers.

Bucko and I ramble back towards his yard and reach the haggart gate. He helps me get up onto it. He opens the hasp and slowly pulls the gate backwards so that it looms above the new waterfall coming out of the tar barrels.

I look down at the fast-moving stream of water and my latest friend gently pushes the gate forwards and backwards. I can't help crying out with delight. I have never had a swing on a gate like this. Bucko seems happy that I am happy.

156

I get off and we travel into Gret's yard. She has baked a few spuds in the hot ashes round the fire. She places them in a towel so they won't burn our fingers when she gives them to us. She helps me get up on the ditch at the edge of the yard. I sit alongside Bucko while she cuts the spuds into smaller chunks. 'Let them cool down a bit in case they burn yeer mouths,' she warns us, using the old language like Grannie does sometimes. We find ourselves having a real feast and not a pretend one like we've just had as guests in the cubby house. It's as good as a Christmas.

A little while later, I stroll home, thinking about my swing on the gate and of the fine time that Rosie and Daisy gave me in their cubby house. The warm spuds have gone down well too.

As part of my growing education, I have been forbidden by Grannie ever to eat a meal at Gret's house, for this good woman has a big family and it is very wrong of me to take food from her. I am not fool enough to tell her when I get home about the delicious spuds I've just been eating on the ditch with Bucko. I know she'd be extremely cross with me for not having heeded her advice.

As I approach our flagstones, I see Jack Scissors and his mare, Betty, trudging up the lane at Brindley's stile. Betty is no longer high-stepping it the way she was when I last saw her galloping down the hill past Jack and me. Poor Betty! She looks quite worn out after her long walk up the slope from Gerry's shop below in Dolla.

Jack Scissors is a gentle giant and I watch him walking alongside his mare. He hasn't the heart to be riding her home after making her gallop so fast down to the shop and showing off in front of Jack and myself. But now he keeps whispering words of endearment into her ear. Though I am a young child, I can see how much he loves her and that she is quite sick these days. She hasn't many more days left to live.

In between all the fun and games I've been having with Gret's children, I still find time each morning to accompany Jack to the Bull Paddock to fetch back the cows and bring back water from Brindley's well for tea.

Now that I am almost four, Jack is inclined to take my education a good bit further. He recently showed me the rabbit runs leading out from the wood and into the Bull Paddock, out as far as the pine tree with the fir cones that I use for my berry farm. He pointed out the little black rabbit-droppings and assured me we'd be having plenty of rabbit soup and flaky white rabbit pieces for next Sunday's dinner. The three of us are sick to death of eating mutton every Sunday. But, in case we should ever forget, these are war years elsewhere where few people have enough food to warm their bellies, let alone get the chance to turn up their noses at the sight of a fine joint of mutton!

I am going on a rabbit hunt next week. I can't wait to get started and to travel into the hills with Jack. I am far too excited to tell Grannie how I feel.

Jack has no remorse for killing rabbits. Already this year, they have eaten two fields of Mick the Herd's cabbages and the poor man can't think of enough swear words to curse them with. Shy Denis and Ellie's father, Rody, feel the same way. They haven't a single cabbage left undamaged.

Next to the hob, behind Lightning's winkers and Moll's harness, Jack keeps two rabbit-traps. They once belonged to his father, Will, but he loathes using them and hates to find a rabbit caught in one of them. Last year, he saw an old buck rabbit trying to bite off its leg before the fox or weasel could get close enough to end its life.

He keeps thinking of yesterday's rabbits from the woods. He has decided to make a few snares and capture one or two of them for Grannie's pot. It's too good a chance to miss. I watch him whittling away at some hazel wand stakes with his knife. He's making stakes and attaching wire rings to them. He holds them up to the light to examine them. He sighs with satisfaction at each new snare. He'll space them out along the rabbit run today when he goes to fetch the cows. 'Snaring is a better death than the trap,' he says. 'A rabbit chokes to death soon as it runs its head through the wire ring and starts struggling to get out. This only tightens the wire's grip round its neck and the rabbit dies a second later.' Jack's words are a big mouthful for me to take in and I'm not sure I've understood all of it.

That was last week and today I hear Jack whistling to himself at the half-door. I steal out of bed and peer out at him from inside the bedroom. My eyes are still full of sleep. He's holding his gun up to the light of the half-door to see if the barrel is clear. On the front table are six blue cartridges. They have gold and shiny tips on them. These will be his killing instruments today and a young rabbit, who hasn't had the sense to run to its burrow, will end up on Grannie's table before the day is out, ready to be skinned of its fur and dressed for the cooking pot.

Jack's gun is the double-barrel one, the unlicensed one belonging to Tom Hayes. In case his aim is not good enough the first time, it can fire a second bullet immediately after the first shot. That might not be necessary. He has a great aim. I have seen him pitching pennies from the half-door to the tin mug next to the press cupboard and filling the mug with them before I'd finished drinking my first mug of milk. I have tried to pitch his pennies into my sweet-gallon. It's big enough to catch all of them. But, so far, I have never been able to succeed. One day, if I keep my hand and my eye steady, I hope to aim Jack's pennies into my sweet-gallon. That would put a smile on his face. I know it would. He wants me to succeed in everything I do.

I am wearing only my shirt and have yet to put on my britches. Grannie is too busy to notice that I am up and awake. She is down on her knees in front of the fire that she's just lit. Once more, she's using the lid of my sweet-gallon to fan the flames. She is almost blinded with smoke and, worse still, a strong wind is blowing down the chimney directly at her and ruffling her hair. I hate to see poor Grannie so troubled with the fire's smoke but the morning's bright sunlight will soon drive my sad thoughts out of my head, for Jack tells her that this is the day he promised to take me hunting.

I tiptoe back for my britches and put them on. I join Jack and his gun at the half-door and see Lord Dunally as he passes our yard. I've seen him often before. He always dresses the same: in his plus four trousers, his deer-stalker hat and greatcoat and his gun tucked under his elbow. This morning, he's heading up to Curryquinn and the hills beyond in search of a few pheasants. He is different from our men. He is posh and never hungry. His belly is fat and his nose is red.

He is different from us in other ways too. He hunts for fun and sport, whereas Jack and the likes of Fiddler Joe or Shy Denis kill rabbits to put food on the table. It doesn't matter how they kill a rabbit – be it with the ferret or the trap, the snares or the gun, even with the brilliance of the flash lamp at night, as long as their wives and children get fed.

My one regret today is that I didn't get the chance to go fishing with Jack a few days ago, the day he came home with his three trout and his pockets full of mushrooms. There's still a lot I don't know. Although he was tempted to take me fishing, he decided not to – not until I'm old enough to enjoy it and nearer to five years of age. A day's fishing (he thinks) is not as pleasant as walking across the fields to dig up spuds while he amuses himself pelting worms at me and listening to me raining down curses on him. What on earth would I be doing while he spent the day fishing? Just sitting on his waistcoat and staring at the back of his head. That's not the sort of life for a child who has recently been indulging himself in cups of pretend tea with Gret's little girls and eating hot spuds with Bucko on the side of the ditch.

It rained during the night and the dew of the early morning has been heavy. The grass in the hills is going to be soaking wet with the richness that young rabbits love. They'll be out early around Mucklin, their noses twitching and their mouths buried deep in the soggy grass, enjoying its delicious taste.

Jack puts the chair back under the front table. He takes out the cartridges from his pocket and lays them on the oilcloth. He rolls them round in his fingers. He lets me roll them round too. I feel their smoothness. I know they will bring death to some young rabbit today. I know they will put an end to its frolicking round the field.

160

Grannie gets up off her knees at the fire and follows us out the half-door. Jack hoists his gun onto his shoulder. He hands me Grannie's walking stick, the old one that she uses to chastise her cow at milking time when it hits her across the jaw with its shitty tail.

I place the walking stick on my shoulder like Jack with his gun and off we go to kill a rabbit or two. 'Let two-men-of-us take a walk,' says Jack. That's what he always says when he goes off rambling with me: 'Let two-men-of-us-take a walk.'

'Wait a minute!' shouts Grannie. She races back into her bedroom for her bottle of holy water. She pelts a shower of it across our faces so as to bring us good luck. We cross the stream and Jack wipes a few drops of the holy water off of my nose as we walk on. I try to match Jack's manly strides as we head up the lane. By the time we pass Gret's gateway, I am half-running, but Jack doesn't seem to notice, so anxious is he to reach his rabbits. We meet no-one on our way, nor hear a sound from anyone either, not even a cow bawling. The mountain breezes stream down to welcome us from Bog Road and the sunlight dazzles my eyes.

I am anxious to be of use to Jack and it isn't long before I am on the look-out for the white fluffy tails of rabbits and (the little liar that I am) I tell him that I have already spotted a few. I continue to carry Grannie's walking stick proudly on my shoulder. There's a hatpin pierced onto the end of it. I don't know why it's there – not until Jack explains the reason amid bursts of laughter.

There was a day long before I was born when Grannie found herself getting into an unusual state of desperation. She was driving Lightning to Gerry's shop when he heard another ass calling to him from inside Maher's field. The little devil stuck his hooves on the ground and wouldn't budge another inch. Grannie wasn't prepared for such bad behaviour. She got more and more angry with him as the time went by and was in danger of getting to the shop after the doors were closed at dinnertime.

No matter how much she whipped him, the blasted animal refused to budge. If Jack was to have sugar in his tea, this situation

161

required some sort of urgency. He never drinks tea without three spoons of it stirred in his mug.

She took the hatpin from her hat and fashioned it into the end of her walking stick. She lifted up Lightning's tail and gave his surprised bum a savage prod with it. Ouch! In no time, his hooves were hopping off the lane. There was no stopping him and, true to his name, he moved at lightning speed. Seconds later, he reached Gerry's door, almost knocking it off the hinges and much to the surprise of the lady customers and the regular afternoon drinkers.

Success at last, thought Grannie! In her future shopping trips, she knew what she'd do to get to the shop in time for Jack's sugar: make use of her deadly hatpin if Lightning didn't behave himself. Grannie always knows best what to do, whether it's for me or for her ass.

Jack and I pass Ellie's gateway. She is giving her bowlee wheel a rest this morning. Maybe she is out in the haggart, devouring another bag of her father's sweets. Maybe she'll get another black tooth.

He stops outside the entrance to Shy Denis's haggart. Denis is busy painting the outside walls of his barn. He painted them two years ago, but he's a man who is never satisfied. This week, he has finished painting the top three quarters of the front wall in the colour he loves best: buttercup yellow. He plans to paint the lower quarter in black. When the paint dries, he will dip a horseshoe into a bucket of red paint and stamp the horseshoe onto the yellow paint. The barn's front wall will look very fine indeed when the red horseshoe marks combine with the buttercup colour.

In addition to Denis's natural shyness, this bit of artistry is yet another side to him. It is no surprise to anyone. For his father was known as the Tasty Man and did the same thing with the horseshoes, dipping them in paint every two years, right up till the day he drowned in the river.

But Denis goes one better than his father and before the day is out, he will have completed his latest bout of artistry by stamping white horseshoes onto the black section at the base of the wall. Everyone will go up and stand outside his gate with mouths

162

open wide in admiration of his handiwork. It'll be talked about for weeks on end.

'We have reached the Bog Road,' says Jack as he looks back at me and my weary sandals struggling behind him. It took him a bit of time, but at last he sees how much my legs are hurting me.

Though I am not heavy for my age, I am still a bit cumbersome for Jack to be carrying. However, he is every bit as soft-hearted as Ellie's father, Rody, and the sweets he gives her, or as Fiddler Joe making his daughters a cubby house. He lifts me to his shoulders, where I'll stay perched for the rest of the journey.

'You'll be able to see in over the ditches, Ned,' says he. 'Let me know when you catch a glimpse of a real rabbit and not one of your imaginary ones. And one more thing,' he warns, 'from now on, the two of us must be quieter than a mouse. Rabbits have long ears. They can hear a man's voice a mile away.'

We slow down our pace. Jack won't admit it, but he's beginning to feel how heavy a load he is carrying – me on his shoulders and his awkward gun under his elbow. He's starting to feel pins and needles in both arms.

'One day, I'll take you out to the bog to save turf,' he whispers. Not another word do we speak from then on, all the way up to Mucklin. I hear Jack sighing. Maybe I might cheer him up by whispering in his ear and telling him I've seen a real rabbit inside the ditch. Or maybe I'm getting too heavy on his shoulders. Still, it's not that. At these quiet moments in his life, he has nothing to do but occupy his mind with the war news coming back daily about the Germans and their bombing raids.

Perhaps he's wondering how long it's going to last now that the Americans have entered the scene. It's a huge worry for him. He knows that when the war is over, I'll be wrenched away from him and his mother, that I'll be taking my little suitcase back to Nell and Patsy, the parents I've never known. He can see hard days ahead, especially for me. *I can't let them have Ned back* (he thinks) *after all these years. It's far too late. We're a happy family now with all that we've experienced together these recent years.*

He trudges along, his mind still at work. He can't make sense of it. A dark cloud has come over him, intensifying his frown, and he covers his eyes with his hand. He must shake off this dreadful misery and get back to thinking about the rabbits that are waiting for him at the end of the journey. We are high in the hills, with just the light sound of his wellingtons. There is silence even in the trees and bushes and I begin to feel the enchantment and mystery of the hunt. Jack is careful not to tread on any snapping twigs.

We are close to the top of the highest hill when he stops for a second or two to get his breath back. He lifts me down off of his shoulders and pats me on the head. He bends down and whispers in my ear, 'Ned, my lad, let two-men-of-us go shoot a few rabbits.'

He hides the barrel of his gun underneath his coat in case an overzealous rabbit might catch a glimpse of its shininess. He has seen so many rabbits in his lifetime that he can distinguish the older ones from the young ones and not by their size alone. They are the first to spot danger and to rush off to their burrow despite their slowness and their old age with its limping ailments.

He raises his nose above the ditch. He lifts me up on my tiptoes. Do I believe my eyes? I never knew there were so many rabbits in all the world, tons of them. Some of the younger rabbits go on nibbling the grass. Other young ones stretch out their hind leg to shake off the dew. Their mothers stand still and cock their ears. They sniff as though sensing danger, for they are forever mindful of their young. They turn their head towards their burrow, making sure they can find the proper entrance if they have to make a run for it.

Jack points out the rabbit he has chosen. He puts his finger to his lips and directs my eyes in that direction. No rabbit has yet stirred. The older ones have no need to feel dread – not yet. They are not aware that we're about to pay them a visit.

Jack puts his gun to his shoulder. He doesn't want to kill an old rabbit, knowing that its meat might be unsuitable for our table. Nor does he want to kill a young one. An adolescent rabbit is the best rabbit of all. Its flesh is as ripe and tender as a juicy pear.

One or two of these adolescent ones have strayed into the middle of the field, far away from the adults. They are playful and full of their antics – just like Sweeney and Bucko and other young lads below in Dolla when they are out at play.

Jack smiles to himself. He loads two cartridges into the double-barrel of his gun and rams them home.

Suddenly, I am aware of what's going to happen and I watch him in awe. There's a determined look in his eye like when he eyes his axe before splitting logs in pieces out at the woodpile. Death is on its way – the death of one poor rabbit who until now has been hopping about in the clover.

Ah, foolish rabbit, unaware of Jack's gun peeping from behind the bushes. By this time, it's far too late. Jack whispers a prayer that his gun will not miss, that we'll not go home empty-handed with our day in ruins. For, as soon as the gunshot is heard echoing off the hills, not a single rabbit will be seen for the rest of the day.

'I normally aim for the head,' Jack says to himself. 'I must not ruin the rabbit's pelt.' He turns to me and whispers, 'When I give the signal, Ned, you must clap your hands three or four times. It'll give the rabbits a sporting chance to escape from the gun.'

My excitement has now been replaced by an unexpected fear. There is no mystery left, just this miserable fear for the rabbit that Jack has picked out for our dinner plates next Sunday.

He nods his head and I clap my hands.

'Here comes man. Here comes his big gun. We must run like hell,' the rabbits seem to say. The field suddenly becomes alive with rabbits speeding for their lives, the young ones scattering in all directions and tumbling over one another.

'Crack-crack!' roars Jack's gun. The noise of it shakes the hills to their roots. There's not so much as a squeal out of Jack's chosen rabbit. It leaps into the air and drops down dead. It happened so fast. The field is at once as silent as the grave. I almost die with fright and cover my ears with my hands. It's the loudest bang I have ever heard, louder even than the thunderclaps

165

over our fields in September and I realise that the birds have all flown away.

Before we rush across the field, we see a second rabbit nearby. It is lying beside the first one, as if the bullet has bounced off of the first one and into the second one's forehead. But Jack knows better. The second bullet entered this one directly and lodged there. The rabbit is shivering – shaking and jerking its last few breaths before dying. Jack clips it behind the ear in case it is still suffering from the bullet-wound. It is now dead like its comrade.

He lifts both rabbits into the air triumphantly. He lets me stroke their soft fur and I see the blood from the gunshot wound on their foreheads. It is dripping down into their eyes as thick and red as the haw berries in our yard.

Jack dabs a little of the rabbits' blood onto my forehead. 'Now you're the real hunter, Ned,' he laughs and he stretches the two rabbits close together. He searches for the two cartridges and hands them to me. 'Grannie will be as pleased as punch,' says he with a smile.

I look into the rabbits' dead eyes. They are sad, no longer soft like the eyes of our sheepdog, Rose, when I stroke her back home. Jack reaches for his penknife and makes a cut in one of the rabbit's hind legs. He puts the rabbit's other feet through the cut in the leg. He places both rabbits on the barrel of his gun and the two of us march out the gate and hurriedly sweep our way home. My legs are no longer aching. I no longer feel wobbly and I can't wait to get back and tell Grannie what fine hunting we have done today.

We are back in our lane in no time. The only time we stop is outside Gret's gateway. Jack takes one of the rabbits off his gun-barrel and loads it onto Grannie's walking stick (the one with the hatpin). He arranges it on my shoulder and tells me to take it in to Gret.

It's impossible to recount her joy and the look on her face when I hand it to her. She is a kind woman, always ready to help Grannie if she's ever short of anything or if there's nothing left over inside the lid of Old Harpy the piano.

166

I run back to Jack and race on ahead of him to tell Grannie how we have shot two rabbits and have given one of them to Gret. I have never seen Grannie look so happy and she places our rabbit on the front table.

She sees the blood-stain on my forehead for the first time and is about to rub it off with her spit when Jack pulls her away from me. 'It'll all be gone by tomorrow, Mother, never fear.' She steps back and nods her head. 'Let Ned enjoy his day's hunting – it's his first,' he whispers. Then he takes me over to sit down by the fire alongside him. We take a look at one of Grannie's old picture-books and I try to learn a few more words with him so that I can tell my friend Ellie how well I am doing.

That evening, Jack and I travel down to the Bull Paddock to fetch back the cows. They are huddled together in the middle of the field underneath the oak tree, the tree that gave me the acorn berries for my farm. It's as though they are expecting a shower of rain. This often happens. They are the most reliable messengers of rain or wind, but especially during storms when they are afraid to stay under the oak tree. On such occasions, they get fairly lively and trot over to the far corner of the Bull Paddock. Once there, they keep close to one another for bodily warmth midst the overhanging bushes next to the crab tree. They haven't time to feast on the crab apples, so intent are they on their own safety against the oncoming storm.

Our present thoughts of summoning them from under the oak tree are interrupted by the clanging sound of a bucket banging against the railings of the metal bridge that spans the river at the end of the field.

We can hear the voices of Fiddler Joe's older lads, Dan and Shawnee, loudly directing the bucket down into the river. It is tied to a rope and the rope is tied to the bridge. They often go down there to fill their barrels with water in dry weather.

There's a small sally hole, barely 3 ft deep, situated in the centre of the river and directly under the railings. Sweeney and Bucko are knee-deep in the sally hole. Their eyes are on the bucket and they're waiting to catch it as it is dropped down to them.

Slowcoach is his usual self, totally disinterested in this spectacle, his mind preoccupied. On his cart are two tar-barrels. He knows what's going to happen. The barrels will be half-filled with several buckets of water. Even when half-filled, they will be heavy enough for him to struggle up the lane with. Had they been filled to the top, there would never be enough people to lift them off of the cart and they'd be standing there till the day of judgement.

Jack knows the reason why Gret's lads are down at the river today with the ass and cart. He tries explaining it to me, even though I'm young and can't follow all his words.

Up until now, Fiddler Joe and Gret have been delighted with the way the stream has been redirected. Everyone has been talking about it even more than they have about the war, how Joe buried the stream inside the barrels and covered them with grass clods mixed with cement. Gret said it was a miracle the work was completed in a day and she thanked the helpers a thousand times over. They had pitched in to work from dawn till dusk. In no time at all, the dry weather hardened the cement around the barrels.

A few nosy neighbours came down the hill that evening and put their ear to the ground to listen to the musical sound inside this unheard of contraption. No longer will Gret fear her stream travelling up the yard and reaching her door on stormy days. She, too, has been spending her time listening to the sound of the stream inside the barrels and watching it gush out at the lower end before dropping into the dyke and dashing off towards Old Pat's ditch.

But yesterday, when Fiddler Joe bent his ear over the tar-barrel tunnel, he heard hardly a drop of water running through it. Rosie and Daisy are not nearly as pleased about the tar-barrel tunnel as their parents. They have seen their stream glistening up at them for the last time and now have no stream to paddle their feet in and give their legs a wash.

Worst of all, their flagstones have disappeared and have been taken away and smashed. Where on earth are they going to draw their pictures of the church or of Rosie's schoolhouse? It's enough to make an ass cry. But this doesn't worry Shawnee or Sweeney. All they have to do from now on is leap over the ditch

168

with their buckets, creep down the dyke, capture the water coming out from the barrels and fill up their buckets for their mother. It's an easy task for them. It's far better than the way Jack has to spend his time travelling all the way down to Brindley's well every day.

Dan and Shawnee continue lowering their bucket into the river for Bucko and Sweeney to fill them up out of the sally hole. They don't mind lifting its heavy weight up out of the river and they don't spill a drop before tipping the water into the barrels on Slowcoach's cart.

Jack and I listen to the shouts of Bucko and Sweeney ('swing the bucket a bit more to the left... over a bit more to the right') as their big brothers throw the rope back down from the railings. They place the bucket in the centre of the sally hole.

Jack marshals the cows out as far as John's Gate. Rose gainfully helps to speed matters up till we get back up to the cow shed. As soon as the cows are chained to their posts, Grannie and Jack take their stools and get down to the milking, their bucket tucked firmly between their knees in case of spilling the milk. To this day, I can hear Jack softly humming one of his rebel songs so as to get more milk out of his cow.

I get tired of standing at the cow shed door and am anxious to go off adventuring again. You'd think that, having spent my day hunting rabbits in Mucklin, such a day would have been enough enchantment for me. But no. From where I am standing, even though we are more than half a mile away from the metal bridge, I can hear the shouts of Gret's boys. They'll be at least another hour pelting buckets of water into the barrels.

Slowcoach must be the most patient ass in Tipperary, just standing on the bridge without bothering to cast off the annoying flies from round his eyes and between his legs. He is thinking of the tremendous load of water he'll have to pull up the hill when the boys have finished with the rope and bucket.

Grannie has left a towel to dry next to the fire. I take it away with me and rush across the yard. I head down the lane as far as the river. On the downward slope, I spot Rosie and Daisy. They seem to have deserted their cubby house. Like me, they have heard all

169

the commotion coming up from the bridge. I have grown to love playing with them and I feel that they've the same cheerful idea as myself this afternoon. Namely, to spend our time paddling in the cool water of the river.

As soon as we arrive, we see Bucko and Sweeney busily filling the barrels with water. They scarcely notice the three of us. I take off my sandals and socks and roll up my britches as high as I can so as not to get them wet. I'm not sure how deep the river is. Rosie and Daisy do the same and tuck their skirts into their knickers. They never wear shoes. Nor do they take notice of thorns, for Fiddler Joe is the best man for removing them with his goose feather and bottle of iodine.

'Cripes! This river's cold as ice,' cries Rosie as we edge our way to the middle of the waves. We balance on the wobbly stones of the riverbed and stand a good bit away from the sally hole so as not to confuse the sterling work of Bucko and Sweeney.

There are many fine trout living in this river, as Jack well-knows. It's not long before we spot a shoal of trout swimming towards us, none more than four inches long. They look so small but they are far from frail. We bend our knees and make a desperate attempt to capture some of them but they meander their way skilfully through the swift water and most of them hurry past us. We manage to catch one or two. The shouts of the boys filling the barrels are no match to our screams as our fingers struggle to hold onto these tiny fishes. They're as oily as an eel and they slip out of our clutches before catching up with the other little fishes.

In my desperation, I am tempted to use the adult word 'shite' again and show the girls what a fine manly fellow I am. For I am almost four and nearly as old as Daisy – and she's going on five. However, I am smart enough at my age to hold my tongue opposite her and her big sister. A new feeling, shame, has come over me and stopped me from using this filthy swear word like I once did. Added to this is the thought that Grannie might find out and get herself into a towering rage like she did the time I swore at Jack when he pelted worms at me.

The next hour passes dreamily by. It's as if we have known each other all our lives and not just from recent days when we drank our pretend tea in the cubby house. How we'd love to climb out onto the bank and drop a few little fishes into one of the barrels before retrieving them later this afternoon and showing everyone what fine fishers of fish we are! But no such luck.

END OF PART FOUR

WIDER HORIZONS

The Summer of 1944

I have seen a rabbit shot. I have looked into its dead eyes and witnessed its final sorrowful moment. I have seen a second rabbit lying next to it, kicking and jerking its legs frantically in an effort to escape death. But I still don't know that there are other deaths – those of fellow children, some of whom lie beneath the rubble back in London after a night's savage bombing by the German planes.

My horizons are about to be expanded by Jack. He's going to kill yet another creature, one far bigger than a rabbit – namely, Shy Denis's pig. Jack has a number of talents, such as cutting the hair of one or two neighbouring farmers with Grannie's scissors. This happens the day before they travel to Nenagh to sell some of their cattle. They like to look their best on these days, especially those old prospectors who are searching for a young wife. It'll be such a relief to have their hair trimmed by Jack before setting out to town with their cattle.

From my seat on Lightning's cart, I have seen a number of men hurrying to the flagstones and perching themselves on one of Grannie's better chairs. Jack wraps a towel round their neck. Then I watch him cutting their hair and fussing over them like a hen with her chick. It's one of the most intimate moments when men can exchange views with Jack on all sorts of subjects as he clips away at their hair.

One morning, it's the turn of Ned Needles to get his hair trimmed. Ned is the rogue who tried to steal our pig, though it was in jest and just to hear me raining down curses on him at the time. But now it's Jack's turn to be the humourist. Snip, snip, snip. He doesn't say a word but concentrates on shaping Ned's hair and distracting him from what he has planned to do with the scissors. However, he finds it difficult to suppress his laughter and it's not long before he has left poor Ned so well-shorn that he's almost bald. Ah, Jack, you're such a mischief-maker!

Jack looks over at me on the cart and smiles. 'That'll teach the rascal not to try stealing our precious pig again,' he whispers. He is so glad he's got no mirror to show Ned his scalped head of hair.

Jack and I run out the lane and watch him racing round the bend beyond Gret's gateway. He's as sprightly as a young ass. But what a surprise is in store for him when he gets home and takes a look at himself in the mirror! Ned won't be back in a hurry for another haircut from Jack.

'Why,' laughs Jack, 'I've left him bald as an egg.' Grannie takes a fit of laughing too. The news of Ned's haircut is enough to keep the neighbours smirking for the rest of the week.

Jack's prime talent is for killing pigs, but he thinks it's a great misfortune to have such a gift as this. He's a gentle soul at heart. This means he'll try to kill Shy Denis's pig with as little pain as possible. It's far from easy and no pig has ever come back to thank him. Jack would rather be invited to a neighbour's house-dance to sing one of his rebel songs or to the graveyard to dig a grave. He'd rather spend time trimming a piece of bog oak into a walking stick for an old lady like Mrs Collins or be asked to train a young ass the way Shy Denis does, anything rather than spend the afternoon killing a sad-eyed pig, a pig that never did anyone the slightest harm.

Unfortunately, pig killing is what Jack does better than anyone else. To dispatch a pig the way he does requires every ounce of his strength, all his keenness-of-eye and slight-of-hand.

It's early on Thursday morning and Grannie is her usual busy self. I watch her on her knees at the fireplace. She hasn't had time to say a prayer. She has loaded the grate with a bagful of twigs, thin ones which she and I collected in her shopping bag the previous week. She has covered them with half a dozen furze bushes to get a lively blaze.

It doesn't take long before I see the smoke curling up the chimney, followed by the first bright sparks of flame. I have seen her do this a thousand times before and I never get tired of watching her and listening to her humming to herself.

I haven't heard Rusty the cockerel crowing. He isn't awake yet. I'm sitting on the wobbly stool by the side of the fire and watching the flames growing hotter by the minute. Behind me, the bright sunlight is streaming in over the half-door, filling the room with its own type of warmth and beckoning me to come outside.

I feel my bones getting stronger these days. Grannie tells me I am now four years old. She says she will bake me a cake for tomorrow full of apples and blackcurrants and that I can invite Ellie to share the cake with me. I feel I'm becoming a man – almost a man like Jack, though still little.

With the fire now raging, I know what will happen next. Grannie won't spend time sitting me on her knees and dressing me. Gone are those far-off days when I sat in my pram abroad in the yard for the passersby to look in at me. Gone are my days struggling to walk with Jack's fingers guiding me. I begin to realise who I am. I'm no longer Grannie's little man. I am four and I consider myself to be a fully-fledged child, like Gret's children.

But there's more, much more. At last, I realise that I'm different from the neighbouring children – a child born far away – a child almost killed by the bombs that almost destroyed the house where Nell and Patsy lived with me, their newborn son.

Grannie did her best to tell me this a few weeks back while we were sitting on the ass's cart after collecting our eggs. She felt I was old enough at this stage to take in some of what she said – how my parents loaded me inside a big suitcase and carried me down to the railway underground station where I cried and roared the livelong night as the bombs rained down over our heads. I'm unable to understand all that she was saying. I don't know what the word 'parents' means. The only parent-figures I've ever known are Grannie and Jack.

I am dressed and ready for my egg and milk. But first of all, I kneel down and say my blessing prayers beside the fire for Grannie. This is the year when she will teach me a list of what she calls 'proper prayers'. She will show them to me in her prayer book and point out the words and I will try to recite them back to her: prayers like *Hail Mary,* the *Our Father* and *Glory be to God.* This is the year when I'll learn at least another six or seven prayers while I'm kneeling beside her. I won't understand what many of these new words mean. But I'll get to understand the holiness in

175

Grannie's eyes and on her lips as she winds her way through this complex list of prayers.

I have always wanted to please her and I will have learnt enough long prayers by this time next year to flabbergast the likes of Father Speed the Plough. I am also anxious to please Jack and keep the smile on his face. I will never again allow the visiting card-players to teach me how to use swear words.

Jack walks in the half-door and I run to greet him. We dip our mugs into the bucket of water and he offers me a mugful of milk from the jug on the press cupboard shelf. It's fresh from the cow and still warm.

Grannie has put our three eggs into the tin saucepan and placed it in a nest of twigs on top of the fire. Jack is busy cutting thick slices of soda bread and layering them with heaps of butter. I take my place at the front table – the usual place under the St Brigid's wicker cross.

Grannie brings our eggs to the table, each one boiled to her liking. Jack adds lots of butter and salt to my egg and he stirs it round and round for ages without saying a word. I could be gone to the well and back again before he stops stirring it to his satisfaction. This morning's ritual of the egg and the accompanying mug of milk (my second one of the day) is a great start this morning and I swallow the egg in no time at all. It's much better than pretending to swig down a thimbleful of imaginary tea in Rosie and Daisy's cubby house. It even beats those mornings when I join Ellie for a day playing with her and her bowlee wheel and spinning it from the crossroads all the way down to Brindley's stile.

Grannie is clearing away the table and I am sitting on the hot flagstones, burning my britches and staring down into the stream. I am looking for fishes like the ones that slipped from my hands recently at the river. I know that there are no fishes in Grannie's yard stream. I'm not a fool. But I can dream for a while and contemplate catching a small fish like the trout Jack caught a mile upstream from the metal bridge.

176

Jack walks out the half-door and across the yard towards me. He has just filled Grannie's tea chest with logs. They'll last at least today and tomorrow. He creeps up behind me and stands looking over my shoulder.

'Ned, my lad, you'll get a rash from looking at yourself in the stream,' he laughs. I haven't the foggiest notion what he's talking about. I am half-expecting him to make a grab at me and swing me up on his shoulders like he does when we come out from Sunday Mass. He does that just to hear my shrieks of laughter – like Bucko's laughter when Shawnee and Sweeney tickle him half to death over in the Thistle Field.

However, I remember what Grannie told me – that I'm now four and that she'll bake me a cake. I think I'm too old for Jack to be swinging me up on his shoulders. I think Jack knows it too.

Something unusual is about to happen today. I have a strange feeling about it, though I can't explain it. Perhaps it's the unusual look I see in Jack's eyes. He beckons me down to the ass's cart and we sit next to each other for a chat, the way we do at other times, like when he and I are resting on the headland after he's dug up the spuds.

'I'll be away for the best part of today, Ned,' says he. 'I can't take you with me, even though I'd like to.'

'Why can't I go?'

'No, Ned, it's not possible. For the past week, Shy Denis has been begging me to go and kill his pig for him. It's not the same thing as you and me going off to shoot a few rabbits.'

I realise that killing a huge pig is a dangerous job. I know that Jack was up at Bill Buffalo's place the other day and that he had some difficulty killing Bill's pig and had bruised his shoulder. I feel sad for not being able to go with him. I have always gone everywhere else with him – whether to the well or the fields for spuds. The only other thing I've not done with him is go fishing but he has promised that I'll go with him when I'm a little older.

I wish it wasn't like this. The excitement of killing a pig is something I've never seen before. I have heard a pig squealing in the distance but I never knew why. I recently heard Gret's pig

177

squealing and I heard Old Tim's pig also squealing a day later. Perhaps their pig got into a fight with a gander or with one of those wild dogs that forever go killing lambs around the hills.

To make sure I understand, Jack says, 'It's not a place for a child to be seen and it's not a place for you either, Ned. You don't know the cruelty that a pig has to put up with when it's about to die. And another thing,' he went on, 'it's not uncommon for a frightened pig to escape and spend the day running round the hills. A pig is a fierce creature when cornered, far worse than a rat, and you might get trodden on or even killed if I take you with me.'

There's to be no further argument. Jack has put the fear-of-God into me and I will have to stay behind with Grannie and try and make a card-house instead. This is one of the few times when I feel sad. But I am even sadder for Shy Denis's pig and I am relieved that I won't have to see him die.

Apart from our Sunday mutton and the occasional rabbit, we often have a plateful of ham along with our cabbage and spuds. There's always a few fletches of bacon hanging on the hob above the fire. They are the gifts given to Jack after his pig killings and are left there to get smoked from the heat of the fire. That's what Grannie tells me. She told me this before but I'd forgotten it. Now I understand why Jack is going to Shy Denis's place this morning – to help put food on Denis's table – enough that will last him for the next six months. He'll bring us home a few fletches of meat once the pig has been cut up and salted.

'But please, Jack, why can't somebody else kill the pig?' I ask.

'It's because I'm the best man for this sort of job – just like my father was before me.'

He sees the sad look in my eyes. 'But Ned,' he says as he tries to re-assure me, 'I hate myself for having to do it.' And I can see that Jack is sad for having to go and kill the pig.

He brings a chair into the yard, the same chair Ned Needles sat on recently. In his hands, he is holding two knives. I don't know why he needs to have two knives. Surely, one would be enough. I can hear him whistling and trying to put a bit of cheerfulness into himself over the task that lies ahead of him.

He starts to sharpen the knives, holding them up to the light occasionally and testing the blade with his thumb.

I continue to watch him from the ass's cart. The gleam of the sun puts the colours blue and silver into them. The hens run back into the haggart, looking for a safe spot to hide. The dazzle of the blades has frightened them. The knives might well signal their own death if they're not careful. I avert my eyes and look towards the stream where one or two young ducks are spinning round merrily in the water.

I am spellbound by the knives. It's no use asking Jack what he'll do with their sharp blades. I can picture what's going to happen to the poor pig – a pig that was once a wobbly-legged piglet living in the dark recesses of the pig house. That was a long time ago. And then the old sow propelled him out into Shy Denis's haggart and introduced him to the great big world.

I feel another surge of pity rising up inside me. I have never felt such strong feelings as this before – not even for the rabbits killed by Jack's gun. It's the thought of Jack's sharp knives killing the pig today and the fact that there is nothing I can do to stop it.

So overpowered am I with these sad thoughts that I cannot sit on the ass's cart any longer. I keep my eyes averted from Jack and his cruel knives and make my way out past the hen house and on towards my berry farm. I sit there, hidden under the tree. I don't even look at the berries lying in front of me in Jack's shoe box. I'm in no mood for playing with them. I'd like to whisper my feelings to them, but it's no use.

Like the pretend tea in Rosie and Daisy's cubby house, my berries are useless playthings and I feel thoroughly alone, just me and my sorrow. I have a great deal to think about. I am about to cry.

It's time for another visit to my little friends' cubby house and I venture out over the flagstones and on up the lane. Jack hasn't even missed me, so busy is he with sharpening his knives.

Rosie and Daisy are sitting on the side of the ditch inside their yard. Each of them is munching a hot spud they've filched from Gret's burner. They see the sad look on my face and the recent tearstains on my cheeks. I tell them how I feel about Shy Denis's pig and how I watched Jack as he was sharpening his knives and the way he was whistling to himself as though to give himself a bit of courage.

They don't seem to understand what I'm saying as I pour out my sorrow and go on unburdening myself. They tell me they once saw a pig dying up at Old Tim's place.

'Seen it with my own eyes,' says Daisy.

'There wasn't so much as a squeak out of Tim's pig when it was dying,' says Rosie.

But I know they are lying. A pig killing is no place for children as young as us. They are simply trying to wipe away my sadness and bring back the smile to my face like before.

Rosie becomes serious. She tells me how Old Tim gave Jack the pig's bladder and how he cleaned and washed it in Tim's stream before handing it to her as a plaything to take home. I can see that she is not telling a lie this time. I'm beginning to understand the importance of a pig's bladder, though I have known nothing about it until Rosie begins explaining it to me. She tells me how Fiddler Joe blew up the bladder with his bicycle pump for Daisy and herself when he got home from Bill Buffalo's pig killing, how he tied it with a piece of long twine and how Gret wrapped it round her wrist and then Daisy's wrist the following day, how they spent the entire day racing round the Thistle Field with it.

I immediately forget about Jack and his knives. I can only think about the wonders of a pig's bladder and my eyes light up. My little friends are happy when they see me smiling again and if Jack brings me back the bladder, I don't think I'll ever again play with my sock-ball.

As if she has read my thoughts, Rosie says, 'Shy Denis will give Jack the bladder for you. Don't worry, Ned, I'm sure he will. You can spend hours chasing round the Blue Button Field with it

180

and frightening the life out of Jack's calves when they see you racing at them with your bladder.'

'Maybe the Rotten Tree will fall down and collapse from the sight of you and your bladder,' laughs Daisy. I didn't know that she could be so clever with words.

What on earth is she talking about? The two of them are beginning to get themselves overexcited. I think about what Daisy just said about the Rotten Tree. A tree has no feelings, especially a rotten one. I don't have to be four years old to know that much! But a pig – Shy Denis's pig – has feelings like we have.

Now that his knives are well-sharpened, Jack gets up from the chair. He goes back inside the half-door and fetches his bloodstained apron from the bottom of the press cupboard. From above the hob, he brings down half a dozen hazel wands that he lately whittled down. They have sharp points at either end. He throws them into Grannie's little bath pan. The wands are to keep open the dead pig's belly once he has slit it open from top to bottom and hung it on the half ladder in Shy Denis's living room.

This last hour, Grannie has been watching his progress from behind the net curtains. And now she dashes out after him and sprinkles holy water on his forehead in the hope that the killing will be swift and as painless as possible. Jack stretches out his hands towards her and she blesses them too.

He marches out towards the gap between the half-door and the pig house. He reaches up to the pig house roof and brings down the reins for tying the pig's legs together. He brings down the shiny new bucket that he bought in Heffernan's shop in Barrack Street to replace the old one. It's to collect the pig's blood in. With all the other stuff – the apron and the wands – it's an awkward load for him to carry. The other helpers will bring new and clean buckets with them too: Jack Scissors and Mick the Herd, as well as Shy Denis and Ellie's father, Rody.

Jack carries on up the lane towards Shy Denis's place. He has been walking slowly and reluctantly, his thoughts full of the pig and its final confrontation with death. On other farms, men have made use of a sledgehammer to stun their pig before killing it. Jack thinks this an added cruelty and a way to spoil the pig's bacon. His own way of dealing with Shy Denis's pig won't have the same effect.

The men are already there, waiting for him. They are smoking their pipes inside the cow shed so as to clear away the flies with the smoke.

Shy Denis has brought out his horse's cart and lowered the jambs onto the grass just outside the pig house door. He has an old barn door sloped up onto the cart and tied onto the jambs so that his pig can make a run up onto the cart the minute Jack Scissors gives it a few darts of his hayfork up its backside.

The previous evening, Shy Denis borrowed four high boards from Rowanberry. They needed to be high in case the pig tries to leap out over the side of the cart when he sees Jack and his knives approaching.

The cart has been scrubbed clean by Mrs Fidget. Shy Denis has put mountains of fresh straw on it to soak up the blood when Jack starts the killing.

Jack Scissors has the shoulders and chest of a wrestler. He has brought his hayfork along with him and he knows what he has to do with it. It's always the same. He strolls over to the pig house with a bucket of mash and smiles in the doorway. He spreads the mash evenly along the pig's tray, all the time whispering words of endearment into its ear.

He stands behind the doomed pig and waits for the signal. Now that the boards have been sloped up onto the front of the cart, the pig will have no trouble running up onto it and settling himself down comfortably in the middle of the fresh straw.

All is now ready for the sacrifice of the pig to begin. Jack Scissors raises his fork and gives the pig a sharp dart into its bum. The pig gives a loud squeal of anger. He forgets about his breakfast of mash and makes a hurried dash out the door.

Jack, Rody, Shy Denis and Mick the Herd have formed two lines from the pig house door out as far as the cart so that the pig is hemmed in between them. Such precise detail is not needed since Jack Scissors has given the pig an almighty fright and his fork has drawn the first blood, a little red river running down the cheeks of its bum.

The pig leaps up onto the cart with the nimbleness of a steeplechaser. The high backboard and sideboards of the cart have already been hasped onto it and now that the pig is on board, the front board is hasped too. The pig is trapped inside the cart and ready for its death.

The men are in no hurry. They return to Shy Denis's living room and light their pipes a second time. Shy Denis pulls out a pack of cards from his pocket and starts dealing them out for a game of 'Beggar me Neighbour.'

The pig has settled down in his new home on the cart. I wonder what he is thinking. *This is a cosy straw bed. Maybe I'm off on a journey today. Maybe I will see the market cross inside in Nenagh.*

Meanwhile, us three children in the cubby house are happily drinking our mugs of pretend tea. We are interrupted, however, when Bucko calls Rosie and Daisy from the haggart gateway. 'Mother wants ye to go down to the well and fetch back water for the dinner.'

A smart woman is Gret. She intends to distract us from the lion-like roars of the pig on realising it's about to die.

Rosie and Daisy step alongside me to the well. They know how sad I have been and they try to put my mind on other things. They bang the bucket off of the sweet-gallon to make a musical rhythm and they laugh at one another. Daisy starts singing one of her Table songs, starting off with 'five and five make ten-ah'.

I have my mind on the bladder. After the pig is killed, I am hoping Jack will bring it back to me to play with. Already, I think I hear the pig's shrieks above at Shy Denis's place. Am I dreaming?

It's time for the men to get to work. They put their pipes away and stroll back to the pig. Jack stands on the wheel of the cart and peers in. The pig is snoring blissfully – but not for long. Jack gets down and beckons the men towards the cart. They perch themselves on the wheels: two on one side and two on the other. They each have a rope.

Jack Scissors gently loops his rope round the pig's trotter nearest to him. There's not a murmur out of the pig. From the other side of the cart, Shy Denis loops his rope round the hind trotter. They pull the reins tight. Rody and Mick the Herd prepare to do the same with the front trotters.

The men quickly tie their ropes to the corner-posts of the cart. The pig is firmly trapped and cannot move a muscle. They speedily roll the pig over onto its back. The work is hot and heavy. But, stretched on its back, the pig is at last safely secured.

The pig's fear comes alive, followed by a sudden hatred of its surroundings. Had the poor creature a moment to think, what might have been in its mind?

I am a pig. There is no one here to help me. I have known this fear ever since I was a piglet – a fear of wild things – a fear that some cruel beast might one day come skulking after me and take away my life – a fear of an irretrievable fate – a fear of Man.

Jack steps up on the jamb of the cart and takes a look at the pig to see if everything is to his liking. The poor animal looks peculiar, lying on his back and decorated with so many criss-crossed ropes. Apart from the ropes, its position is made further awkward – the front of the cart being sloped down so that it's merely a foot off the ground. Once the blood starts to flow, it will run smoothly down the pig's belly and be easily collected in the buckets.

The men step down off of the wheels. Jack stays where he is, looking at the ignominious pig and examining it. This lasts but a minute. Shy Denis brings out the knives and lays them on a chair next to Jack, who puts on his blood-stained apron. It's time for the pig to die.

He studies the pig with the eye of a surgeon. He searches for the death spot that will let the chasm of blood flow. With his index finger and thumb he marks out a small triangle of flesh. Shy Denis hands him the brown-handled knife. With the flat, thin flash of its blade, Jack pierces the pig's throat, puncturing the soft gullet before removing the blade. Shy Denis hands him the long, black-handled knife and Jack plunges it into the pig's heart to hasten its death.

The geraniums in Shy Denis's window box are red indeed. But redder still is the pig's steaming blood and soon the straw on the cart is drenched and so is Jack's bespattered apron. The pig's eyes are mournfully bleak in the loneliness of its shivering death.

Rosie and Daisy sit with me at the edge of the well. It's only for a minute or two that we hear the pig's screams. It's a cry for help and I feel sad all over again. In spite of themselves, so do Rosie and Daisy. The three of us are near to tears and to this very day, I can hear the screams of Shy Denis's pig. Had it not been for the promise of the pig's bladder, I think I'd have died of fright on the spot.

Shy Denis prepared his eight-rung ladder earlier this morning. He has a long rope attached to it and he brings the ladder out from the half-door. Jack and his friends will need all their strength to bring the dead pig down off of the cart. The boards are removed from the cart. The men take a short break. There is no need to hurry. They know the pig is dead.

It's not the same as when Gret's son, Dan, was wheeling the pony and trap round the yard. The men need the strength of Samson to lift up the jambs of the cart and pull it across to the half-door. Once there, they push the pig sideways, rolling it out onto the ladder. They tie its legs firmly to the top and bottom rungs.

They struggle in the doorway with the pig and the ladder. If only they had a few more men with them! Even Jack Scissors is praying for more strength to his arms. Finally, they manage to prop the ladder up against the back wall of the living room, the pig's front legs tied to the bottom rung.

Shy Denis places the buckets round the ladder so that as little blood as possible gets lost. Every drop will be needed by the women: Mrs Fidget, Molly Hughes and Gret. They have already arrived and are ready to make the black puddings. Gret has brought her caraway seeds to spice up the puddings, like her mother taught her to do.

The pig is a good one and its blood is still flowing down into the buckets.

Jack cannot take off his apron yet. He has more butchering to attend to. He makes a long incision down the length of the pig's belly from the neck to the groin. It's time for him to attend to the ropey entrails of the pig and remove them out of its belly. He pulls them out and winds them round his arm like a skein of wool before handing them to Rody.

Rody stretches them out in the bath of hot water that the women prepared earlier when the men were busy round the cart and working on the pig.

Shy Denis hands Jack the hazel wands and, with the help of the other men's fingers, he stretches them across the pig's warm carcass. The men will get a fletch of meat each and Jack will get an added one because of his experience with pigs. They are all happy. There'll be meat enough left over to last Shy Denis till Christmas.

They can now rest. The day's work has been a success. They pull out the chairs and sit round the table. They treat themselves to a few bottles of stout at Shy Denis's expense. They light up their pipes once more and put smoke to the heavens.

Much later, Mrs Fidget and her crew of women spend their time filling up several kettles of water and boiling them on top of Denis's blazing log fire. They continue to pour the boiling water into a huge bathtub so that the pig's flesh is thoroughly scalded. After a short while, they scrape off the pig's thicker bristles with the men's cut-throat razors and light up their church tapers to singe away the thinner bristles.

Grannie has been listening at the window all day, scarcely breathing, so as to get wind of the pig's fate. So anxious is she that she has forgotten which chores she should be attending to till she hears the pig's last screams.

'Ah-ha! Jack has finally killed the pig,' she cries, 'and the poor creature can now rest in peace.' She blesses herself so as to ward off evil. It's one of her old traditions like skimming the cream from a jug of milk before letting a tinker have a mug of it – in case the ghost of the pig should return to haunt them all.

The afternoon is getting late. She hears Jack's weary footfall coming down the lane. She has been worried sick in case the pig got loose and gave him a fierce kicking in its attempt to escape. She runs to the half-door to greet him.

By this time, I have been home a long time after playing with Rosie and Daisy. I am sitting next to the fire, me and my thoughts about the bladder.

Jack enters the yard. He stands in the doorway and nods to his mother. 'Yes, we killed the pig,' he whispers as he looks across the floor at me. He reaches for his mug and takes a long drink of water from the bucket.

Grannie heats up the kettle on the crane and Jack gives his hands a good clean as if to wash the stench of the pig's death away.

'Ma'am, put a few records on the turntable till we cheer ourselves up,' he cries. 'I'll throw a few sods of turf on the fire.'

Suddenly, I'm aware I haven't eaten all day. Grannie sees this also. Jack hasn't eaten either. She pours each of us a huge bowl of rabbit soup with lots of flaky rabbit-flesh in it. I drink two mugs of milk and look wistfully at Grannie to see if there's any more rabbit soup left over.

We listen to the records for a while. Then we kneel down in front of the fire and say our prayers. I pray for the pig but I don't tell Grannie or Jack. I am not sure what happens to a pig when it dies. I know that we are going to heaven when we die – that is, if we behave ourselves and I never again steal Grannie's icing-sugar from inside the lid of the piano. It's something else for me to think about. Perhaps there is a life elsewhere for this pig to enjoy. I hope and pray there is.

Jack throws a few mugs of water on the fire and quenches it. It makes a hiss of steam. He and I hop into bed and wrap our legs round each other so as to get ourselves warm and drive away the bed's dampness. I can hear the last of the bees as they return to the laurel leaves in the empty fireplace near the bed. They keep me awake a while longer.

I soon hear Jack snoring. He has had a much tougher day than me. I'm beginning to understand a lot more. Like Shy Denis, we will have plenty of meat for weeks to come. We will feast ourselves like kings until the pig's flesh is gone. Then Jack will go somewhere else and kill another pig and we'll have more fletches to hang on the hob.

Next morning, Jack goes up to Shy Denis's place to collect his fletches of bacon. Denis must have been up all night. He has cut up his pig into several pieces and placed them in his pig barrel. He has salted them well and layered them with greenery and cardboard. He has sealed the barrel tight as a drum at the top.

The bladder is lying on the table and Shy Denis says, 'This is for Ned.'

Jack thanks Denis for his fletches of bacon and with scarcely another word, he hurries out the door and heads home. He is anxious to give me the bladder.

Grannie has a ball of twine hidden in the bottom of the press cupboard and, like Jack, she is ready for this great day, my race with the bladder through the bulrushes in the Bull Paddock.

Meanwhile, Ellie has brought down her bowlee wheel to let me bowl it down as far as the metal bridge – and away we go. Soon, we are quite a way past Brindley's stile. I have my eyes firmly glued on the bowlee wheel as I tap it further and further towards John's Gate.

Suddenly, we hear Grannie banging her tin tray. We have to return to her at once. Her tray is an obstacle that has to be obeyed.

I see Jack stamping his boots down the slope towards us. He is waving the bladder in the air and I remember what Rosie told me yesterday. 'Nothing compares to playing with a bladder,' she said, 'not even our cubby house nor Bucko's rotten orange that Mother brought him back from town to hurl round the yard till it burst.'

How excited I am to hear her say that! My sock-ball's springiness is no match for a pig's bladder. Oh, the adventures I will have with it! Neither can my two berry farms of animals compete with it. They will have to rest in their shoebox for at least another week.

Ellie and I follow Jack in the half-door. The scissors and twine are on the table. So is the bicycle pump. Jack takes the bladder and with the pump's nozzle, he slowly pumps it up. It takes a while. Ellie and I hold our breath.

When the bladder is a foot long, he cuts a length of twine and lays it on the floor. It stretches from the press cupboard to the half-door. He takes me by the arm and wraps the twine round my wrist. He secures it with his fingers, leaving a length of 4 or 5 ft exposed so that the bladder can fly high above me once I get out to play with it. If it were any longer, it might get caught on thorny bushes and burst.

Jack sees the joy in my eyes and Ellie has never seen me look as happy as this. The three of us head for the lane, Grannie again running after us to bless the bladder with holy water. I clutch it to my chest. I can scarcely wait to reach John's Gate and extend the twine and bladder before shaking it into the sky.

The Bull Paddock is Jack's biggest field with only the oak tree and the pine tree in my way. Ellie climbs onto the gate to watch me play. Jack is behind her.

Free! Free! Just me and my bladder, locked together and the wind behind us! How fast my heart is hammering!

Ahead of me lie the bulrushes. It's time to unravel the twine and race my bladder round the field. I stand for a moment in front of the smiling faces of Jack and Ellie before shaking my wrist.

Off, off and away! I hurtle myself and my bladder across the bulrushes from the gate to the crab tree and back. I can almost hear the bladder laughing with me as my sandals speed ever onwards, the bladder making strange patterns in the air as I continue to shake it. If Jack's cows were not busily nibbling the grass beyond the Danes' Hill, they'd be so alarmed at the speed of my legs that they'd have dashed into the river in fright.

One or two rabbits at the edge of the wood scatter to their burrows behind the fence. A flock of crows in the pine tree fly off to Bill Corcoran's cornfield, leaving the place to myself.

At last, I have to give my bladder a rest. I find a patch of grass beneath the pine tree and sit myself down, my bladder close beside me. The air suddenly comes alive with Ellie's laughter and

Jack's clapping hands. They share in my joy as I ponder this wonderful moment.

Did I really race my bladder the length and breadth of this huge field? I realise how much I am sweating. I hope to play with my bladder again soon, for I have never experienced so much freedom and fun as I have today.

I suddenly feel the slightest touch of sadness, knowing that my bladder will one day burst on me. Then Jack will have to go and kill another pig. But I am not as sad as when I saw Jack first sharpening his knives.

The field soon becomes silent. The world has returned to its old ways and it is time to go home. The crows have returned to the pine tree. The rabbits have come out from the wood. The cows have started bawling again. We travel up the lane and Jack keeps his eye on the bladder.

'Well done, Ned!' he whispers. 'Let's go tell Grannie about it.' And while he is talking, he unwraps the twine from round my wrist and, much to her surprise, twists it onto Ellie's wrist.

I don't mind a bit. Ellie has been kind enough to let me bowl her bowlee wheel most of this morning. It is her turn to race up the hill and into Grannie's yard with the bladder flying behind her.

Jack and I take our weary legs home after her. We are a long way back. I am too tired to say anything to him. Both of us are far too excited.

Grannie comes out to the flagstones to welcome us. The minute I set eyes on her, I am bursting to tell her my news.

Meanwhile, Jack has unwrapped the bladder from Ellie's wrist. He won't place it on the hob beside the horse's tackle. The heat of the fire would ruin it.

He'll hide it in the visitors' room next door to Grannie's room, where it can lie on the bed, imperiously, till the next time I've the pleasure of playing with it. Jack will keep an eye on it to make sure no air escapes from it.

It's another Saturday. These last two weeks have been even hotter than usual. It's the year of '44 and the German army looks as though it's getting the worst of the battles. At least, that's what Herald the Post says when he delivers the odd letter from my mother to Grannie.

The sadness of the pig's death and the joy of the bladder are replaced some days by the enticement of the river. Rosie and Daisy will take me with them as soon as they've done their Saturday chores for Grannie. Grannie and Jack know it's safe to go down there and kneel in the water without getting myself drowned.

Long before we arrive, we hear its merry murmuring and we hurry even faster. When we reach the river, we see many other children already in the water. Some have come from as far away as Killeen. There are no big boys here; they are too busy helping their fathers on the land.

Me and Daisy know none of these new faces, for we are not old enough to go to school. Even Rosie doesn't know all of them. Some of the girls have left school recently but they are not too grand to come down and play their games alongside us. They'll make sure we smaller ones are safe. Besides, it's a chance for them to take a break from helping their mothers bake the weekly soda-bread or helping them with the ironing and darning.

I haven't seen many big girls like these before except at Mass. The older ones soon disappear and stroll along the riverbank till they get to the big sally hole a mile upstream. It's not a deep sally hole like the one out in Glown. The water is no more than 3 foot deep and has been partially blocked off by a few fallen trees from past storms.

None of these girls can swim a stroke. They spend time in their usual frolics and games, splashing each other with cupped hands until they are totally soaked. Then they climb out onto the bank and enjoy an hour or two with nothing else to do but dry off and watch the big yellow sun smiling down on them.

Apart from my friends, I also know Sadie and I know her rosy-cheeked younger sister, Apples. They are two of the big girls that I see at Mass when I'm kneeling next to Grannie. They live in the Silvermines village and have brought a small bucket with them to try and catch a few small trout. They would love to show them to younger children like us, just to see the look in our eyes before dropping them back in the river.

They spend a while watching us paddling round beneath the metal bridge. Then they stroll along the riverbank towards the big sally hole. When they arrive, they have the river to themselves, for the girls from Killeen have gone home for their dinner.

Sadie and Apples are shy girls and in the sheltered privacy of the pool where no boys can spy on them, they twist out of their dresses and leave them among the ferns. They dash into the pool and jump up and down. Their shrieks of laughter echo through the glade. If there are any crows nearby, they have now surely fled.

Meanwhile, the day hurtles on. By now, even the most timid children no longer spend time paddling alongside us three. All race up and down the river except me with my tender feet. Even Rosie and Daisy churn up the water in an effort to see who'll make splashes higher than the others.

I sit on the bank and watch them. They climb out and race each other up and down the bank and through the ferns, rubbing their hair with fern leaves to make sure that they're thoroughly dried. After all their fun in the water, they are as clean as a whistle, especially their legs, which are often less than spotless from running barefoot all day.

I wish I was like them so that I could run among the stones in the river without the pebbles hurting my toes. My sandals protect my feet too much. They are a nuisance at times.

Rosie and Daisy come and sit beside me. The three of us have time to relax. We sprawl on the grass and the next hour passes dreamily by. We close our tired eyes and the sun lulls us to sleep.

I have enjoyed all my toys, from sock-ball to pig's bladder. But the river in Dolla seems almost magical. It's as though it's leapt out from one of Grannie's storybooks.

It's the last Sunday in July. We've been to Mass and we've had our breakfast. Rosie, Daisy and I are on our way back to the river. Bucko is joining us. He has been given orders to look after us and see that we come to no harm. After our recent visit, the little sally hole under the bridge will cause us no trouble. We can even kneel down in it. Me, too, if I don't walk around too much and hurt my toes.

The three of us spend time searching for shiny stones like the rusty and lavender ones or the blue and black ones, so that we can draw on Grannie's flagstones. Bucko says we will never be able to draw good enough with smooth stones. He says it's better to look for stones with rough edges. He is a very clever boy.

When we get tired of paddling and searching for stones, he takes us for a stroll through the ferns. It's something I'll remember – the smell of the shrubs that we pass through on our way upstream.

The hills that surround the riverbank seem to hem us in. These hills are well-known to Rosie and Bucko when they walk the 3 miles to school. But for me and Daisy, they are a magnificent marvel and we can't stop gawping up at them as we stroll behind Bucko. The ferns are nearly as high as ourselves. We find a place to sit down under an oak tree above the river where we can gaze down at its sweeps and curves.

Bucko has brought with him a few roasted crab apples and hot spuds. We are enjoying our mid-morning feast. It's much tastier than the make-believe tea in the cubby house. We eat in silence away from the rest of the children and listen to their screams in the distance, especially the shouts of the bigger girls up round their sally hole.

We walk down to the edge of the river. We see a bunch of girls a little older than ourselves and realise that, in spite of ourselves, we are close to the forbidden sally hole. This stretch of river is still shallow enough for us to wade along behind them.

I join Bucko and his sisters in the river. I try to be brave about my tender feet and not to scream. We paddle among the other children. Some of them wave back at Rosie and Bucko.

The river is getting deeper but not yet deep enough to frighten us. We enjoy the cool chill of the water round our legs. Ahead of us, between us and the sally hole, are big girls older still. They have been walking through the river like us. Their legs are so clean that they remind me of the white statues in church. Some of the girls are able to run along the river and their feet seem to feel no pain. I can't tell Rosie and Daisy that the little pebbles are sharp on my feet.

The day moves on giddily towards the early afternoon. The older children race out of the water and up the bank. I watch them playing hide and seek. I hear them screaming as they run towards the highest oak tree in an effort to reach 'home'. Their screams get even louder when the chaser is about to grab hold of them before they reach the tree.

By now, some of us little ones are getting tired. We find ourselves a patch of grass where we stretch out. The sun bears down on us and we cover our eyes with our arms. Our feet are soon dry.

For the rest of this day and for many days to come, we will spend half our time in the river. Come September, once school starts for all except me and Daisy, the children will be back behind their desks, captured and enslaved in front of Mr Flanagan.

For some of them, school is a nuisance to put up with, but for others, a chance to learn new and exciting things about the world they live in. For all of them, the river is their best friend – ours too. Its charms surpass everything else and the hills around it add to our happiness. It's as though nature is laughing alongside us throughout these river days.

But for now, we have to go home and we rouse ourselves off of the grass. Even the big girls are getting tired like us. Like us, they are also a bit sad to be leaving their merriment behind them in the water. They'll be back again next Sunday.

As we stroll up the lane, we are quiet and I have time to think. It's one of my moments of uncertainty. Whilst I was playing with my friends, I had forgotten everything else, even the joy of playing with my bladder and with my berry farm and my go-cart the day before that. I fear I'm too late to go with Jack for the cows. Poor Jack will have to fetch them on his own, just himself and Rose the sheepdog.

My guilty heart catches up with me and tells me to get home quickly so that I can be in time to take my usual walk with him to the Bull Paddock. There is so much I have to tell him – and tell Grannie, too. They'll have another pain in the ear for the rest of the evening if I don't stop gabbling on about my time in the river. I can't help it. It's the only news I have for them – the river, the river, the river. I've even forgotten my bruised toes!

It's Tuesday morning. Before Rusty the cockerel has crowed, Jack is into his wellingtons and heading off to fetch the cows with faithful Rose. I am still in dreamland and splashing around in the river. But Grannie has already thrown her candle pieces onto the fire and it is blazing up nicely. She has said her prayers in front of her bedroom altar, asking God to keep me safe and praying that I won't have to go back to England for the next year or two.

She tiptoes down to the hen house and lets her hens and ducks out. They are hard to shift. Most of them are still asleep. How they keep perched on their roosting sticks, I'll never know.

She goes out to the cow shed to check on her geese and let them out. They are much noisier than the hens and ducks. They rush past her and fly out into the Blue Button Field.

Jack enters the Bull Paddock and throws off his socks and wellingtons to air his feet. He heads across the field to look for his cows. They often hide from him behind Danes' Hill. It's a game they like to play.

An hour later, when milking is over and the creamery tanks are full with milk, he tackles Lightning. The ass is anxious to get today's visit to the creamery over and done with so that he can get back to Moll and continue nuzzling her. They have always been best friends.

Jack taps the whip gently on Lightning's back and they set off. By the time he reaches the cross of Dolla, there's already a number of rumbling carts jogging their way towards the creamery. A little further on, the queue meets another queue coming down from Lisnageenlee. When they reach the creamery gate, there's a long line of carts standing there, waiting for their turn to get in.

The men jump down from the carts and take out their pipes. Early as it is, their conversations are brisk and their laughter warms the air, all of them striving to talk at one and the same time.

Jack gets home from the creamery by 11 o'clock. By that time, I have joined Grannie at the fireside, said my few prayers and listened to her reading me a story from her school storybook. I have had a drink of water from the bucket and my mug of warm milk along with my egg, Grannie has wiped my face with the dishcloth and made sure to clear the sleepiness from my eyes. She stands to look at me and brushes my cheek with her lips.

My day is about to start. It's not another pig-killing day for Jack. He is taking Moll up to Mick the Smith's forge for a set of new shoes. Lightning will be as miserable as sin while she's away. Jack is going to take me with him and I am quickly in my socks and sandals. Once again, I am giddy with excitement.

Before we set off, I watch him tending to Moll's cart wheels in the yard. He has a tin of axle grease in his fist and is pasting it liberally in and around both ends of the axle to make sure the wheels run smoothly. Moll's cart, also Lightning's, are precious objects and have to be kept in proper order. It's not only the two cart wheels, but the safety and lives of Moll and Lighting that are also precious. We depend on them having a set of good shoes on their hooves.

Jack tells me to hurry on or we'll be last in the queue when we get to the forge. I am anxious to see Mick at his work. I know our blacksmith well. He always has a line of white frothy foam round his mouth, for he is the only man who has a set of false teeth. He is a jolly fellow with a round red face and when he laughs, the white foam seems thicker than ever.

We travel past Mrs Fidget's gate. There is no sign of Ellie. She must have gone out the fields with Rody, her father. We go on towards the crossroads at Mountisland and on past Shy Denis's place. His haggart gates look dazzling. The ones he painted sky-blue and with white tips at the top. Ah, the artist in him!

As we get near the forge, I am every bit as excited as when I was paddling in the river with Bucko, Rosie and Daisy. The boards of the cart make a trembling noise and when Jack starts singing, they make his voice quaver as though the wind is getting stuck in his throat.

The cart rounds the hill above the crossroads and we hear Mick banging his hammer on his anvil. He is already hard at work.

We reach his forge and Jack reins in Moll next to two piles of turf and logs. There are several wheel hoops nearby. They are of various sizes to suit the cart wheels of ponies, asses or horses.

We enter the dusky doorway. Black clouds of steam and smoke rise up to the roof of the forge. It's even warmer in here than Grannie's blazing fire.

Mick looks different inside his forge. He is dressed in his butcher's apron and, thanks to his busy work, blowing on his bellows and the continued hammering on his anvil, he hasn't seen us yet. I have nothing else to do but look and stare. His face is covered in sweat and blackened with soot. There's a frown on his forehead. I have forgotten about his frothy lips and his bursts of laughter. My eyes are full of the glory of his warm forge and the smell of red hot iron.

Mick is the son of Ned the Smith, who started off his blacksmith work with nothing but a clawhammer, an anvil and a rasp. Within his first year among us, however, he became the talk of the lane when he was seen fixing the driving rod of old Tom Scissors' mowing machine. Tom's son (Jack Scissors) has the best mowing machine among us to this day.

Mick is every bit as fine a smith as his father and is able to heat the metal for the rim of a cart wheel to the right temperature – not a fraction too hot or too cold – in case the metal might break. His work is so detailed that no one has ever been able to see where he joined the pieces of their cartwheels together.

He doesn't take long tending to Moll. He places each hoof between his knees and pulls out the old horse nails with his pincers. He pares her hooves with his knife and hammers in the new nails, bending the sharpened ends before rasping the new shoes and fitting them onto Moll. Her hooves are now as cosy as a glove.

At last, he has time to smile at us and to share a laugh with Jack over a job well done. When he laughs, I see that he's not wearing his false teeth – just showing us his gums. He must reserve his false teeth for special occasions. Maybe he fears they might drop out of his mouth and into the flames of his furnace.

Jack and Mick see the look of horror on my face at Mick's toothless mouth and they laugh loudly. I can't understand why.

But I'm having an exciting time this morning. None of the other children are here – just me and Jack and the mighty Mick. I wonder if Ellie, Rosie and Daisy know what they're missing and the great work that Mick has done for Moll and her hooves.

There have been times, however, when money might be scarce and men like Jack are unable to go to the forge. That's when they have to do their own repairs to the hooves of their ass or horse.

When I was much younger, I saw Jack clawing out the old nails and rasping home the new ones.

It was an eventful morning. While his back was turned and he was talking to Grannie, I knelt under Moll's belly. I grabbed Jack's hammer in an attempt to tend to her hind hoof and give Jack some help by trying to nail a few of my own nails into her shoe. Moll must have been the quietest mare on earth that she didn't kick me to bits when she felt me hammering at her hoof. But, faster than an eye blink, Jack whisked me out from underneath her legs and into safety.

Grannie walks up to the half-door to look out. Light rain together with sunshine fills the yard and lands on the fuchsia bushes round the pig house. 'The Devil is beating his father,' she says to herself. But I can hear her. I don't know what on earth she's talking about.

The rain doesn't stop the two of us heading for the haggart and making our daily search for eggs in the nettles and the hens' other hiding places behind the hay reek. It's still a little early in the day and the ghost of fading night still hangs round us in the overhanging trees. My two berry farms of animals – the cows and the kangaroos – are still sleeping soundly and I'm determined to give them an outing in my go-cart today. I notice that their resting place in Jack's shoe box is covered in silver cobwebs that shine out at me.

Meanwhile, Jack has gone down to the Bull Paddock to fetch the cows. He has big plans rolling round in his head for me and himself this morning. He'll be taking me to help him save the turf abroad in the bog and bring a load of it home. That's the reason we went to Mick's forge yesterday, to make sure Moll's shoes are fit for the long journey out over the hills. That's why he was busy with his tin of axle grease, to make sure the cart wheels are strong enough when facing the current of the river in the bog. This river can be treacherous for cart and beast alike, for the flood water can be deep and fierce, depending on the rain. Huge boulders sometimes get swept down at the spot where farmers have to cross into the bog.

The journey is three miles. Women seldom go out there – just the men – not only to save turf but to swim in the giant sally hole on Sunday afternoons. It's ten times the size of the sally hole in the Dolla River.

The furthest away I've ever walked is down to Dolla with Grannie. That's less than a mile away and even with her stooped back, she can walk that far with me and give Lightning the ass a welcome rest. We walk and talk all the way to Gerry's shop. Then I help her carry home her message bag. It's not too heavy for me, but all the same, we do little talking on our way home.

Of course, we go to Mass in the Silvermines every Sunday (two miles further on from Dolla), but we travel in Moll's cart to get there.

Jack makes his way back with the cows. Moll is coming with him, hurrying along and in great spirits. She has a new set of shiny shoes on her hooves and she stamps them on the lane triumphantly to let anyone passing know that she's the owner of such fine objects as Mick's new horseshoes.

Instead of one egg for breakfast, Jack is having two eggs and so am I. I have an extra mug of milk while Grannie gets busy, roasting a few spuds in the hot ashes for us to take on today's journey. She boils four more eggs in her saucepan over the fire. It's her usual preparation for Jack's trips to the bog and I'm beginning to see why she is fussing so much.

I don't yet know how long the journey will be or how hard today's work will be for a little chap like me. But Grannie knows that both of us will need the extra nourishment while we're working. By noon, we'll be starving.

Jack is busy cutting up thick slices of soda bread and layering them with butter and blackcurrant jam. He pours milk into two small bottles. We are going to have a feast today but I'm still not sure where Jack is taking me.

'Jack, are we going somewhere important?'

'Indeed, we are, Ned. We're off to the bog. There's no place on earth like it. It stretches for miles and miles. I'll tell you more as we get nearer to it.'

Grannie will have the house to herself. It will be a chance for her to spring-clean all round and polish the crockery on the press cupboard. She is ever-mindful that the war might end soon. She has no idea when her daughter Nell will be taking me back to England but she keeps hearing how badly the Germans are doing. She knows that the best way to banish her sad thoughts is to occupy herself with housework – lots of it. One job she won't have to do: she won't have to worry about the fire. She has it heaped up higher than ever with half a dozen fresh logs. They will last her the rest of the morning.

Moll is soon tackled and harnessed to the cart. One of our neighbours (Rowanberry) has lent Jack a set of high boards from his cart. He brought them the other day. Jack has already fitted them round the sides of the cart so that we'll be able to bring home oceans of turf – enough to warm Grannie's fire till kingdom come.

I hear Moll stamping her new shoes, telling us to hurry up and get ourselves out to greet the lane. The earlier mixture of sunshine and rain has given way to a few more glimpses of the sun from behind Gret's cow shed. Jack squints up at the sky. He is never sure of the weather when he's out in the bog but tells me we'll see enough sun to let us work at the turf without a break. I think he forgets that I'm still only four and not five till next summer. However, I am prepared to work like blazes if Jack needs me to help him today.

Grannie showers us with holy water – showers Moll and the cart as well – and we head off across the flagstones. It'll take the best part of an hour to get to the bog. Our high-stepping Moll knows the way and spurs us on. We pass Gret's gateway. Then we take the same trail as we did when we went hunting rabbits with Tom Hayes's gun, at least for the first bit.

We pass the cross of Mountisland and from there, we travel on to Curryquinn. The sun has just pierced through the last remnants of dark clouds and the sky's greyness has finally given way to blue. But the day is not yet warm.

Some men go off earlier than others. It all depends on the work in hand and what turf remains to be dried and saved. Shy Denis works as early as six o'clock – that is, after he's finished the work that he does with the hay during the night. On our way, we might even meet him coming back home with a full cartload of turf. Oh, the shame of it, to think that we are only now setting out to do our work!

The road beyond the crossroads opens out in front of us. We pass Mucklin and Logg on the right before proceeding higher into the hills. The sun has at last got warmer and we are beginning to feel its heat. The flies and midges are busy round Moll's ears and Jack rubs the sweat from his brow. He continues to talk to Moll, all the time encouraging her. He never raises his whip. He knows she'll need all her good humour when we're out in the bog. She'll have nothing to do all day except munch from the load of hay that he's brought with him in the cart.

Up here, the land is different. There are fewer fields of meadowland and more of heather. The hillside is rocky. The surrounding woodland seems sad-looking and the trees at the side of the lanes look sinister and black.

I have little to do but contemplate. I listen to the rattle of the cart and the rumble of the wheels. I listen to the sound of Moll's shoes and tackling. I watch the raucous crows cawing as they work and play. I feel the whispering breeze in my ears and watch Jack puffing on his pipe. The smoke will keep the flies away. That's what he tells me. Volumes of it rise up around his head.

We have reached higher ground still, having passed out Jack Scissors' well and the red-berried rowan trees. Some of the fields are mustard-coloured with ragwort. They look golden when the clouds pass overhead.

Standing up in the cart, Jack has a magnificent view of the hill slopes and deep valleys. My eyes keep looking up, searching for the two eagles that he told me about. Their nest is a long way off, deep in the clefts of Keeper Hill. If I keep looking at the sky long enough, perhaps I'll spot them later on when they leave their nest to go hunting young rabbits.

It's so quiet up here, almost lonely, in places where there were once more than a dozen thatched cabins before people went off to seek their fortune. Gone are the black cattle for which men of the hills were famed. Mick the Herd and his brother, Phil, along with Johnnie Sherlock, are the only ones living out here now.

'We'll be there soon,' says Jack and though he continues to whisper words of encouragement into Moll's ear, her steps are not as lively as they were before.

The lane ahead has grass growing down its middle and our cart twists and turns round one bend after another. I think I can hear the sound of the bog river in the distance. I wonder if Jack can hear it too.

When he's away from Grannie and alone like this, he has time to ponder on my future and what sort of life I might have had, had I been let stay behind in London with my parents. What sort of lives are other children having this very day compared to mine? What are they doing in the back streets this morning? Playing leap frog, hop scotch or skipping their rope along the pavement, the older ones roaming the bomb sites in search of gas masks? That's what I'd be doing had I stayed in Paddington among them.

We are now a long way from Grannie and close to the mighty river. Jack steers Moll down through a winding lane on the left. It's surrounded by rusty rocks and scraggy bushes that might have turned into trees were the land good enough. Moll is careful and takes her time crawling her way down towards the river. Her new shoes won't let her slip.

The lane grows narrower. The briars grow thicker, almost covering the sides of the cart. Jack reaches for my hand without looking back at me and he lifts me up onto my feet. I have never seen anything like this before – not even on the banks of the Dolla River. I see oceans of purple heather in front of me. It's as if no one has ever been here before. Far away and towering above all else is the immense mountain, the top of which is hidden in the clouds. It is like a wall reaching up to heaven.

'That's Keeper Hill,' says Jack, pointing his pipe in that direction and he steers the cart to a stop.

We can't yet see the great river but we hear its raging roar. 'We'll soon be at the river,' says Jack. 'We'll have to cross it to get into the bog.' He seems to have no fear of the river's fierceness. Like Moll, he has made this crossing many times before.

We leave the briars behind us along with Jack's curses when one or two of them scratch his face. At last, we reach the river. Moll's legs are steeped in the spray even before she steps into it. There's far more sand here than there is in the Dolla River.

To the left of us is a rocky gorge where the river edges its nose forward amid grey boulders. I can see how angry it looks – not a bit like our merry river back home. It's as though it wants to attack the mouth of the gorge before tumbling its way on towards Limerick.

It looks very deep to me and I'm not at all sure how we will get across and into the bog. And another thing – there are no pink or lavender stones in this river for me to take home and draw with. Jack's voice is gentle and almost musical as he urges Moll into the river. For a moment, her shoulders tremble. Then she lowers her head and drags the cart forward. The water splashes up along her legs and tail. As she soldiers on, it soon rises up to her chest, glistening her coat with foam. To coax her forward, Jack starts humming to her. His voice is strange, a voice that I've not heard before, and the wheels of the cart rumble their way forward.

We are fortunate this morning. Though rocks have been thrown down around the crossing on previous stormy days, making it troublesome for farmers to drive their way round them and get up on the opposite bank, there are no rocks in the river today to bar the path of the wheels.

Ahead of us, we see the pink trail that twists uphill towards Jack's patch of bog. My eyes are wrapped in attention. I don't know which way to look: the pink pathway, the purple heather or the high wall of the mighty mountain. But I don't yet see the two eagles. They must be hidden among the clouds that crown the mountain top.

Moll splashes her way up onto the bank. The cart jolts forward towards Jack's patch of turf and water is still dripping down from its wheels. It is dripping down from Moll's sides too.

At the bend of the slope, she comes to a stop beside Jack's patch. To the left of us is Rowanberry's plot and to the right is Old Tim's. Both men have been working hard during the previous weeks. They have lots of turf dried out and ready to bring home.

Behind Jack's plot is that of the Gog – an old-timer with little help from anyone. His family crossed the ocean to America long ago. It's a shame to see his turf so neglected.

Jack frees Moll of her tackling. With his fork, he makes a nest of hay in between the upturned shafts of the cart. Moll stamps her foot approvingly or it might be to shake off the orchestra of flies and midges that surround all animals as soon as they arrive in the bog. She begins eating the hay quietly. I could almost hear her singing with joy.

It's time to get down to work. Jack has set aside the best part of an hour for gathering in the turf sods that he previously cut with his wing-slayne. Several of them are spread around his plot, some lying on top of others and not well-drained of water. Together, we collect them. Some of them are heavy, depending on the number of days they'd been drying out after the rain.

Jack marks out two long rows the length of the plot and places a few sods at either end. We gather the sods and place them in batches of four until both rows are filled. He asks me to count the batches. There are twenty batches in each row. He shows me how to make a little tent out of four sods. I find it easy work. This is to let the air get in among the newly-made tents and allow them to dry out quickly between the showers of rain that often visit the bog.

We work fast along the first row and hardly have time to say a word to each other. 'You're a great little man, entirely,' says Jack.

I don't understand what the word 'entirely' means. It must be one of the old expressions that he and Grannie often use.

While I continue making my tents of turf sods along the second row, Jack is busy scraping off the top soil at the far end of the plot. He takes his wing-slayne and with his right-footed wellington, digs deep into the bog.

His first two digs bring up the brown turf. 'Not much good,' he says to himself and he casts these sods aside. When he reaches down to the black turf, he smiles at me. This sort of turf has always been like a jewel to him. It will please Grannie too. There's an unusual smell to the newly-dug turf, not unpleasant, as he throws the sods onto their sides to dry.

'Black turf is good enough to burn down the walls of a house,' says he. 'Such blazing fires it'll make for us.'

He comes back to take a look at my tents, his eyes appraising where I'm up to. He nods his head at the ones that I have made. 'Not bad for a lad of four,' he murmurs. Any water on these sods will drain off quickly as a result of the upright position I have placed them in and he explains this to me a second time.

I walk down the row to see his newly-dug sods of turf. They are at least twice the size of my sods. But, seeing the puzzled look on my face, he says that, in time, they will shrink back to half that size. By now, I notice that a number of other men have been busily applying themselves in different stretches of the bog, their backs stooped down to the ground. They have been working hard like us and a few of them are settling into a well-deserved mug of tea.

Parts of the bog have spring wells where the workers can fill their kettles and make themselves a pot of tea like they do back home. I see little columns of smoke rising up here and there as they kindle bits of heather to heat the fire when they've lit it. Jack says there's no fear of them setting fire to the bog, as they always keep their fires neat and tidy. They have been well-practised in this since the days of their childhood.

So hard have I been working that I am almost sick with hunger. I now know how hungry a place the bog is and how the cold breezes blowing across from Keeper Hill will make a small child like myself get this way.

Jack takes out a newspaper and lays out the roasted spuds and hard-boiled eggs as well as his doorstep sandwiches. He pours me out a bottle of milk and keeps the other one for himself. We tear into our sandwiches and give them an unmerciful mauling with our teeth. I forget about my success with my turf tents (what Jack calls 'my footings'), so busy am I attending to my sandwiches. I have my greedy eyes cast on the spuds and eggs as well.

After devouring the last of the floury spuds, Jack tidies up the egg shells and rolls them into a ball of newspaper. He sits down with me on the shiny side of his waistcoat. It's cosy and warm. He lights up his pipe and sucks in his jaws to get the smoke going. Then he puffs and puffs contentedly, looking at the work we've done. I can see that he's as pleased as punch with my tents of turf and the way I followed his lead.

As I have no pipe to smoke, I spend my time looking at the view, at the colours of the heather, at the little fires of the workers drinking tea and at the blue of the sky marred with just a few fluffy clouds scudding by on the wind towards Clare.

I continue to squint at the mountains in the hope I might see at least one of the eagles. But I see no eagles. There are times when a child doesn't get all that he wishes for. It's something new to be learning.

At the other side of the cart is a low wall of turf sods, what Jack calls his 'plank'. It's a good bit taller than me. In previous weeks and when I was too young to help him, he dismantled the old rows of turf tents (the footings) and turned them into a huge mound, this present plank.

The next half hour is spent in carrying sods from the plank over to the cart – I pass the sods to Jack and he loads them into the cart. He has taken off the nearside board of the cart so that the turf can be quickly fired into it. He will not overload Moll but will fill the cart with only as many sods as he thinks she can drag across the river. She can't be overladen in case she might topple over in the unpredictable rush of the water. A horse ending up on her back with the wheels in the air is something that has happened to others.

Jack sees that Moll has been hungry like us and has eaten all her hay, thanks to the cold and the wind. There's been nothing but boredom for her these last two hours and she's anxious to get back to the Bull Paddock and rub noses with her old friend, Lightning.

It's time to get moving. Jack tackles and harnesses Moll, making the bellyband firm after steadying her backwards under the cart. My job is an easy one: to stroke Moll's nose.

Like poor Moll, Jack is anxious for the road home. The bog is no place in which to linger. He knows that heavy rain can come down over the mountains at great speed and unexpectedly.

There have been times when the first thing he knew of the storm was hearing the thunder booming behind Keeper Hill, quickly followed by fingers of silver lightning. But even before that, he saw the black clouds hovering and felt the fury of the raw wind plunging across the heather and crumpling everything in sight. Even a fool would know it was time to escape and race home.

The only other choice was to brazen out the storm and hide under the cart in the hope that the bad weather wouldn't last too long and that his poor drenched Moll wouldn't bolt across the heather and get sucked down in a bog hole. But hiding under the cart was a gamble. It could be ages before the storm ceased.

None of this is going to happen today and we finish loading the turf into the cart. This has been our main task and our little feast has given us a renewed burst of energy.

When Jack is satisfied that enough turf is in the cart, he tidies up the plank and puts back the heap of straw that previously covered it. He lays some rocks on top. He lifts me up into the cart and makes sure I have a space where I can kneel down and hold onto the front board. I can poke my nose up whenever I see anything interesting, maybe the two eagles.

Jumping up from the wheel, he stands high in the cart beside me and without once having to use his whip on Moll's back, he steers down the winding trail at a snail's pace and on towards the river. Moll struggles through the current safely, then onto the lane.

I am tired and weary but Jack, knowing what a fine day's work we have done, is softly humming to himself. There's an air of serenity and satisfaction about him.

By now, the sun is slipping in and out of the clouds and the daylight is fading. One or two crows are already returning to their nests. They have done a great day's work like ourselves.

The lane twists its way towards Logg before dropping down over the hill and on to Curryquinn. I am almost asleep by this time. All I can hear are the wheels creaking and the sound of Moll's new shoes on the lane.

As we reach the cross of Mountisland, Jack sees Nenagh in the misty valley below. Its silver lights are just coming on and sparkling. A few minutes later, our cartload of turf reaches the flagstones and comes to a stop in the yard. I won't be the only one tired. Moll's hooves are aching from all the pulling and dragging she has done to get us across the river.

Jack still has energy enough to jump down into the yard and smile at his mother. How glad she is to see the pair of us home safe and sound! She looks down into the cart and sees me asleep. 'Ah, the poor child!' she cries and turns away.

I blink my eyes open and Jack lifts me down from the cart. His cheeks are aglow. He has so much news to tell Grannie. He carries me in his arms into the bedroom and tiptoes over to our bed. He lays me down and covers me with the blankets. I don't even say my prayers and I'm soon asleep. In my dreams, I am flying over the bog along with my new friends, the two mighty eagles.

END OF PART FIVE

THE AFTERNOON SUN

The summer of 1945

It's Saturday and Sweeney and Bucko have come down to Grannie to help her clean out the dung from the pig house. It's a lengthy job. They are just a small bit afraid of the two big pigs but Jack is there to supervise the operation. It's all part of their life-training and they make a reasonable job of it.

Jack has a cartload of ferns from Clonmore Wood stored behind the hay reek. The boys layer the pig house floor with these, giving it a sweet-scented perfume. The pig house is now like a palace and the pigs grunt their approval.

Rosie and Daisy have come down, too, to help Grannie around the house, tidying the crockery on the press cupboard shelves, separating the cutlery in the press drawer and making smart the back table with the gramophone and the records neatly arranged. They cast an envious eye at the gramophone and wish they could have one like it.

Once they have completed the work inside and out, Grannie gives the four of them their customary reward of humbug sweets from the drawer beneath her bedroom altar. They are just about to skedaddle over the flagstones and into Sam's Grove when Jack calls them over to the stream.

'There's something I want to show ye; something I've been meaning to do for a long time, to amuse ye,' says he.

He knows how much I hated the pig killing that he performed above in Shy Denis's yard. Yet he knows how much pleasure I am having these days with the pig's bladder. And now, he wants to please me even further with his 'tree antics'.

Gret's children and I sit down on the flagstones. The drawings of a church and a schoolhouse by Rosie and Daisy are still visible there from the day before. They are getting better each time at using the rough edges of their coloured stones like Bucko told them to do.

I wonder what Jack means by his 'tree antics'. It's not long since I saw him somersaulting in the Blue Button Field and encouraging me to do likewise – much to the amusement of the passersby.

211

He takes off his waistcoat and throws it onto the ass's cart. He ambles over to the stream. He stands back and takes a long look at the ancient sycamore tree that grows alongside the flagstones – the tree with a great black rift in its trunk.

He looks up at the main branch projecting out over the stream. We've heard tales of his bravery before and how he once did his acrobatics on other trees in the days of his youth. None of us, however, have ever seen it with our own eyes. We don't believe a word of all these rumours.

He runs out into the lane and climbs onto the ditch. Then, using the stronger scrubs of grass and the wedges of his wellingtons, he hoists himself up and sits across the branch, gazing down in triumph at us. It's a sight to behold – a big man straddled on the branch above us – his arms waving at the sky and the shining stream 10 ft beneath himself and the branch.

'Does Dolla graveyard want another corpse?' whispers Sweeney to Bucko.

'Maybe they'll put Jack in the Duffy Circus if he succeeds in his tree antics,' mutters Bucko and they smother their laughter behind their hands.

As for Rosie, Daisy and myself, our voices fail us, so scared are we that Jack will get himself killed.

I look at Daisy. She is young like myself. I have heard that when anyone is frightened enough, their eyes fall out of their head. This hasn't happened to Daisy – not yet anyway.

Jack grips the branch in front of him. He swings his wellingtons back and forth. He bounces up and down on the branch as though he were testing the saddle or the tyres of his bike but, above all, to see if the branch is strong enough to support his weight when he performs his trick. Ah, a man and his faded youth! Ah, a man and the sparkle of magic still in him!

He circles his wellingtons underneath and round the branch. May Heaven come to the aid of his two heels! Yes, Jack and his magic and the wide open space now in his power, or is it?

Slowly... slowly. Oh, the suspense!

Slower still... he twists his body down towards the stream – a stream that has never before seemed as menacing or as serpent-like as it now appears.

He continues to sway and writhe, still shaking the branch dangerously and testing its weight.

Will he... won't he? For a moment, we are as awestruck at the sight of him as at the sight of any small bird we've seen captured in a cage. Jack reaches down his arms to see if he can touch the stream. And when, at last, he grows tired of his own villainy – and feels that he has kept us in a sweat of suspense long enough – he gives a final sway to the branch before plunging down and touching the stream with his fingertips.

This is the greatest event we've yet seen in our lives. We clap and we clap and we keep on clapping till, at last, Jack swings his legs back over the branch and his hands grip onto it before he clambers down onto the ditch and jumps into the lane.

And while all this has been going on, Grannie has been peering nervously out behind the net curtains and twiddling on her rosary beads.

'Ah, the devil that's in this son of mine,' she cries. 'Will he ever get a stem of sense?'

Jack's tree antics are something I am not going to forget in a hurry. They have stayed with me to this day.

Thanks to Jack's tree-climbing stunt, the next week is taken up with nothing else except climbing trees. At the lower end of the Blue Button Field is the Rotten Tree. It's been dead for many years without a leaf or a berry on it. All of Grannie's children climbed it at one time or another without ever breaking their necks.

Today is a sunny day and the sky is brightly coloured. My friend Ellie is visiting me this morning. We will take a trip to the Blue Button Field to run up and down through the wild flowers. Ellie will strap the pig's bladder onto my wrist so that it can chase along after me all the way down to the Rotten Tree.

She has other plans in mind this morning. But first of all, she lets me have a good few runs up towards Old Tim's ditch and back down with my friendly bladder. She and I fill the air with a series of war whoops.

I can hear the rattle of a cart's wheels and the two creamery tanks hurrying down the lane. Old Tim is taking his milk and our own milk to the creamery. He is singing loudly to his ass, Lock-Jaw, to get the poor creature into some sort of good humour. I wonder what he thinks of us two mad hares when he hears our war whoops as we race round the field with the bladder from Shy Denis's pig.

We soon get tired. Ellie finds a young alder tree near the gap leading into the field below us, the field we call the Deer Field, even though no deer has ever been seen in it. When Grannie was a child, she saw herds of deer sprinting down the hillside on their way to the wood. She watched them jumping from Old Tim's ditch into the Blue Button Field. She watched them clearing the ditch into the next field where they stopped for a while to graze, thereby giving it the name the Deer Field. There is a ditch, 6ft high, between that field and the Bull Paddock. Grannie couldn't believe her eyes when half a dozen deer leapt clean out over this insurmountable obstacle before racing on into the wood.

Ellie ties the bladder and its twine round the alder sapling (it'll be safe there) and she takes me by the hand to the Rotten Tree. She helps me up on the ditch and we sit there, looking out at Jack's cows beyond the Danes' Hill. We have a sunny spot beside one another where we can contemplate the scenery in our own childish way.

Rosie and Daisy are nowhere to be seen this morning. They're playing in their cubby house. Bucko has gone off with Sweeney, searching for birds' nests even though Gret has forbidden them to go anywhere near birds and their nests. Shawnee is off on his own. He has gone down to John's Gate to take a look at the tree that only he knows how to climb. He has done it before. It's the Difficult Tree, as opposed to the Easy Tree at the metal bridge, which children since days gone by have found easy to climb on their way back from school. However, not even Shawnee's big brother, Dan, has ever tried climbing the Difficult Tree.

'Next Sunday after Mass,' says Shawnee to himself, 'me and mee friendly tree will shake hands with one another once more.' Then he strolls slowly up the lane, his mind full of this mighty tree and how he might safely climb to the top of it.

Ellie and I are still sitting on the ditch and admiring the Rotten Tree. 'Stay where you are,' says Ellie and I do exactly that, for I have always taken heed of what she says. She spits on her hands so they'll let her get a firm grip when she starts climbing the tree. I am astonished. I never knew she could climb, especially a rotten tree.

There are nine branches on it and they are all bare as though someone has peeled the bark away. Four of them stretch out towards the Blue Button Field on one side and four more stretch out to the Deer Field opposite it. The other branch, the largest one, stretches out towards the lane. Ellie has climbed this tree more than once, long before I met her and her bowlee wheel. Her sandals have a sound grip on it and her mind is full of concentration as she reaches up towards the sky.

I am not sure whether to pray for her or to cry for her. I don't want to lose my friend or see her get herself killed. I watch her as she makes steady progress, carefully selecting which branches to put her sandals on. Finally, she reaches the top and sits on the branch pointing towards the lane. She can see Old Pat's hay shed on the far side of it.

At last, I can rest easy and stop holding my breath. I can see how happy she is and I am eager to join her. I ask her to let me climb the tree. 'Just onto the first or maybe the second branch, Ellie,' I plead.

She climbs down and grips me by the shoulders. She is thinking hard, wondering if I'll be able to attempt this latest venture along with her. She knows I am not yet five years old, whereas she is already eight.

She shows me how to get up on the first branch and after that little success, she reaches down her hands so that I can follow her up to the second branch. We sit there contentedly and I am not one bit afraid. I am never afraid when I'm playing with Ellie. We are as happy as two young magpies.

From our perch, we can see Jack's cows more clearly now. They are heading towards the river, following one another in a straight line. It looks like they are going for a dinnertime drink to quench their thirst. We seem to be miles away from the rest of the world. I feel very grown up. I only wish that Jack could see me now, so high up in the sky.

Grannie bangs her tin tray on the flagstones. It's the signal for us to get down onto the ditch. Ellie leads the way, all the time holding tightly onto my hand until I'm safely on the ground.

It's her turn to race with the bladder. She makes a loop out of the twine and puts her fist through it. She frees the bladder and gives it a vigorous shake into the air behind her. The two of us race towards the haggart and the yard, scattering the geese and their goslings.

Grannie has already poured us out two mugs of milk and Jack has cut the soda bread into slices, layering them with butter and blackcurrant jam.

I have so much news to tell him. I am not sure whether I should tell Grannie. I think she might get cross when she hears how I've been climbing the Rotten Tree. I think she might be cross with Ellie too.

Climbing trees is something that Gret's children never tire of. It started during their early years after Fiddler Joe had filled the barn with cartloads of turf brought home from the bog. That's when they all – from Dan down to Daisy – spent a good deal of time in the barn, climbing up to the top of the turf and enjoying their game of 'I'm the king of the castle'.

They played it two at a time: between Dan and Shawnee or between Sweeney and Bucko or between Rosie and Daisy. The heap of turf was almost 10 ft high. It was an awkward obstacle to climb up – especially for little Daisy. One of the pair of climbers was sure to be first to reach the top of the heap and shout down, 'I'm the king of the castle!'

The game of climbing up the turf led to later games, especially racing down the Blue Button Field to see who would reach the Rotten Tree first: who would climb to the top first and who would spot the home of the leprechauns in Fort Dangerous or the metal bridge below at the river.

Every tree has its summit and no trees are the same. Most of them are too difficult to climb and children keep far away from them or leave such trees to Shawnee, as he is the best tree-climber in Dolla. He loves the Difficult Tree more than any other tree. It's his one chance to show off his mettle and impress the rest of us. The first time he climbed to the top, his reward was great. He could see five miles away: as far as Nenagh, its castle tower and lofty church spire. Both were at a level with his eye. Oh, how tall he felt! And oh, how small he felt when he came back down to earth to renew his life among his brothers and sisters!

For all of us (excepting Rosie and Daisy), our favourite tree for climbing is the Easy Tree down at the metal bridge. Rosie and Daisy spend their time gazing in over the bridge railings to see if they can spot any trout swimming in the river so that Fiddler Joe can take his rod down and try fishing for them.

In the meantime, Sweeney and Bucko race over to the Easy Tree to test its branches. It's only a few steps away from the bridge, just inside Jack's wooden fence at the edge of the Bull Paddock.

This fence is a blessing. It is 6-foot high and has five bars across it. Once they have clambered onto the top bar, no great effort is needed to swing themselves over and onto the lowest branch of the tree. From that point on, their way to the summit is as easy as pie. Rosie and Daisy have not yet learnt how to climb it. They are not strong enough. They feel a bit sad to be left on the ground, looking up at their big brothers. However, their turn will come soon.

The Easy Tree is a sturdy old elm and the best time for climbing it is when some of the leaves have fallen. Then it's easy to spot the layout of the branches and climb to the top. There's scarcely an evening, especially coming home from school, when children don't make it their main task to see who'll be first to race from Burke's Kill and touch the tree, who'll be first to reach its summit and cry out 'I'm the king of the castle!'

Shawnee will have nothing to do with it. It's not nearly as tall as his Difficult Tree. His tree stretches up forever and ever. Daisy thinks it must surely touch the sky. The Easy Tree is not even as high as Old Pat's hay shed and none of the children (except Rosie and Daisy) see any risk in climbing it. To sit on its top branch is the joy of all joys for Sweeney and Bucko, with the sun glistening on their faces and Rosie and Daisy gaping up at them in pure admiration. The recent days of Shawnee searching for birds' eggs in the trees or for Bucko leaping across the narrow parts of the river – none of this can match reaching the top of this tree. When they're up there, they no longer envy the birds.

Now that I'm a tree-climber after my recent exploits with Ellie at the Rotten Tree, I am tempted to take my go-cart for a ramble as far as the Easy Tree as soon as I've had my dinner.

Once there, I like to watch Sweeney and Bucko climbing up along it, branch by branch. If only I could be as brave as them! If only I could follow their lead like I followed Ellie's at the Rotten Tree! If only I could sit beside them at the top! The temptation is great – but so is the fear.

Perhaps when I'm five years old, or maybe when I'm six, I might pluck up courage enough to attempt this mighty task. However, I am smart enough to remember times when I've seen the sad look in Grannie's eye, times when she has been cross with me or worried about me. I don't want to hurt her feelings. I learnt this a good while back. My love of her, something that I can't put into words at my age, has long overcome everything else.

And yet, I know that the day will come when I'm able to climb the Easy Tree, just as it will for Rosie and Daisy, or at least a day when I might be able to climb onto the fence and grab hold of the lowest branch, if only to sit on it and not the branches higher up. What a great success that alone would be! Though I've climbed the Rotten Tree, I cannot count Ellie's tree as a proper tree. It's not a real tree, it's a dead one.

I will have a talk with Ellie. I will tell her of my worries and my fears. I will ask her to walk with me and my go-cart tomorrow morning when no one else is looking. I will ask her if she's able to climb the Easy Tree and, if so, can she show me how she does it, like she did with the Rotten Tree. I know I'll not be able to climb up after her, not for a year or two yet, only to admire her when she reaches the top and to cherish her all the more.

Cool air is roaming round the lane this morning. Shawnee wipes the sleep from his eyes. His guardian angel nudges him to arise and pick up the new day.

Gret has set the table for her children – their eggs and their soda bread, their mugs of milk, warm and fresh from the cows that she and Fiddler Joe have just milked. There's not much chat between any of them; they are still half-asleep. But at the back of their minds, all except Shawnee and Daisy, as well as their big brother, Dan, is the thought of their school in Killeen. It'll become a reality for them in just over a month's time.

Shawnee hurries out the door with scarcely a look from his mother. She has other things on her mind for, in less than an hour, she'll be up on the Heights behind the orchard, digging a sack of spuds and cabbages. On the way home, she'll check in on her apple trees to see if they are getting ripe and she'll snag a handful of gooseberries for herself. None of her children like their bitter taste. She'll pick a few blackcurrants and redcurrants and give them to Rosie and Daisy when their brothers have gone off gallivanting round the hills.

Shawnee runs as fast as he can down the lane. It's as though the Difficult Tree is walking up the lane to summon him, as though it's telling him to hurry his steps towards it. He soon reaches his tree. A family of buzzing bees are chorusing nearby but show no interest in him, only in the odd few wild flowers on the ditch. He examines the tree, his eyes searching for the thicker stems of the dusty ivy clinging to it. He grabs these and tests them with his fists. They are strong and unbreakable and he begins his climb. It will take him a while before he can reach the first firm branch.

With steadfast thread up he climbs, his eyes always intent on the next branch. He never looks down. It's his rule. The leaves are thick around him, as if to trap him on his journey towards the top. He plunges on through them. He is in a world of his own, just himself and the tree, the sky and the heavens. He has no fear. It has never entered his mind, such is his self-assurance when he's climbing trees. Up up he climbs branch by branch, with the catch-holds of a monkey. It isn't easy for him and it gets more difficult as he moves higher among the branches. They are thinner up here and each one has to be tested before he moves onto it.

The sun beams down on the back of his head and, for once in his life, he finds sunlight a nuisance that he could do without. At last, he reaches the top and can afford to gaze down through the foliage at those bits of ground that he can see beneath him. It's a long way down and after all his noble efforts, he's in no hurry to return to earth.

The treetop is his new home for now and he plans to spend at least half an hour enjoying this new feeling of being miles away from the rest of us – miles away from the whole world.

It's his secret place. He straddles himself on the top branch and holds onto it firmly with both hands. He dangles his legs downwards and swings himself to and fro, making the branch sway gently in the breeze. Peering through the fingers of the leaves, he can see the whole panorama of the nearby farmland and the metal bridge over the river. He can see Jack's cows trundling away from the mud at the gate and heading off towards the Danes' Hill. It's not every day that a child can have so fine a view as this.

He realises he's as high up as the crows in Old Pat's rookery nearby. They have just returned from Bill Corcoran's cornfield and as soon as they have settled down, they start squawking like blazes when they see how close he is to their nests. The noise of them makes him feel uneasy and their angry outbursts have encouraged him to take the downward path and go home.

He has something far more troublesome than crows to worry about: his downward path to the ground. This is the most difficult task of all. Nevertheless, he has prepared himself for this, having made sure to remember the various branches and tough bits of ivy which he hand-gripped on his way up.

His thoughts are interrupted by the sound of several bare feet pounding down the lane. It's the rest of Gret's children hurrying to see if he has succeeded in climbing the Difficult Tree or if he's been killed in his effort to do so.

Grannie has been reading her stories to me, but now she is finished. I hurry out the half-door and chase after Rosie and Daisy, who are slower than Sweeney and Bucko in racing down to get news of Shawnee.

The three of us finally catch the big boys up and we all scramble onto the ditch. I am the last to get up there and that's only with the help of Rosie.

I know that Shawnee is famous for his tree-climbing. I know that he is safe in God's hands, something that Grannie told me. I hope that one day I will also be able to climb a big tree like the Difficult Tree and not a tree like the Rotten Tree. I will say an extra prayer to God this evening and ask Him to help me become a tree-climber like Shawnee.

The grey clouds have replaced the sun, pushing her away from us even though it's not yet noon. Their shadow creeps across the fields and the blueness of the sky has also turned grey. We realise that Shawnee's tree climbing is finished for the day. He knows we are standing on the ditch below him even though none of us have dared shout up to him in case he should fall. Sweeney and Bucko have joined their hands together as though praying for him.

Their big brother suddenly interrupts the ongoing racket of the crows. Much to their surprise, he lets out a deafening roar, letting the world know he's now on top of the Difficult Tree. It surely terrifies every duck, hen and goose out of their lives. The cows, asses and horses stop nibbling at the grass and they listen. They've never heard such a roar as Shawnee's.

Gret must have heard his roars, for she is heard banging her tin tray furiously to call her children home and tell her what's happened to her beloved Shawnee.

'I'm coming down now,' says he. 'Go home and tell Mother that I'm safe and sound but it'll be a good while yet before I reach the ground. Go on, go home, all of ye, and tell her.'

We are delighted to hear Shawnee's voice and we race hell for leather up the lane – me, to tell Grannie – Gret's children to inform her of Shawnee's triumphant climb. We are all shaking with hysterical laughter. We can't wait to see Shawnee's face and for him to tell us how he made his wonderful climb and how he got acquainted with the crows in Old Pat's rookery nearby.

Shafts of sunlight stream in through the bedroom widow, highlighting the beams of shivering dust. Jack's space in our big bed is empty but still warm and I snuggle up into its heat. He has already brought back the cows from the Bull Paddock. Grannie is in the cow shed, ready to greet him and waving her stool out the door at him. They are ready for the next hour's milking.

Gret's two wild cats have come down and are standing next to Grannie's skirt, curling their tails round her boots and staring hopefully at the cows' udders. They are waiting for the warm milk to be tipped into their sardine tin.

I tiptoe over to the bedroom window and look out at the yard and the stream. Today is what Jack would call a 'bright, soft morning'. There's a promise of the sun's full heat later on and only a few fat clouds in the blue sky. Their shadows serenely scud across the lane and on into Sam's Grove and the Thistle Field beyond. I am anxious to be on the move. I grab my britches and hurriedly put them on.

Out in the living room, there is the pungent smell of the burning logs, the crackling of the woody cinders and the smoke from the turf. It permeates the whole house, including my bedroom. I'd like to be sitting next to the roasting fire for the rest of the morning but a compelling force draws me towards the half-door and the big wide world abroad.

I put on my socks and sandals. God forgive me. I haven't yet said any of my morning prayers, so intent am I on visiting Gret's big boys and their little sisters.

I take down my mug from the press cupboard and dip it into the bucket of water behind the door the way Jack does during the day. I race off to the cow shed for my first drink of milk. It isn't only Gret's wild cats who love the taste of it. After that, it's time for me to go out the lane and hunt for Rosie and Daisy. I will spend time with Ellie tomorrow and we can take turns whaling her bowlee wheel down as far as the river.

I scamper across the yard. The hens and ducks are, by this time, all out in the yard, each of them busy at their work. One hen is trying to open a snail's shell and pecking fiercely at it with her beak. Two ducks are stationed on the pig house dung heap, happily drinking up the pissy swill.

I will take a trip to the lower end of the haggart and check on the animals in my berry farm. After a hurried look at my berries, me and my sandals disappear up the lane towards Gret's gateway.

Up at Gret's place, there's a little bit of magic in the air today. Slowcoach is a bit of a pet and as the children enter the haggart gate, they hear him bawling from the lower end of the Thistle Field. It's as if he's calling them to come chase after him and jump on his back. He enjoys this sport more than any of them, for they have never yet succeeded in riding him round the field.

They wonder why Fiddler Joe gave him the name Slowcoach, for he can show a tremendous burst of speed if they tease him too much. He knows that if they are planning to ride him this morning, they'll soon run out of steam and the fun of chasing him will be long gone. Not one of them will be sad to see the rascal galloping out the gap and up onto the Heights.

Once more, their arms are laden with spuds and crab apples. They are heading to Rosie and Daisy's cubby house to store their food supply. It will make a pleasant change from the make-believe tea cakes Bucko and I were getting used to with his little sisters.

Shawnee is our leader, at least for another four or five weeks when other children in Dolla will be off to school to enlarge their brains, all except Daisy and me. After that, he'll have to act the part of a real man and help his father save the hay and bring home the turf from the bog. He'll no longer be a child like the rest of us. We will miss him terribly, especially his tree-climbing antics.

He leads us out the haggart gap, followed by Sweeney and Bucko. The three lads do a series of cartwheels round their father's old hay reek. I have difficulty keeping up with them. When I reach the haggart gate, I'm left speechless at the sight of them and their cartwheels. It's just like the time when Jack leaned down from the branch of the sycamore tree to touch the stream with his fingertips. Rosie and Daisy clap their hands and so do I. We wonder what they will do next.

Shawnee suddenly catches hold of Rosie by her ankle and swings her round and round. Her shrieks fill the nearby fields.

'Me too! Me too!' cries Daisy excitedly and Shawnee does the same to her.

Then it's my turn. I am sure I'll wet my britches, so happy am I to be swung round about by Shawnee – high in the air at first – then down low, almost touching the ground. Oh, if only Jack and Grannie could see me now!

But at fourteen years of age, Shawnee is really too big and strong to play rough-and-tumble games with the likes of his brothers. Sweeney is only ten and Bucko is eight.

Shawnee pulls out some sops of hay from his father's hay reek. We rush to help him until we have enough hay for us all to sit down on. The hay makes a warm, soft bed.

He calls Sweeney and Bucko over to him and whispers to them. 'Bucko!' says he, 'I want you and Sweeney to show the little ones what strong men ye are and see which of ye will get toppled to the ground first.'

Bucko is not nearly as strong as Sweeney. He's not sure if he has the strength to tumble him over. Besides, he has always looked up to him – just like he and Sweeney look up to Shawnee.

Sweeney lays his hand on Bucko's shoulder. 'It's just a bit of amusement, Bucko,' he whispers, 'just to impress the little ones.'

They circle round each other, baring their teeth and shaking their fists at one another, the great big actors that they are.

Sweeney then lets out a tremendous roar and makes a mad dash at Bucko. It frightens the life out of me. I can see that Rosie and Daisy are frightened too. The boys grapple with one another's wrists and fingers and they lock arms. They swing their feet round each other's legs and try to trip each other over. I can hear them puffing and wheezing. I can see their faces growing red. No one says a word until finally Shawnee cries out, 'Halt!' and drags them apart. He makes them shake hands. There has been no winner. It's been a great spectacle. What mighty warriors these big boys are – especially Bucko to be seen taking on the likes of Sweeney!

Shawnee now sets me against Rosie and Daisy in a race as far as Old Pat's ditch. It's a very long race for my young legs.

'When ye get to the bottom of the field,' says Shawnee, 'ye are to sit down next to the ditch and wait for the rest of us to race down after ye.'

I have the advantage over my little friends for, I am wearing my sandals.

'Ready! Steady! Go!' And away we fly, all three of us, anxious to impress the big boys with our stout hearts. I try my living best, but all my endeavours are no match for Rosie. Me and Daisy are left many yards behind her and we see her seated cockily on Old Pat's ditch and grinning back up the field at us. It'll be a far different story when we are bigger. Just you wait and see, Rosie!

Fiddler Joe's hay cart is up-heeled next to his old hay reek, its shafts pointing up in the air. From Old Pat's ditch where Rosie, Daisy and myself are perched, we can see what's going on round the hay reek. It's time for the two boys' balancing act.

Bucko and Sweeney lower the shafts to the ground. As they edge their way up along the shafts, they find it handy to be in bare feet as their toes have a firm grip on the narrow wood and they are in no danger of falling off. Inch by inch, they reach the top and leap into the cart.

They start all over again, this time racing at speed up the shafts to see who will be first to sit down in the cart. It's another moment of breathless entertainment and Bucko gets into the cart first. Such skill! So nimble are his feet. So big is his heart.

225

They both join Shawnee on the lower bench of hay. It spreads itself across the width of the hay reek, the result of Fiddler Joe cutting back the upper layers of hay with his hay-saw for the cows' foddering last winter. We three little ones race up the field to sit on the bench of hay alongside them. Rosie has the presence of mind to grab the spuds from the cubby house on the way. Me and Daisy take the crab apples.

Everyone is tired out from all the jack-acting and we sit down with the big boys and serenely consume our feast. There's no place we'd rather be than here on this bench of hay. Shawnee has a serious look on his face – almost sad. He knows his childhood days are lost forever.

Slowcoach has returned through the gap from above on the Heights. We see him racing at speed towards the valley stream. We watch in horror as a swarm of maddened horse bees drive him ever onwards. He topples into the dyke before falling down into the stream. He swings his angry tail in case any horse bees are loitering underneath it. Then he gets up and sits down on the soft moss nearby. He has had a narrow escape. Not one of us has an ounce of sympathy for the poor ass. We laugh at his misery and we wonder how many stings he has received and whether his bum is very sore.

Meanwhile, Gret is busy at her housework back home. She stops and listens to our laughing merriment. She smiles at the thought of her children enjoying their play. Maybe she's thinking of her own childhood days.

While we are having such merry times, Ellie has been on her own, just her and her parents. She is used to being alone and having no brother or sister to brighten up her days, other than me of late. I have been thinking of her and wondering what she is up to when I'm not with her. She can't be playing with her bowlee wheel every hour of the day.

After I get home and have had my dinner, I take a ramble up the lane to see if I can find her and extend today's playtime. I find Ellie sitting on the ass's cart, humming to herself. The hot caress of the sun is shining on her face. She looks a picture of happiness, without a care in the world. As soon as she sees me, she opens her eyes wide. She always does that.

I run across the yard to meet her and to tell her my news – the great times I've been having with Gret's children throughout the morning and the tremendous tree-climbing antics of Shawnee.

I think I see a little cloud of grey in her eyes. But she quickly brushes it aside. She is always full of ideas and she has just had a good one. 'We must do something special to celebrate Shawnee's great work in climbing the Difficult Tree,' she says. 'I have a plan. It'll need a lot of our time and patience.'

I wonder what she means. She seems excited. 'Even though the daisies and buttercups have died, it won't matter,' she says. 'There are loads of wildflowers like the honeysuckle and foxglove on the bushes behind Shy Denis's shack,' she says. 'We will make a garland of flowers, different ones, for Shawnee.'

I see what she has in mind: a flowery garland like the one we made for Grannie's bedroom altar.

'This time, Ned, you and I will shape it into a crown to go round Shawnee's head. A necklace or a bangle would never do, not for a boy as big as Shawnee,' she adds.

I haven't noticed till now, but Ellie is in her bare feet. She quickly puts on her sandals and runs to the half-door. She gives her mother a cheerful wave and the two of us set off to visit the glittering wildflowers behind Shy Denis's shack.

We stroll up the lane as careless as the little birds in the bushes. Nothing encroaches today's task, the gathering of the wildflowers.

Ellie knows everything. She knows where the wildflowers are, loads of them. She spotted them the previous evening while strolling with her father. He likes to walk down that lane and on through the valley below it – out as far as Barnagore. The long walk gives him a chance to smoke his pipe. Mrs Fidget cannot stand the smell of tobacco or the smoke that it makes.

We turn left at the cross of Mountisland. The starlings and greenfinch come swooping in and out from behind Mick the Smith's forge, bobbing up and down as if to welcome us. But no, they are merely after the abundance of berries at the entrance to the lane. These little birds love nothing better than sucking out the sweet juices from these sort of berries. The flies do too.

Ellie knows how many flowers we have to gather. She hasn't brought her mother's shopping-bag with her this time. She wants twelve honeysuckle and twelve foxgloves. Between us, we can carry them back to her place and start twisting their stems into shape. It's a ladylike job and boys like Gret's lads wouldn't be seen dead fashioning garlands like the one Ellie has in mind. What would the boys at school think of a lad making a garland for Shawnee?

We start collecting our flowers. Ellie has brought her mother's scissors in her bib pocket. It's a time for silence, a time for gentle harmony between us, a time for reflection. The honeysuckle flowers mirror the sunlight with their bright colours of white, gold, yellow and pink, each one perfectly formed for us. There are far more foxglove flowers than honeysuckles. Ellie bends them down towards her and carefully examines each one so that she can get the right ones. She loves their purple colours, the white insides of them, the dotted speckles of yellow amid the purple. Foxgloves have always been her favourite.

We haven't caught sight of Shy Denis today. Maybe his shyness has kept him away from us. Maybe he is off somewhere else, painting yet another set of farmyard gates for somebody.

Ellie is busy like her fidgety mother. She can't wait to get home and lay her collection of wildflowers on the bench in Rody's workshop. I keep very quiet and pass the flowers to her when she calls for them – a foxglove – then a honeysuckle – then another foxglove followed by a honeysuckle.

We finish collecting and hurry back down the lane. We haven't time to be listening to the birds. The gentle breezes hurry us on, refreshing our nostrils.

Ellie lays her foxgloves out in a row. I hand her my honeysuckles. She lays them out in another row. Our next hour is spent in deep concentration with Ellie in charge. She is the expert. She tells herself it's like putting beads on a rosary, like the rosary-

228

bead garlands that her mother used to make for children on the day of their First Holy Communion.

She cuts the stems down near the scut. She tells herself she is not making a necklace or a bangle but a crown for Shawnee. His garland will be full of lovely colours, all skilfully intertwined, a suitable headwear for a victor who has climbed the Difficult Tree.

It's taking shape nicely. I can't help admiring the wetness of the flowers. They are still covered in dew and they shine out at us. The crown is finished. It's like a fine jewel and Ellie spins round towards the daylight at the doorway of Rody's workshop. There's a twinkle in her eye. I feel like jumping with delight. Shawnee will be very pleased, I'm sure. He has never spoken a word to Ellie, not even on Sundays after Mass. For the girls sit on one side of the church along with their mothers, the boys on the other side with their fathers.

Boys usually don't give a fig for flowers. Nor do men. They'd rather be abroad in the fields tending to their cattle or hunting rabbits and catching fish. But this time, it will be different. I don't know anyone else who has climbed the Difficult Tree. A flowery crown is a fitting triumph for Shawnee.

We arrive at Gret's gateway. Gret takes the crown from Ellie. It's all done very queenly-like and she bows to Ellie. She calls Shawnee out into the light of the half-door. He has just finished his meal and wipes the milk from his mouth. He is a puzzled lad and yet he can see that Ellie has brought him this wonderful gift.

Gret whispers in his ear, 'It's a crown for you after your great triumph in climbing to the top of the Difficult Tree. I am going to place it on your head the way it was done in days of yore when kings were crowned. When all the clapping is over, I will keep it safe for you on my bedroom altar.'

Shawnee's brothers and sisters stand round him in a ring. Slowly and as though she were crowning the May Day statue of Mary, Gret places the crown on Shawnee's head. It's his happiest moment so far. He is not ashamed of his lovely garland. It's something he'll remember for days to come. We all clap our hands.

We clap and clap and don't want to stop, till at last their mother cries out, 'Whist, let ye!' It's a wonderful scene – Ellie with her eyes open wide and Shawnee with his eyes somewhat moist and the rest of us staring like mad at this new king and admiring the lovely crown.

All eyes are on Ellie. 'Ned helped me make it. He helped me collect the flowers,' she mutters. Not only have I found myself their good friend recently but Ellie also has joined the rest of us in our ring of friendship. And right welcome she is.

Gret lifts the crown off of Shawnee's head and, almost religiously, tiptoes into her bedroom with it. She lays it on her altar as though it were an offering to God.

Sweeney has grabbed a few spuds from the chicken-feed in the burner and heads out the yard. We follow him and sit on the ditch where we munch our feast.

Shawnee says, 'I'll be back in a minute,' and races behind the barn, carefully threading his way through the cow dung. He brings back an apple from his mother's orchard and hands it to Ellie without saying a word. We feel like clapping all over again. From this day forth (at least till school begins), we will spend as much time as we can together. There's never a cross word between us.

The war over in England has now been going on for almost six years and the city where I was born is a messy mass of ruined buildings. How unlike the beautiful countryside in which I have been living with Grannie and Jack for the last four and a half years!

If the fighting should come to an end (and rumour has it that it might be as early as next springtime), I will have to return to my parents' flat in the back streets of Paddington. For Grannie and Jack, this is a terrible thought and they try not to think of it – not even during those quiet moments when the gramophone records are put away and they are chatting beside the dying fire.

The following afternoon, Ellie and I have happy thoughts of Shawnee and his floral crown, of his smiling brothers and sisters and their pride in his tree-climbing. We leave him to his glory and head across the lane and into the Blue Button Field.

Grannie and Jack have already started milking the cows. When they've finished, we will give them all the news about the foxgloves and the honeysuckles and the crown we made for Shawnee.

Though the daisies and buttercups have long gone, the Blue Button Field is still fully carpeted with wildflowers among which the late afternoon bumblebees forage. It's coloured not only in green, but in brown, yellow, red and purple too. The ever blue sky compliments it all. But we know that the afternoon will soon merge into evening. This is a time which makes us a little sad – a time when all children's playfulness comes to an end.

We are in a hurry. We race down to the bottom of the field to the Rotten Tree. I have a hard job keeping up with Ellie's racing sandals. We are both too tired to climb onto its withered branches. We lie down and rest among the puffball remains of the dandelions. We sit close together, ourselves and our thoughts and our one chance for a bit of silence. The wildflowers tickle our legs and we stretch them out in front of us. The breeze is still here, rustling through the nearby briars on the ditch. I stretch my fingers over my eyes as though to hide from the scenery in front of me before widening them to get a better view of the reddening sky beyond Bill Corcoran's hayfield. Rapture in childhood doesn't often come to us but for this once in our lives, it seems to embrace us more than before.

Down below the Rotten Tree we can see the Deer Field and beyond that the Bull Paddock and the Dolla River – and beyond that lies the rest of the world, about which we know nothing. I hear the sound of Grannie's tin tray rapping on the flagstones. Herself and Jack must have finished their milking. It's time to get home.

Once Grannie has scoured the creamery tank with her scrub-brush and left it spotlessly clean, herself and Jack pour their buckets of milk through the muslin cloth into the tank and seal the lid tight to keep out the evening flies.

Ellie races off home. Then me, Grannie and Jack sit by the fire until the kettle starts singing for Jack's mug of tea.

I keep their ears busy, pouring out all my news to them and (the little liar that I am) embroidering bits of it to see them smile across the firelight at me. There are the remains of a juicy rabbit in the pot and we have rabbit soup with it, all washed down with warm milk.

It's the end of another day. The sunset is finally red and there are one or two stars, not yet fully luminous, appearing above the pig house. I will sleep like a log tonight and won't notice Jack getting into bed beside me. The only prayers I'll say are, 'God bless Grannie and God bless Jack. God bless me and God stop the war,' even though I don't understand a word of this last bit. My dreams will be happy ones, like the merry song of the blackbird in the hawthorn tree, lulling me into a deep sleep.

It's another day during this sunny summertime. The sun's fat face appears early, shooting its rays in through the windowpane, brightening up the red geraniums on the window sill and the pink rose bushes that stretch down towards the hen house.

I peep out from underneath the blankets and watch these rays trembling their way across the rafters and crawling down onto my big brass bed. I listen to our cockerel, Rusty, crowing his heart out. I hear the pigeons coo-cooing in Sam's Grove and the crows fussily croaking as they repair their nests after last night's rain. The flies hum and buzz against the windowpane, trying to get in through the glass. They must know that Grannie has stored something good to eat inside the lid of Old Harpy the piano. It will soon be time for the two of us to go searching for eggs.

Gret has an orchard. Only one or two of the apple trees in it are to the children's liking – the rest are ancient and worn away. Behind her orchard is a secret place. It has been the hideout for children ever since Gret's own mother was a child. That's when children called it Castle Eden. No one knows how it acquired this quaint biblical name and throughout late July and August, Gret's children often frequent it even more than they frequent the river.

Rosie and Daisy not only send me invites to take pretend tea with them in their cubby house, they keep pestering me to come and see their castle. I am full of excitement. Today is the day for my first visit.

However, by the time we reach the high gate that leads to the orchard, I realise I'm too small to climb over it and I begin to feel unsure of myself. Gret has placed layers of wire netting in between the bars of the gate to keep out the hens and ducks – but especially the geese, who are more adventurous and might travel too far from the yard and into the clutches of Mr Fox.

The little girls notice my predicament. Rosie lays her hand on my shoulder and wipes my eyes. 'Ned,' she says, 'I am going to help you and show you where to place your hands and feet as you climb.' It's just like the time Ellie showed me how to climb onto the branches of the Rotten Tree and I feel I'm again in safe hands. Rosie and Daisy are not going to scuttle off and leave me behind like some poor lost lamb.

We get over the gate successfully and make our way through the apple trees to reach the second gate that leads to the castle. This next gate is even more cumbersome. It is covered with a rusty old bedstead placed there long ago and meant to prevent any intrusion into the orchard from that side. I am sad all over again. The bedstead is huge. It seems an insurmountable mountain for my small legs to climb up and over.

Rosie and Daisy have been inside the castle a few times already and with Rosie's renewed help and guidance, I eventually find myself on the far side of the bedstead and inside the castle.

My eyes marvel at the unique outlay of the place. Though it's my first time being here, I am sure it won't be my last. Next time, I will bring Ellie along with me. She'll have no trouble in climbing over the gate and the bedstead.

In the last few weeks, Shawnee, with the help of his brothers and sisters, went on a tidying-up expedition to improve their castle.

233

They removed several boxes, crates and unmentionable household objects that had been thrown out in previous years and were strewn around the place. They arranged them on the ditch next to the Thistle Field. It was a great improvement and smartened up the appearance of their secret world.

On the upper ditch and with a little bit more care and attention, they stacked a number of faded pictures of Boar War soldiers that had been discarded by Fiddler Joe's father. The picture now looked very forlorn.

I continue to look around. There's not a weed in sight. The grass has been cut short, the bigger boys taking it in turn to make use of their father's scythe. The briars on the ditches have been trimmed back and last week their father burnt as much of the rubbish as he could in a great big bonfire up on the Heights.

My two young friends are strangely quiet – almost reverent. The rest of Gret's family – Shawnee, Sweeney and Bucko – are already here. They are sitting rather sedately on one of three fallen pine trees that stretch along the side of Shy Denis's ditch. When these trees were still in the ground, they must have stretched as high as the Difficult Tree itself. They make a cosy seat for these big boys to rest on.

I notice something else: the three of them are puffing on fags like grown up men and as soon as they see us, they start showing off and putting smoke to the heavens. Shawnee has a heap of fag-butts in a canister resting between his knees, ready and waiting for their second smoke later in the day.

Since the previous Monday, he has been taking the family's milk to the creamery in Killeen. He's well able for the task, Fiddler Joe having taught him how to strap the milk tanks to Slowcoach's cart and make the reins firm and tight. For (says he) as soon as Shawnee drives the cart past Griffin's Cross, he'll come across a deep fall in the road. This will be followed by a sudden upturn where the slope is steep enough to topple the tanks out from the back of the cart if they're not secured properly. It has happened to other drivers on their way to the creamery, leaving them in a puddle of spilt milk and crying like banshees.

Shawnee is a likeable lad and on his way back from the creamery, he occasionally holds Slowcoach back so as to chat with neighbourly folk and give his ass a chance to nibble on the bushes. It gives him time to hear some of the latest news about the war and how it's going on against the Germans. Maybe he'll have something to tell Grannie and Jack as soon as he gets home. They are always looking for war news and it appears that the Germans are still not doing as great as before. If that is true, then the war might come to an end even sooner than expected.

There is one house where Shawnee stops a while longer than at others. It's the home of Bridgee McCormack. She's the only woman known to enjoy smoking a fag or two and behaving as though she were a man. Her little cottage is known as the Vatican, a quaint name given to it by some of the more humorous lads. It has red velvet curtains on the front windows and it is said that she has red velvet covers on top of her bed and certain unmentionable parts of her under garments are red velvet too. This has not been established as a fact; it's merely a piece of rascally gossip handed out by the wily old lads who are always up to mischief.

Bridgee has another unusual habit and smokes only half a fag at a time. She leaves the other half in her canister for a separate occasion when someone might stop at her door to chat and share a smoke with her. She has built up quite a collection of fag-butts by now.

After coming home from Mass the previous Sunday, she developed a head cold and as a result, the very taste of tobacco became most unpleasant to her. She suddenly found that she had no inclination to smoke at all. It was a sad day, indeed, for her.

Last Wednesday, she brought out her canister and showed the contents to Shawnee. He could see it was full to the top with her unused fag-butts. Much to his surprise, she insisted on presenting this unique treasure to him, telling him it would do him good to have a smoke now and then. After all (she said), if he's man enough at fourteen years of age to drive his ass to the creamery and home again, surely he's man enough to have a smoke from time to time.

Shawnee didn't need much persuading. He snatched the canister out of her hands and drove Slowcoach home at a rather spritely pace.

Consequently, as soon as we three arrive in the castle, the first thing we see is the three boys busily smoking. We can't believe our eyes. But how did they get so clever? They're not grown men yet.

Only Shawnee knows. On the day he arrived home with the canister of fag-butts, he made sure to hide it from everyone and started planning his next move. He took out Gret's box of matches and spent an hour or two hiding himself in the dyke where no one could see him. Then he earnestly began teaching himself the art of smoking.

At first, the fag-butts smelt very bitter and made him cough like blazes. In a few days, however, he got used to smoking them. He began to feel like the rest of the men and to cock his finger in the air and spit at a fly now and then. He has become the grand young fellow indeed.

To no small extent, he owes this to my friend Ellie from the moment she crowned him with her garland of lovely flowers. When he showed Sweeney and Bucko his canister of fag-butts, they kept begging him to let them try one or two for themselves. So much so that he finally gave way.

And now, we little ones can see for ourselves how his young brothers have become great smokers just like him, occasionally examining the glowing red fire at the tip of their fag-butt before gently dabbing the ash off. They never give so much as a cough while drawing in the smoke and they have learnt how to cock their little fingers daintily like Shawnee.

It's very strange to see them acting this way for, apart from today's smoking and blowing the smoke out at us, the only things that Sweeney and Bucko have ever blown up till now have been a few dandelion puffballs into our faces simply to annoy us.

Rosie, Daisy and I sit on the grass in front of the fallen tree trunks and continue to admire the big lads. It never enters our heads to ask if we can try smoking a few of their fag-butts. We are much too timid. What would people think if they saw the likes of us strolling down the lane with a fag-butt stuck in the corner of our mouths? But where on earth did Shawnee learn his recent skills, cocking his finger in the air and spitting at a fly and when did Sweeney and Bucko catch onto this? We'd love to know.

The truth is, Jack (though I have rarely seen him smoking fags, only puffing on his tobacco-pipe) was the one who taught Shawnee how to smoke. He couldn't have asked his father to teach him, for Fiddler Joe would have shown him a far different side to his kindly nature by firing the chair across the room at him.

Until a few days ago, Shawnee's smoking has been a well-kept secret between Jack and himself. Jack was able to show him how to blow the smoke out through his nostrils and let it escape through his ears as well. I would love to have seen such a great event as smoke coming out of Shawnee's ears as though he had turned himself into a dragon from one of Grannie's storybooks. So would Rosie and Daisy.

Sweeney and Bucko are two innocent lads and they always believe whatever Shawnee tells them – on this occasion, the lies about Jack letting the smoke out through his ears. Shawnee, however, is well-known for telling the odd little lie just like the rest of us.

I hadn't seen Ellie for a few days and today, she came down to our yard with one of her mother's large shopping bags and a pair of scissors. She didn't bring her bowlee wheel. I wonder if she's going down to Gerry's shop to do a bit of shopping for her mother. Maybe her mother is sick. But why is Ellie holding a pair of scissors?

After a short chat with Grannie while Jack is out checking on his pigs, Ellie and I sit on the ass's cart for a few moments of contemplation. I tell her of my exciting adventures inside Castle Eden. I don't mention the big boys smoking their fag-butts in case I get them into trouble with their father. I am not that big a fool.

Ellie tells me about her recent evening rambles with her father. They went out as far as Jack Scissors' well. They called in at Mick the Smith's forge to warm their hands at his blazing fire. Then, they went back down the lane and turned in at Shy Denis's place to see was he painting something new, maybe the wheels of his cart or his pig house door!

The shopping bag and the pair of scissors is beginning to make sense. Ellie takes me by the hand as she always does when she has something exciting for us to do.

I run in the half-door and whisper in Grannie's ear. 'Ellie is going hunting for blackberries. Can I go with her?' I know Grannie's answer before she can get a word out and away we go.

An hour later, we return to Ellie's place with her shopping bag half-full with blackberries and not a sign of a white maggot in any of them. Ellie made sure to check each one. Mrs Fidget gets down three of her bigger jam jars and lays them on the front table: one for Grannie, one for Gret and one for herself. With the help of Ellie and myself, she fills the jars to the top and there's still some left over. She gives these berries to us to feast on. Then, she seals the lids on tight and hands one jar to me and another one to Ellie.

'Off ye go and mind ye don't fall over or ye'll destroy yeer berries and break my jam jars as well,' she says. I am used to her old way of speaking by now.

Mindful of her orders, we take our time walking down the lane. I can see none of Gret's children. At this hour of the day, they are all locked away inside their castle.

I stand outside Gret's half-door and I don't venture in. She has a large family and unless I am invited to do so, Grannie has forbidden me to make a nuisance of myself by going in and eating their food.

'Coom in, coom in, let ye!' yells Gret with her usual fat smile and in spite of Grannie's orders, we tiptoe in. Ellie does all of the talking, being older and cleverer than me.

Gret is as pleased as punch with Mrs Fidget's jar of blackberries and she thanks Ellie profusely. I tell her that my jar is for Grannie.

'What a wonderful woman your mother is, Ellie,' cries Gret. 'I must get her some cooking apples from the orchard and bring them up to her tomorrow after Mass.'

This is my chance to take Ellie's hand and lead her towards the orchard and on into the castle. She can see how excited I am. She is excited too and after crowning Shawnee with her flowery garland, she is now one of the family. Their castle will be her secret and they'll be sure to welcome her. Maybe she will show them how to make garlands someday soon.

Castle Eden isn't a real castle like the ones Ellie reads about at school with a princess in a tower and a fine young knight riding to her rescue. Yet, it has something of a castle about it. The high gate and the bedstead are the defences of our fortress and once we get inside, we find ourselves safe from the rest of the world.

All we need (says Ellie) is a ditch full of water to make ourselves a moat. But that would take dozens of barrels of water from the river. How can an ass as slow as Slowcoach be expected to bring back so much water on his cart? The thought is quickly banished. There's no doubt about it, our castle is unique and thanks to Shawnee and Fiddler Joe, it's the tidiest place imaginable, just the way we want it to be.

Now that Ellie is here, we remember that all castles have a flagpole and that no flagpole is complete unless it has a flag on top.

Sweeney thinks up a bright idea. Gret has recently purchased a new pole for her washing line and has thrown the old one out behind the barn. He is quick to seize the opportunity and make use of it.

Bucko and he take Fiddler Joe's two hay forks from behind the hay shed and dig a large hole at the upper end of the castle. They find something else that Gret has thrown out, a brightly coloured flour sack with the words *'112 pounds weight'* printed across it. Shawnee lets us know that not only can he climb high trees but he recognises the words *'112 pounds weight'*. It is the same weight as the eight stone weight outside their barn door. Even Rosie is amazed at his cleverness. He must be an awfully fine scholar.

Sweeney will spend the evening fixing the flour sack onto the old washing line pole. In his mind's eye, he can see his flag swaying to and fro in the breeze. No one else from the real world will ever have the privilege of seeing it and we little ones clap our hands vigorously as always.

Not to be outmatched, Bucko brings back a heap of stones from the dyke and makes the bottom of the pole even more secure.

Shawnee isn't satisfied. They need a symbol next to the flagpole. He finds a dead rat that Gret's wild cats left behind the tree trunks at Shy Denis's ditch. He turns the dead creature over with his toe and comes back. He whirled it round and round in front of our faces, holding onto it by its long white tail and short, stubby legs. I can still hear our screams and it makes me shiver.

He leads the rest of us in a procession round the castle, all the time muttering incomprehensible words of bog Latin much to the delight of Rosie, me and Daisy. He places the dead rat reverently on top of the heap of stones. It makes a grand finish to the flag that's on top of the flagpole.

During the night when all is still and quiet, Fiddler Joe shows his kindly spirit. He finds a pair of dead frogs and when all his children are fast asleep, he lays them beside the dead rat.

Next morning, none of us can work out who has done this. But Shawnee suspects his father. He knows him better than the rest of us. When he tells us of his suspicions, we almost wish that Fiddler Joe was a child like us and that he could join our merry band. But that would be asking too much.

The dead rat made us little ones scream like blazes. The dead frogs make us sad. How often Gret's children have hunted for frogs in the wet corners of their meadows! Like the young trout, how slippery they were! It was a devil of a job to hold onto them and they always let them go. For a while, they watched them leaping about in their search for water, their eyes bulging. These little creatures made them laugh out loud, especially if they saw them catching a fly and swallowing it down whole.

From now on, each day is going to be different. Shawnee is like a schoolmaster, though a pretend one. He's forever scratching his head to find something new to occupy our minds and on the day after raising our flagpole, he begins by teaching us our Tables.

It's my second day in the castle. I am in no way ready for this new lesson. I keep telling myself I'm not even five till next summer.

Shawnee sits us down on the tree trunk. Daisy and I are at the bottom of the row. I feel rather sheepish and so does Daisy. She is not much older than me and not ready till September to go to school with Rosie.

Ellie sits beside us on the tree trunk and I give her one of my quaint little smiles. She smiles back at me and I feel better.

Sweeney and Bucko sit next to Ellie. They have the appearance of important-looking swans. Daisy and I look like ugly ducklings as we wait for Shawnee's Tables to begin. We wonder what his teaching will be like.

'The lesson for today is Doubles Tables and we will be doubling our numbers,' says he.

He starts off with '10 and 10 make 20.' The bigger children know how to chant this and they repeat each bit after Shawnee in an echoing sing-song chant. It's a sound I've heard them making before when they were passing Grannie's flagstones on schooldays. They're like a crowd of humming bees, all the time swaying from side-to-side on the tree trunk and singing in harmony. They start off slowly in an effort to encourage Daisy and myself. Then they gradually quicken the pace. I think they are tremendously clever.

Shawnee prods us on and the bigger children echo his words with 20 and 20 make 40, 30 and 30 make 60, 40 and 40 make 80 until they reach the grand total of 50 and 50 make a 100. This they shout out in a roar that almost deafens us.

They repeat this lengthy list time and time again till the bigger ones are sick and tired of the monotonous chanting. By now, even Daisy and I know the Doubles Tables. I can't wait to repeat the whole exercise for Grannie and Jack when I get home for my dinner. I look across at Ellie. Then I look at Daisy and the three of us smile. Ellie might even make a lovely garland of flowers for me and Daisy like she did for Shawnee. We feel we are now a part of school life and we are looking forward to shaking hands with Mr Flanagan the revered schoolmaster.

Shawnee leads us over to the flour sack flag. He sits us down next to a rusty old pulper, something else that was thrown out by Gret's mother many years ago.

It's time for the second lesson of the morning – time for Shawnee to dress up as a priest and hear our confessions – even mine and Daisy's, though Father Speed the Plough has yet to hear us confess our sins in a proper confession box. Neither of us will be ready for this until we are seven and judged to have reached the age of reason. This is something else that I'm not old enough to understand: an age when children know the difference between right and wrong and know that to do wrong is a sin.

This morning, it doesn't matter if the sins we confess to Shawnee are true or false. The older children (the rascals) are looking forward to telling Shawnee a pack of lies, all of which will be delivered with solemn faces and downcast eyes.

He sits us down in front of him between the pulper and the flag. On top of the pulper is one of Fiddler Joe's old work shirts, which seemed as if it was left there to air and dry. Sweeney helps Shawnee put it on. It reaches down below his knees. He looks rather stately in his makeshift priestly robe. He stretches out his arms and looks up to the heavens. He spins round and starts spouting his bog Latin again, mumbling the same way he did when marching us over to the flagpole.

'Father Speed the Plough is sick this morning,' says he, 'and I'm the new priest. It's time for yeer confession and I need to hear yeer sins. And, if ye haven't any, ye must make up one or two for me. I like to be entertained and am anxious to know what ye children have been up to during the past week.' He says this pile of words with a smile.

Even I know that this has nothing to do with our real church and that we are going to play a game of make believe. I have never played the game before.

Ellie whispers in my ear. 'Ned, if you have never done anything wrong, you can make up a few sins for Shawnee. It's part of the game. He won't want more than three sins from us, I'm sure.'

As for Sweeney and Bucko, the more outrageous the made-up sins are, the more enjoyable the game is and even Ellie is making up a list of horrendous sins such as murdering her pet dog.

'Only three sins, if you please,' says Shawnee. 'My ears won't tolerate any more than that.' Then each of us kneel before him and shout out our sins for the rest to hear. No one will believe my own sins but what I'm about to tell Shawnee is nothing but the truth.

The same way as the others, I start off telling my sins with the words, 'Bless me, Father, I have greatly sinned.' It has taken me a second or two to learn these words. It's part of the game.

'Bless me, Father, I stole icing sugar from inside the lid of Old Harpy the piano and I said the word 'shite' after Jack pelted worms at my face over in the potato field when he'd finished filling up the bucket with spuds.' I have no more sins to tell him. Aren't I the little angel!

It's the afternoon now. Shawnee suddenly whispers in Sweeney's ear and suggests that himself and Bucko entertain the rest of us with another bout of wrestling.

The two wrestlers jump up and slowly circle each other, making snarling noises before pitching into one another. This time, the wrestling is far fiercer than it was before – clawing at each other and tackling with arms and legs until finally Sweeney hooks his right leg round Bucko's heels and sends him sprawling on his back over near the pulper.

Poor Bucko! But he is not hurt in the slightest and takes his downfall manfully.

From behind the stump of an old tree, Shawnee produces his mother's shopping bag. Inside, it is a supply of her best red apples, half a dozen spuds (one for each of us) and a package of biscuits from Gret's hidden store at the bottom of her press cupboard. She'll never miss them.

For the next half hour we are silent, our teeth munching and chomping. We cannot explain how we feel in sharing such an addition to a meal. The peace and quiet is delicious.

Sweeney breaks the silence when he asks each one of us if we are able to kiss our elbow. I have never heard of such a thing. He must have asked the others this before and now each of us tries desperately to deal with his question. Ellie sidles over to me and tries to twist my arm back far enough so that my mouth may get near enough to kiss my elbow. I fail hopelessly.

Rosie takes a large leaf from the side of the ditch and begins to whistle on its edge. It makes a double whistle. The next few minutes sees us all with similar leaves, even me, and trying to whistle on them. But we all fail. It is something new, the way Rosie can form her lips to make the double whistle. I hope I'll get better at it.

That ends our play and for the rest of the day each of us goes off in different directions to do our household chores: helping to sweep the chicken dung off of the yard, forking out the dung from the cow shed, all this for the older ones to do, and for me and Jack to go down to the well and fetch back the water, something that Daisy, too, has to do for her mother. It's a chance for us all to show our mettle when it comes to an afternoon's solid work in addition to learning our Doubles Tables and confessing our few miserable sins to Shawnee this morning.

Next day cannot come quick enough. After Shawnee's game of hearing our confessions in which Sweeney and Bucko confess to a number of murders and highway robberies, the day starts off with a pause and a moment for reflection.

Now comes the time for Rosie and Daisy to entertain the rest of us by telling us their sins. But they have been struck dumb on hearing their big brothers telling their supposed sins to Shawnee. They can't think of any sins to tell. They can't say they stole the spuds from the chicken's feed in the burner. No, it's always boys who do the pilfering – even me, their little friend – stealing icing sugar from Grannie's old piano. Perhaps I should not have been such an innocent as to admit this. But then I'm not too clever yet.

Though they have no sins to tell, Rosie and Daisy have something else to entertain us with. Rosie is a fine singer and so is Daisy. They are ready to burst into song at the drop of a hat. Shawnee stands them up near the pulper while the rest of us stay seated in front of the flagpole and wait for them to start singing.

As well as learning our prayers at the fireside, all of us have learnt to memorise a few songs even before starting out for school. Dolla is a place full of songs and fiddle music – set dancing too at weddings and wakes and after the harvest.

Rosie sings the first verse of '*No one to welcome me home*'. It's a sad song about an emigrant coming home from America – only to realise that his former school friends are now resting peacefully in the graveyard.

She is a little bit timid at first. But when Daisy joins in with the chorus, her confidence grows. You'd not hear a pin drop as the two of them hymn their way through all six verses.

Like Ellie, I sit amazed at the beautiful sound coming out of my little friends' mouths. It's as sweet as a bird and the rest of us clap and clap them for their gift of singing.

How surprised are we next minute when we hear the voice of Fiddler Joe from behind his barn, shouting, 'Glory to the pair of ye! Glory to ye yet again!' This song was always his mother's favourite.

Shawnee marches us over to the tree trunk by the ditch. He stands before us and claps his hands for our attention.

'I'm the king of the castle,' he says.

Sweeney answers him with, 'Get down you dirty rascal!' It's the signal for us to leap up from our knees and make a mad dash at Shawnee to try and topple him from his perch. Rosie and Ellie grab at his feet. Sweeney and Bucko run in behind him and try to pinch his bum. Shawnee, however, is far too strong and he playfully taps us here and there to frighten us off.

We are like a band of playful puppies, tremendous fun, till he cries out, 'Stop, let ye, I'm well beaten,' and he topples from the tree trunk like a drunken man and lies flat on his back.

There's not a move out of him, the rascal, just like a corpse at a wake, a scene we have all seen before, even me. Once again, I find I'm not sure of myself or if Shawnee is hurt. That is, until he suddenly leaps into the air and, with a lion-like roar, chases us round and round the castle. Our screams are enough to frighten the dead. I am sure it brought back childhood memories to Fiddler Joe inside the barn, listening to us.

After our bout of amusement has stopped, we lie down exhausted on the grass. A moment of silence follows. I gaze up at the streaks of sunlight slicing in through the trees on Shy Denis's ditch. I see Gret's two wild cats lurking a foot or two away from a wagtail's nest. There are times for laughter and fun. There are also times for me to be sad as I watch the wild cats striding towards the nest.

Saturdays are often different from other days. Gret's children have always liked coming down to help Grannie with odd jobs: Sweeney and Bucko around the yard and Rosie and Daisy inside the house. This Saturday, the boys are dealing with filling the tea chest with enough logs for the weekend and replenishing Grannie's stock of turf underneath the wobbly stool. Rosie and Daisy are dusting with the goose wings – the larger ones for tables and the press cupboard, the smaller ones for those little cobwebs that visiting spiders like to weave.

By dinnertime, they are rewarded with Grannie's humbug sweets, which she keeps stashed in her bedroom drawer. I get a few sweets too, even though I have done none of the work and am often abroad with Jack – either taking the cows back to the Bull Paddock or visiting Old Pat's spring well in the hope of seeing Mrs Methuselah again, the lady who takes her daily walk as far as the avenue.

I have had my dinner – pieces of rabbit and thick stew with a healthy helping of spuds, all washed down with my mug of milk and a few mugs of water from the bucket behind the half-door.

I am ready to roam with nothing in mind but Gret's exciting children in their castle. It's now my secret sanctuary as well as Ellie's. She will bring down some red currants from her mother's bushes behind the house. I have never tasted them before. She will add some blackberries, which she collected from Shy Denis's garden. The other children love to see her now that she has shown her skills in fashioning flowery garlands.

Sweeney and Bucko have selected the best apples from Gret's orchard, testing a good few of them first (the rascals). The rest of us will have plenty to eat after we've had our next bout of energetic games.

There is something else. Shawnee's favourite food is a heap of potato skins. No one ever eats potato skins. They are always left to be mixed in with the pig's food. But Shawnee has slyly gathered hordes of them and today, he will tempt each of us to warm our bellies in scoffing a few with him.

By now, I have learnt to climb in over the orchard gate and I even make my way across the wire netting round the bedstead. Shame has made me do it ever since watching Daisy flying her legs out over these obstacles and she's not much older than me.

Once inside the castle, my friends welcome me and Ellie for their next session of playfulness. The sunlight sparkles cheerfully and doesn't slice into my eyes.

We all sit down in a row on the tree trunk. Our tables for today are the well-known ones:

1 and 1 make 2
2 and 2 make 4
3 and 3 make 6 – and so on until 12 and 12 make 24.

We love singing this. We make a humming noise with our joint voices, something like the bees among the laurel leaves in the bedroom chimney where Jack and I sleep. When we reach the

247

words '12 and 12 make 24' we recite these words with a deafening roar and an even greater roar when we add the words 'shut your gob and say no more!'

I can't wait to repeat this last bit to Grannie and Jack when I get home. I love saying it. I know Grannie will laugh her socks off.

12 and 12 make 24
Shut your gob and say no more!

Shawnee takes us over to the ditch next to Fiddler Joe's hay shed. He lines up Daisy and myself at the alder tree and gives us our orders. We race each other twice round the edge of the castle. The first one to race back and touch the tree will be the winner.

Once again, as with my former attempt to climb over the gate and the bedstead, I fail miserably to match Daisy. She and I have to shake hands like hurlers after a hurling match (says Shawnee).

Bucko and Sweeney are next on his list. They have to hop across the castle from the alder tree to the fallen tree trunk. Sweeney, though bigger and older, is no match for Bucko, who can hop as good as a rabbit. And, once again, the gentlemanly handshake follows.

Shawnee climbs over to the other side of Shy Denis's ditch to make his water. Maybe he'll puff on a sly fag-butt whilst he's over there.

Meanwhile, Sweeney introduces us to a game of leap-frog like the game children play at dinnertime in Killeen's school playing field. This game is followed by 'feet off ground', a game that Ellie likes to play in her own school in the Silvermines. There are one or two tree stumps to leap onto as well as the ditches themselves and onto the bedstead, too, so as not to get caught by the chaser. I struggle to keep up with it all, so dizzy am I from the speed of things!

It is noon now. Ellie and Rosie do the housewife work and hand out the roasted crab apples, the orchard apples and the red currants and the blackberries. Shawnee adds the potato skins. It's a proper feast – delicious – and it's also a moment of well-earned silence as we all get busy munching. We give a final lick to our fingers and lips like Gret's wild cats when Grannie and Jack give them their milk at milking time.

Shawnee produces Bridgee McCormack's canister of fag-butts. He has replenished it with some of his father's recent fag-butts. He and his brothers have a fine old time taking deep puffs and jetting the smoke out from their nostrils. They have learnt to smoke as good as Fiddler Joe himself, sitting up straight-backed and looking grand and important in front of us young ones as we watch them throwing plumes of smoke across our astonished faces.

The suspense is killing me as I wait to see if the smoke will escape from their ears. I fear it'll be a long wait. But the stately feast (especially the potato skins) – the fag-butts too – make this a time of dreamy reverie. It's as if the rest of the world no longer exists.

By mid-afternoon, the sun has grown from warm to hot. We lay our backs down on the soft grass. Some of us close our eyes. Others hum with pleasure. I gaze up at the sky, searching for clouds but I can see none.

We hear Shy Denis calling his cows to follow him up the field *(Cow-cow! Cow-cow!)*. We run over to the ditch. We see the cows' long shadows spear out in front of them as they march up the field behind Denis, dutiful as ever.

It is almost time for us to end the day's play. Shawnee gathers us into a ring in front of the flag. He sits on the pulper with his arms folded. With our legs crossed, we look like little tailors. We smile up at him and wait for his final instructions. He is a bright fellow. He is our schoolmaster, at least our pretend one.

This is today's final act: News Time, where each of us stands up in turn to give out our news. Like our confession, it can be true or false news and we have to guess which it is: true or false. Some of Bucko's news makes us shake with laughter, like the time he stole apples from Old Pat's orchard and the old fellow leant out his window and fired his gun out over his head so that he wet his britches in terror.

Unhurried, Shawnee tells us about the day he went to Old Pat's orchard and how the old fellow threw the contents of his piss-pot out the window, drenching poor Mary Gollmoy, who was standing on guard while he himself was up the apple tree doing his robbing. This great bit of news has us in a further fit of laughter.

After we've all held court with our news, it's time to take a last lazy rest. I listen to the stealthy sound of the crickets in the long grass behind the pulper. It'll soon be time to go home and I know that the two tin trays of Gret and Grannie will soon be ringing in our ears, telling us that it's tea time.

Shawnee (the rascal) cannot end the day without being a bit mischievous. He asks us to close our eyes. 'Keep them shut tight!' he orders.

Slowly and in a whisper, he starts to unravel his tale. It's the ghost story of Shy Denis's mother when she died and how she came back in the middle of the night, riding on Passion, her ass, to fetch her cardigan from the press cupboard before going back to meet God. Shawnee has hardly stopped to take a breath.

I don't know whether to believe him or not. He is so convincing with his words and I'm not sure of myself again.

'Many men, including my own father,' says he, 'have seen the old lady riding back and forth around the hills in the night of a full moon.'

Ellie gives me a gentle smile when she sees the sad look on my face and I am no longer frightened. All ends well and it's time for us to bid farewell to our castle and start back home to our soda bread and milk.

I cross our flagstones and run into the yard. Grannie has the fire well lit. I can see the smoke coming out from the top of the chimney and sailing off in a puff of wind.

I was expecting to find all the hens and ducks gone into the hen house by now. Only the hens have gone in. The ducks are still in the yard. Some of them are sleeping on one leg with one eye open. I am careful not to kick any of them over as I race towards the half-door.

Jack has gone off to the Bull Paddock with his matronly cows now that they have been milked. I find the living room so quiet after all the excitement of my day and I feel a little sad once more. The sky outside the half-door is beginning to turn grey. The evening breeze is a little bit cold. It'll be dusk soon.

Grannie didn't hear me come in. But now she rushes from her bedroom to the half-door to greet me. 'I'll put on the kettle for our tea,' she says and her smile, as ever, fills me with happiness. I can't stop chattering. It's always the same. I'm worse than the fluttering crows who are forever mumbling to one another in Old Pat's rookery when they get back to their nests.

Jack isn't long away. When he comes in, I start dishing out my news all over again about the day I've been having, especially the tales of Bucko and Sweeney and the ghost story of Shawnee.

The firelight sends a glow around the room. Grannie's kettle hisses and splutters on the hob. The last of the sunlight peers in over the half-door and penetrates the dark corners of the room. It'll be night-time soon. Grannie lights the lamp and its flame quickly rises up from dim white to bright orange. It's time for us to kneel and say our prayers and for me to finish up with the words, 'Please God, stop the war.' I am beginning to understand that there is a war going on somewhere across the sea but I've yet to learn what it will mean for me – what it will mean for Grannie and Jack if it should ever come to an end. Perish the thought!

August is the month for the haymaking – the mowing, the airing and drying out of the hay-rows and the tramming and reeking when the hay is brought back safe into the haggart. The neighbours come down to give a helping hand and there are often half a dozen men in one and the same field with their sturdy hay forks when it comes to drying out the rows of hay.

The first cockerel has crowed. Our own Rusty joins in and the little birds have started to chorus the crowing of the cockerels. With the lid of her sweet-gallon, Grannie reddens the morning fire of hedge-clippings. She is down on her knees amidst the smoke as usual and waiting for the sparks to rise up.

Jack gets up stealthily so as not to awaken me. He knows his mother will moan and groan (unlike her usual self) to get him to shift his body and fly into the work like other farmers. It's the same as earlier in the year when it was time for him to go ploughing.

'Will she ever stop nagging?' he mutters as he puts on his britches. 'Do women ever stop complaining?'

But Grannie's nagging is only half-hearted. Once Jack has finished reading the latest chapter of his Zane Grey novel, he will race out the door and be as good at the hay as any man.

Grannie gets up off of her knees and mumbles a prayer that the hay-making will turn out good and God will not send the rain. She needn't worry. The big yellow sun seems never to have left us and it will brighten the work of the haymakers today. It was like that last year as well, scorching the whitewash walls outside our little house with its fresh light.

Grannie's older brother, Mikey, has sent down his mowing machine. It's the one with the 8 ft width and the double-edged cutter. He is a neat and tidy man like Shy Denis and has oiled all the mower's parts, treating them as he would a child with love and tenderness. His mower is now waiting patiently behind our cow shed for Jack to come and attend to it.

Grannie gives him a mug, not of his usual strong tea but of leftover rabbit soup from the burner. She gives him a thick soda bread sandwich, not filled with blackcurrant jam but with a thick wedge of ham. His stomach will be well-lined for the rest of the day. She sprinkles him with holy water so that his work will turn out well.

Moll is stamping her feet outside the half-door, anxious to be off mowing. She has been listening to the sound of the other mowing machines where the reapers have already started their day's work.

Jack steps out to the Blue Button Field. He doesn't take me with him. He won't let me go anywhere near the mower. Grannie and I tiptoe across the haggart to take a peep at him round the corner of the cow shed. He is sitting on the mower seat. It has the same shape as his bum and it fits him nicely. For our benefit, he rocks himself up and down on the seat. He's enjoying himself the way we children do. I hope to heaven he doesn't fall off and get himself twisted in the blades. 'Look at the little show off,' mutters Grannie to herself.

Jack goes back to the yard and brings out Moll. He links her onto the mower. They head across the field and into the second field. They drive on to the third field where Jack will start today's mowing. By the afternoon, he may even have time to steer Moll down to the Deer Field below the Blue Button Field.

He kneels down and inspects the cutting bar and the scissor teeth on the mower's blades. Mikey has used his edging stone well and the blades are as sharp as a razor. Their diamond-shaped edges are already catching the sun. Jack now gives them a few drops of oil from his oil can. He checks the height of the blades and makes sure they are close to the ground for a good, clean cut to the grass.

The morning dew has long left the fields and away goes the mower. Jack is steering Moll round the edge of the meadow. The skimmed grass falls back behind the cutting blades. The rattling noise of the other mowers re-echoes back to him from far across the river. By midday, his mower's clattering noise will have scythed down a good few acres of hay.

There's a light breeze coming across from beyond Bill Corcoran's well. It fills the air with the blossoming fragrance of the newly mown hay. Little field mice and rabbits are alarmed by the noise of the machine and they race to the centre of the meadow when they hear it getting near them. Up above is the blue sky. Will they live long enough to look at it again or will the blades cut them to ribbons? They keep perfectly still, not even a bolt of lightning will shift them.

While Jack is out mowing, Grannie and I have our own work to do this morning. It's Monday, washing day, but it's also the day for getting the pension – not for herself (she has had her widow's pension since her dear Will died in '28) but for her brother Mikey the owner of the mowing machine. Mikey is the oldest of her four brothers and farms the old place in Curragarneen where all of them were born and grew up. It's a short distance away, up along Old Tim's two fields and out past Fort Dangerous, then further up the lane.

It will be a pleasant walk for Grannie and myself today as we stroll through Old Tim's field flowers and on across the Hill of the Goldfinch. We will tiptoe round Fort Dangerous where the little leprechauns live. They have been there since history began. Grannie tells me no one has ever set eyes on them and that their hiding place is covered with briars so that no one can get in and get a look at them.

Today's the day I'll be seeing Mikey for the first time. I will also be as near as I've ever been to the little leprechauns. I am so excited. I already know a good deal about them since Grannie is always making up bedtime stories for me before tucking me in under the blankets – stories like the leprechauns' nimble feet when they come out to dance in a fairy ring at midnight – and how they keep wearing away their buckle-shoes from all their energetic dancing and how they are the finest of cobblers, always hammering new shoes onto their feet or repairing old shoes for the younger leprechauns. How I'd love to see them dancing!

Today is Mikey's very first pension day. He would have gone down to the post office himself to collect it had he had the strength to do so. But it was only last Wednesday that he returned from hospital where he had half his ear cut off. The operation left him weak as a kitten. He's far too wobbly to get out of bed at this stage of his life. It'll be at least another fortnight (says Doctor Glasses) before he can lift a muscle.

So, Grannie is going to drive Lightning down to the post office instead of him and bring his pension up to him. On the way, I will sit on the last board on top of the cart next to her. She may even let me hold the reins and drive Lightning for a little bit. I can't wait to be off on this latest adventure. I have never been to the post office before.

Before we set out, Grannie has to lay out the bedsheets on the bushes in the haggart to air them and make them fresh. She had no time to wash them – only air them – such is her hurry to get Mikey his money.

She starts to get ready. I watch her combing out her long locks of hair. She spends a good while at it as though she was preparing herself for Sunday Mass.

Jack wasn't just reading his novel this morning. He made sure to tackle and harness Lightning to Grannie's cart. He left him down near the hen house, waiting patiently for his mother to prepare herself. On hot days such as this, he likes Lightning to get a bit of shade and escape from the flies. He has thrown an armful of hay in front of his nose so that he'll have nothing to do except munch hay till Grannie and me are ready for our trip.

Grannie pins her wedding day brooch in her coat lapel. I am wearing white socks and my sandals are glistening with polish.

We are ready and off we go. Lightning trots merrily down the lane towards the quietness of Brindley's stile, then on to the metal bridge before reaching the crossroads at Dolla. Not once has Grannie used her stick on his back, the stick with the hatpin stuck on the end of it in case she has to prod him under his tail.

Occasionally, our charming ass blows a little wind out of his rear end, a sign (says Grannie) that he is experiencing a happiness of some sort which no humans can understand. She often uses big words like these, which I cannot make head nor tail of.

Inside the counter at the post office sits Nora. She is wearing a dark green dress and her lips are painted deep red. Her hair is as black as soot and combed back neatly behind her ears. She is a pretty lady and I cannot take my eyes off of her. She is far too busy and business-like to take any notice of me even though I am the strange child who came over from England when I was born.

She bids Grannie good day and hands her a brown envelope with Mikey's pension money inside it. There's no one else here and Nora invites Grannie to walk in behind the counter and into the parlour. She pours her out a small glass of port and a second one for herself since Mikey's first pension is a special occasion.

Grannie has never drunk strong drink before. But today, with Mikey's brown envelope stashed away in her handbag, she feels she cannot object. This is something to celebrate and she pours it down her throat in one quick swallow.

Half an hour later, she staggers out the door and gets ready to mount the cart. She finds it difficult to get her foot on the wheel and she mutters under her breath that impolite swear word ('shite') which she thinks I cannot hear. But I can. She is a little bit tipsy, I'm sure of it.

I don't remember how we say goodbye to Nora or how we get home. But, after bidding good day to Lightning and returning him to join Moll, we hurry off to give Mikey his money.

We head up the lane to the Easy Stile and throw our legs out over it. It leads into Old Tim's meadows, the one with the many-coloured field flowers.

We move round Fort Dangerous and into the other field known as the Hill of the Goldfinch. We struggle over the Difficult Stile, the one made of flat slates, and head up the lane towards Mikey's place. Grannie wants to thank him for giving Jack the use of his mower and tell him how Jack has already started mowing with it this morning.

I find it difficult to keep up with her in spite of the few drops of port that she swallowed at the post office and the fact that her back is stooped from the sciatica she developed after the birth of her son Tom. I beg her to slow down and wait for me. I ask her why she's able to walk so fast and she tells me her stoop helps her move all the more quickly as her head is nearer the ground than mine and it's that which helps her move with speed. This is another strange thing she has taught me and like a lot of other things, I cannot understand it.

She's as quiet as a mouse all the way up the lane – thinking of poor Mikey's bad ear and praying silently that he will make a speedy recovery. The healthy envelope of pension money will do a lot to lighten her brother's burden and with greater speed than ever, she hurries on towards his house with me left gasping for breath behind her.

Mikey's wife, Anne, is all friendship when she sets eyes on us. She pats me on the head the way old ladies do after Mass when they're chatting with Grannie.

'How is the little man from England this bright sunny morning?' she laughs. 'Are you going to help Jack with the hay?'

I gaze at Anne and I'm about to get into one of my long-winded tales about the castle behind Gret's orchard when Grannie puts her finger to her lips and gives me a nudge. I realise I'm on a visit and that I have to know my place and act accordingly. So I hold my tongue and smile up at Anne. She rushes to her apple box and hands me a juicy red apple.

She takes down from the cupboard her best willow-patterned crockery and we eat a piece of fruit cake with our tea. I have never had fruit cake before. Then we tiptoe into the bedroom to see my granduncle. Mikey is snoring lightly in the bed. He has a cheerful look on his face as though he is dreaming of happier days. We keep quiet but he opens his eyes and waves his arm in the air. He smiles at Grannie.

I have never seen a man as old-looking as himself. He looks as old as Mrs Methuselah even though he was born in the 1870s and a good few years later than she was.

Grannie notices everything. Her big brother still has that stark serenity about him like he had before. But he has greatly aged and is just a shadow of himself since she last saw him.

I can't help staring at him. His face is grey. So are his eyes and he has two bright red cheeks. He finds it hard to speak as though his brain, unlike Grannie's, is fogged up after the pain of his operation. The room's silence lasts a little while longer and Grannie and Mikey continue to stare at each other. It's a time of adult solemnity, something I'm used to since I spend much of my time with Grannie and Jack, listening to their serious conversations. Mikey again waves his arm, weakly this time and slowly like a snail. We can see how difficult it is for him.

I can't help thinking of Grannie and how she can milk her cows twice a day and how she's able to kill a chicken for Sunday dinner. Poor Mikey hasn't the strength to pluck a feather out of a chicken, let alone milk a few cows.

When all the staring is done, the two of them smile at each other once more and the bedroom fills with their warmth for one another. A small bit of moisture runs out of Grannie's eyes and down her cheeks. I think it's a tear. They have so much to think about – memories of the past – memories of their childhood days.

Grannie points at me. 'This is the little man from England – the child who escaped The Blitz,' Mikey raises his arm as though to salute me. Grannie gives me another nudge and I step forward and make Mikey a bow.

Grannie and I don't stay long in the bedroom. She places Mikey's pension money on the table next to his bed and his eyes sparkle. He gives his young sister another big smile and then nods off to sleep.

When we return to the living room, Anne is busy rattling the teaspoons and washing up the dishes in the pan. She watches us getting ourselves ready for the road home and, once more, she gives me a pat on the head.

'God almighty, but aren't you a fine big little man,' she laughs just like the old ladies do after Mass. I still don't understand what a 'fine big little man' means and, once more, I think how much more I have to learn.

She and Grannie whisper quietly at the gate, confiding to each other their thoughts about poor Mikey.

Anne watches us trace our footsteps down the lane and she keeps on waving her handkerchief until we become a tiny speck in the distance.

Grannie is silent for most of the way home, reflecting on the way her big brother has aged. Perhaps she's listening out for the leprechauns and their dancing feet or to hear them cobbling their buckle shoes.

By this time, Jack is covered in clouds of dust and insects are lodged on Moll's back. She shudders all over and swishes her tail to drive away the flies. He steers the mower through the lower gap and out into the Deer Field. On the left of the Deer Field, the next field Jack is mowing today, lies a very damp spot, almost a pool, and he can't drive the mower across that part. It's the home of a family of frogs.

By late afternoon, the day's mowing is done. Jack gazes down the field, well satisfied. Both fields are as trim as a man's shaved face. He drives the mower back home with Moll. She is worn down with tiredness. In the yard, he takes one of Grannie's old towels and wipes the sweat off of her back and shoulders. With a second towel he dries her off, her sides as well. 'You're the best mare in all Tipperary,' he whispers in her ear.

In a few days' time, he will need her again when it's time to draw the rows of hay across the field to build his trams. The work will be tough for Moll and even tougher for himself as he gathers the hay with the wide hay-rake to make heaps of them for the trams. It'll be hard, too, for the other men, who'll be here to give Jack a hand.

Now that today's work is done, Jack takes me for a walk towards the Deer Field to see the frogs' pool.

At other times, when Jack and I are whispering to each other in bed, we hear the frogs booming and croaking far into the night to such an extent that it has been hard to get asleep. Such a racket. 'It's their way of singing to the stars,' says Jack and I realise that it isn't only Grannie who has the lofty words in her head.

We arrive at the pool and stop still. We're as quiet as the grave until one or two inquisitive frogs raise their heads and swim around, prodding their crooked legs back behind them. 'Lovely swimmers,' says Jack, 'aren't they, Ned?'

A family of cranes live in the nearby wood. They never go hunting at night, even though the frogs make so much noise. It's a difficult life for the cranes as the frogs never croak during the day in case these birds come by and gobble them up.

Jack and I look over to the far side of the pool where a few frogs are resting. He picks one up and hands it to me. It is sticky and clammy. It is very frightened, the way I am frightened at times when I'm not sure of myself. As with the young trout in the river, it's a devil of a job to hold onto it. I place it on the ground and let it go. I watch it pause before it trundles off, leaping in bursts towards the ditch. It has disappeared for the rest of the day.

With the mowing done, Jack needs only a few days of good weather for the rows of hay to dry out. In years gone by, if the weather was unreliable, it might be a race against the clock. Airing the hay was a hot and tiring task as the men had to move their forks at lightning speed before the rain came on and ruined everything. This year, the hay-tossing will be finished long before Sunday Mass, thanks to all the sun soaking into the newly-mown grass.

The usual trusty helpers are here for today's hay-turning, their hayforks neatly balanced on their shoulders. They'll be tired by this evening but I hear them laughing good-humouredly this morning, banging their forks on the flagstones and telling Jack to hurry up so they can shove into the work.

I race to the bedroom window and in front of me stands our kindly neighbour, Rody. He has left Ellie at home to look after the house and tidy the cupboards. Next to him stands Tom Goggles (Jack's first cousin), the only man to wear glasses (except for Doctor Glasses). He's the youngest of Mikey's sons. Though Tom's as thin as a candle, he's a mighty hard worker. Last (but by no means least), I see Shy Denis. He has brought that huge smile of his along with him.

Isn't Jack the fortunate man? Denis has the strength of a bull. Tom can do twice the work of any man. Rody is the neat and tidy one and will keep the hay rows as straight as a plumb line.

There's no sign of Fiddler Joe. He is lost amidst his own newly-cut hay in the field above the Heights. Shawnee, Sweeney and Bucko will help him toss his hay and make sure it is dry today. Fiddler Joe has made their work easy by shortening the handles of their forks so that they can turn the hay with speed. There's no time for them to play in the castle this week or the next. The three of them feel like real men and are eager for the work. It's not only smoking fag-butts that make them feel this way.

Shawnee will soon be shaving off his new moustache (says Jack) and if he doesn't take to the razor soon, he'll have a beard as long as Moses's and be the laughing stock of the lane. Not even Jack Scissors wears a beard.

With a nod and a bow to Grannie, our welcome helpers follow Jack across the haggart and on to the third field. Moll is having a well-earned rest today. They take a row of hay each and have a lot of ground to cover. As they pace along the rows, not a word is spoken. Their shadows lengthen out in front of them.

The grass is already turning grey. With their forks, they pierce as much hay as they can and toss it high in the air to let the dryness into it. It's hard work but the fragrance of the hay fills their nostrils. By dinnertime, their faces are drenched in sweat and their shirts are wrinkled and wet. But their caps have done much to keep the sun's heat away off their heads.

Grannie always thinks of everything and last night, she prepared the dinnertime food for them and covered it with a potato-sack. This morning, Jack took the sack across the fields. Inside the sack, he had a few small bottles of milk. He left them in Corcoran's well to keep them cool. He hid the sandwiches under his waistcoat on the headland.

As soon as this morning's hay-tossing is done, the men lean on their forks and admire their work. It's time for them to rest. They throw off their caps. There's a pink ring line high on their foreheads where the sweat under the caps has mapped out a clear line between the brown skin of their faces and the white skin under their caps. The sky is now serene and there's a little breeze sighing over the meadow. They make their way over to Corcoran's well for a drink of cold water and to retrieve their bottles of milk. They sit in the shade of the ditch and smoke their pipes, as contented as any men on earth.

It's a new day. Jack is anxious to get busy and he leaps into his britches. The morning air is cold, clean and clear like the waters in our yard stream. He is determined to make as many trams as Rody, Tom, Shy Denis and himself can manage in case the dark clouds put an end to their efforts today and later in the week. In his mind's eye, he can see the trams of hay that he and his helpers will make. He can see Moll and her fully-laden hay-cart trundling into the haggart again and again to make this year's reek. All that's needed is the hot weather to hold tough and not let the rain drive out the sun.

Like she did yesterday, Grannie has prepared the meadow food for today's tramming: the bottle of milk and soda bread sandwiches of ham slices with a newly-opened tin of corn beef, all wrapped in newspaper. The three helpers have brought with them three hard-boiled eggs apiece to add to the sandwiches. They made sure to put them in their coat pockets this morning.

But first of all, there's Jack's breakfast to consider. Inside the skillet pot are the leftovers from Sunday's rabbit, a fine healthy soup. She cuts Jack three slices of bread. He butters each slice lavishly and Grannie ladles him out a big mug of soup for him to dip his bread in.

As he goes out the half-door, she gives him a shower of holy water. He blesses himself and heads out to the cow shed to meet the men. They put out their fags, spit on their fists and head off with him to take a look at the rows of hay.

Thank God none of the hay has been blown around the field. The sun is already whipping its beams through the tall trees on Old Tim's ditch and out along the field. They breathe in the sweet scent of the newly mown hay.

Moll is already there, stamping her feet to greet them. Early on today, Jack had yoked her to the wide hay rake with which she'll drag in the hay from the hay rows and make a heap from which the men can build their first tram. Jack gives Moll a playful tap on her nose. He wraps her long reins round his waist and stands well back behind the rake's sharp metal prongs.

Moll pulls ahead into the first hay row and Jack steers the rake towards the spot where they'll start building the tram. The field seems to have an echo in it, the merry sound of Moll's tackling and the jingling of the rake. So fiercely is she pulling on the rake that Jack feels she might run away on him and drag him along the ground after her. She is merely trying to escape from the pesky flies as the sun gathers pace.

262

When Jack thinks he has enough hay brushed onto the front of the rake, he pulls back the wooden lever to raise the handle and rotate the prongs out in front of him, leaving a heap of hay behind the rake. He is well-used to tipping forward the prongs, but it requires split-second timing and good horse control, for he has to keep one hand free to lift the lever whilst his other hand guides the reins. If either Moll or himself don't time their movements to perfection, the hay-raking will be to no avail. Jack is a man not given to swearing but, if the work of today's tramming is held up, he'll rain down curses on the rake and on Moll as well. There may be a few rainy days ahead and the hay might be left on the ground and turn from grey to brown. No one wants brown hay.

The men walk along behind Jack and, with their hay forks, rake the remains of any hay left behind after he tips over his pile of hay.

Jack and Moll work on and on, making as many piles of hay needed to build up four or five trams this morning. As soon as the hay has been gathered to where the tram is to be built, the men get busy laying out the base of the tram. They make it 12 ft across and build it higher and higher. After the first 3 or 4 ft, they begin to taper it into a more conical shape till it reaches a height of 8 or 9 ft. In a few days' time, it will have settled down to 6 or 7 ft tall.

The wind from Kerry can be savage at times. Men have got used to seeing it speeding over the fields and Jack is aware of the damage it can do to his trams. Each tram has to be balanced carefully against the wind and also the slope of the field. When the tram is complete, Jack throws two long ropes of hay (his sugans) criss-crossed on top of it. He firmly pushes the lower end of each sugan deep into the base of the tram to keep it safe and secure.

I am spending the morning with Grannie. She says it's best not to get in the way of the men while they're working at the hay. I'm to go nowhere near Jack and his hay rake today. She stands on the chair in the Big Cave room where Jack and I sleep. She brings me a set of his cigarette cards from the ledge beneath the thatch. Jack has several sets of these cards up there. He must have smoked a lot of cigarettes when he was young before he took to the pipe.

The set Grannie brings down is the one called Wild Flowers. I know she loves flowers. Her little garden is full of them. Most days, she marches me out the half-door with her walking stick to chastise any drake that has the nerve to waddle in among her Sweet William flowers in search of snails. As quick as a flash, she leaps in over the hedge and frightens the drake half to death. A drake might be useful for killing a few snails but not for treading over her flowers and breaking their stems.

For the rest of the morning, I have a wonderful time at the front table, kneeling on the chair next to the St Brigid's cross.

Grannie lays the cards out in rows and gets me started on my morning's education with these wild flowers. She asks me to choose the red ones first, then the yellow ones, and so on. She picks out her own favourites. I pick out mine. She picks the wild roses. I pick the honeysuckles and the foxgloves, the ones Ellie and I gathered to make Shawnee's garland.

I spend the rest of the morning studying all the colourful flowers. I ask her can she bring me down Jack's set of bicycles. I have seen them before and I don't need any help with these. There are so many different bikes. When I grow up, I will get myself a shiny new bike and cycle all round the world.

Grannie has her bolster ready for the men's teatime in the meadow. She takes down the mugs from the press cupboard. She pours tea into small bottles. She half-fills my sweet gallon with today's milk. As an afterthought, she adds a few slices of rabbit, knowing that the men will be ravenous with hunger by one o'clock. She will carry the bolster. I will carry the little gallon of milk.

I am delighted to be going over to the meadow. I want to see what Jack and his mower did yesterday and what his hay rake has done this morning. I run ahead of Grannie with my sweet-gallon of milk. She quickly catches me up as we pass through the potato field. The men drop their forks as soon as they see her. They take armfuls of hay and sit on them on the headland. The sun is on their backs but they don't mind. They squint their eyes and scour the distance. They have a fine view of the meadows on the far side of the river.

I sit next to Jack. I can hear the voices of the haymakers in Ned Buckley's meadow. They're as clear as a bell, though it must be half a mile away. Jack points out the Buckley brothers at their work. We all stop what we're doing and we listen to them. Jack seems to know what the Buckley brothers are saying to each other, even at this great distance.

Grannie sets out the food and the men dig into it. I will have my own dinner when she takes me home and she has told me not to ask for any of the food, not even a sip of milk. Tea in the meadow is a happy moment – just the men slurping their tea and the little birds and bumble bees making music among the briars in the ditch.

I hear our dog, Rose, yelping in the field behind us. Maybe she's been feeling lonely. She comes racing to the headland to greet us, her tail flapping wildly.

Among the helpers, Shy Denis is really like a child. He watches Rose chasing her tail and enjoying her time snapping at the midges. He gets up and chases her round the tram. I chase after him. The three of us are having a splendid time chasing one another round in circles. We are like the white butterflies doing their own dance steps nearby and Jack laughs when he sees me looking back under my legs – something he taught me recently – and seeing the whole world upside down.

'Mind ye, don't kick the trams over,' says he. But I see Grannie smiling. She likes to see me jigging about and running myself wild along with Rose and Shy Denis.

We have soon used up all our energy and are exhausted. I come back and sit down next to Jack again, my tongue gasping and my legs aching. Yes, it's a hard life for a child with nothing else to do but to play in the meadow.

The men finish their tea. Grannie packs everything back in the bolster: the newspaper wrappings, the mugs and even the sweet-gallon. She sits down next to me. I can feel her heat. We are not going back to the house yet.

It's another moment of sleepy contemplation, different from the time when the men were tramming the hay. The sky is cloudless, pigeon-blue in colour. There's not a puff of wind or the stir of a leaf. There is something dignified about it, like the lovely colours inside the church, the priest's vestments, the altar flowers and the merry light of the candles.

Moll is resting in a shady corner of the field and swishing her long tail against the flies to sweep them away.

Jack and the men collect up the hay they're sitting on and throw it into the heap. They don't want to waste a scrap of it.

Grannie walks round the five trams that have been made so far. It's her chance to inspect the way they've been built and the way the men balanced them, forking most of hay on the upper side of each tram.

She and I are ready to go home. We stroll off through the potato field. A solitary cloud appears out of nowhere, like a smoky swan all tinged in silver. Behind us, the rest of the sky is flawless.

It'll be time soon for the men to shove back into the work, but not yet. They take out their pipes for a smoke. They have a few more moments to rest their limbs and their tongues. This is not a time for yarns or stories. They firm down the tobacco in their pipes and light up, collapsing their sunken cheeks in and out with plopping sounds. The honey scent of their pipe smoke banishes the flies who have dared to come near them at the smell of the food.

By the end of this afternoon, five more trams will be ready to be tied down with the crisscross sugans. In a few days' time, there'll be thirty trams decorating this field and the Deer Field.

It's time to go home. The day's work is over. The men gather up their waistcoats from the headland. They rake in the last few sops of hay and head down to the river to free themselves from the itch and scratches clinging to their sweat. They lay their forks on the edge of the river and strip off their shirts, plunging into the icy water with nothing on but their britches. They don't mind if passersby see their bare white bodies. They are too tired to worry.

266

By now, it's early evening and the sun, full of blood at this hour of the day, begins to set. A great band of crimson streaks across the sky.

Meanwhile, I am delighted to see Ellie running into the yard. She has come down to fetch her father, Rody, home after all his hard work. She races in to say hello to Grannie. She sees my cigarette cards still laid out in rows on the table where I left them. 'Have you any others?' she asks.

I get Grannie to bring me down Jack's set of the royal kings and queens of England. I have heard the word 'England' rammed into me so many times ('Is this the little man from England?') that I realise the kings and queens on the cigarette cards are the past rulers of England. It's what Grannie says. She now spouts on for a good bit and in the end, even Ellie has learnt something about England's royal leaders that she never knew before.

Tom Goggles and Shy Denis take their leave of the river and head down to Gerry's pub for a few glasses of stout. Rody takes the road back up towards our house, for he never drinks a drop of strong liquor.

Ellie hears his boots. She runs from the front table and races to meet him just as he reaches the flagstones. Jack is with him. When he sees me and Ellie, he has an idea. 'Would the two of you like to help me make a few sugans before you set off home, Ellie?'

Rody nods his approval. Making the sugans will be a further part of Ellie's education, as well as mine.

The three of us – Jack, Ellie and me – walk back to the hay field. Jack takes the sugan-twister with him. It has a hook on the end of it.

We reach the first tram of hay where he helps us make two sugans from the hay that's at the bottom of the tram. He kneels on one knee and pulls out a length of hay from deep inside the tram, making sure it has no thistles in it. He ties a fistful of it onto the twister's hook and hands it to Ellie. He shows her how to turn the twister. He tells her to walk away from him slowly so as to keep the sugan thick. She does as she is told, all the time twisting slowly as he continues to add more and more hay to the hook on the end of the twister.

Ellie stops twisting when Jack thinks the sugan is long enough. Then he unhooks it and wraps it round his elbow while Ellie advances towards him. She soon has twisted two long sugans.

It's my turn for the twister and I have been watching Ellie – watching Jack too. I repeat the way she walked backwards and how she twisted the hay slowly so as to make her sugan thick. We work on and on for the next half hour till we have twenty sugans made. My wrists ache from the work. It has been difficult for me.

Jack throws two sugans criss-cross over the first tram. He pushes the lower ends into the bottom of the tram to secure it. The tram is now firm and sound. It will not move an inch until it's time to bring the hay into the haggart.

Before we have finished twisting, we will have made all twenty sugans, two for each of the ten trams, five that the men made this morning and five they made this afternoon.

Ellie's work and mine was easy enough but it was back breaking for Jack, who was all that time kneeling on one knee and pulling out fistfuls of hay to make the sugan and keep it thick enough not to break. He must have been doing this since he was a child.

The day of the tramming is over and all ten trams are safe. In a few days' time, all thirty trams will be complete and ready for drawing home.

It's late in the day and all creatures are returning home – bees and wasps to their nests and Old Pat's crows to the rookery. Our half-door is still letting in the last of the daylight. I can hear the little birds twittering in the fuchsia bush near the pig house and the crows squawking in the high trees.

These summer evenings are long and it takes time for the light to grow pale. Jack is standing at the half-door. Though his muscles are tired, he seems happy. His day's work has gone favourably. He watches the shadows of young men going down to Maher's Mill to while away the last hours of the day, playing pitch and toss.

Grannie has already lit the lamp. She has lit the two candles – one for the front table where, once more, she can better read the Messenger with its tales of black Africans and their new lives as Christians. The other candle she places on the back table next to the gramophone. She selects half a dozen of her favourite records from the bacon box and checks the little nest-hole of needles to see if the needles are good enough for playing the records.

Meanwhile, the spuds are boiling over the fire along with the cabbages. Jack and I sit by the fire and keep an eye on the burner. He throws a few more sods of turf onto it and we sit there quietly. It will be time for our evening meal before we know it. Grannie inspects the dinner plates to see are they clean enough and she lays the table for the three of us.

With other creatures now fast asleep, including Grannie's ducks, hens and geese, all we hear is the ticking of the clock. It's ticking away our lives together. Will we still be together when this wretched war comes to an end? Jack can but wonder and Grannie always blocks the thought clean out of her head.

In the meantime, while Shawnee, Sweeney and Bucko are helping Fiddler Joe load their trams onto the cart and bring them home, Rosie makes herself busy collecting wisps of hay to make a small pile out of it for her father. Daisy has little or nothing to do and stays at home to help Gret around the house. For once in her life, she is at a loss for what to do without Rosie by her side.

'Why don't ye go down to little Ned and see what he's up to?' suggests Gret.

Jack has spent time the previous week using his billhook and axe at the woodpile. I have had time to watch him, something I like doing. He holds aloft four stout branches of trees that he sawed off below in the wood. Out of these, he makes four poles for Moll's cart. They are necessary for trapping the hay inside the cart so that he can fetch it home securely and safely. With his billhook, he pairs off the tougher bits of the branches. He thins down their ends into a pointed stake so that the poles will fit easily into the corners of the cart.

Daisy has come down the lane to meet me. We have no time to play in her cubby house today. Jack loads us up on the cart behind Moll and off we go to the meadow. The galvanised sheeting rattles musically on the floor of the cart and the smoke from Jack's pipe fills the air. Rose pads along beside us.

Rody, Tom Goggles and Shy Denis are already out in the meadow to help Jack load the hay into Moll's cart. When he arrives, they see that he has fixed the poles into the corners of the cart. They are long enough and sloped at least 10 ft upwards into the air.

The men get busy with their forks, lifting heavy forkfuls of hay and firing them into the cart. Moll shudders as the weight in the cart increases. Her back is quickly covered in hayseeds. The men balance the hay carefully against the slanting stakes, filling the corners first before filling in the middle when the load is almost complete.

Moll is usually passive and obedient, but now she becomes irritated as the load gets heavier. She shakes her head from side to side and rattles her tackle to dislodge the flies. Her tail is trapped inside the harness and she can't make use of it.

When the load is almost two trams full, the men rake the sides down to make it compact so that none of it will fall off on the way back to the haggart. Jack throws the reins across the load and makes a double slip-knot onto the cart to secure it.

Daisy and me are fascinated to see how heavy the load is and how sad the face of Moll is. How can she possibly walk a step with so much hay to carry?

Suddenly, Jack catches hold of me and Shy Denis catches hold of Daisy. They throw us up on top of the load and send us scurrying into the middle of it in case we should fall off. Jack urges Moll forward with the usual words, *'Coom oop!'*

As soon as Moll begins to trudge towards the gap at the potato field, he tells us to lie on the side nearest the hill. If we don't do as he tells us, the hay will topple over and the cart will have to be loaded all over again.

We reach the gap and pass through successfully. We come to the gap leading to the Blue Button Field but this gap is awkward. There are several hoof holes there made by the cattle.

'Hold tight!' shouts Jack, 'And don't wobble about or ye'll tumble off into the briars and that'll be the finish of ye.' He frightens the life out of us.

The cart makes its way slowly through the gap. I have never been as high up as this before. Nor has Daisy. We are so close to the branches of the ash tree that I can almost reach out and snatch its red berries. The ground is a long way off and everything seems so small down there, even Rose our sheepdog. I feel dizzy with joy, as though I'm about to fly away.

Moll makes her way along the curve of the Blue Button Field. We are close to the ditch where long tree shadows overhang the cart. These trees are also within reach and the sunlight pours through them.

Moll struggles on, in and out of the shadows. More red berries – holly and ivy also – reflect the sun. The branches lean down like monsters' hands to grab at us and we duck our heads to avoid them.

'Mind yeer heads!' shouts Jack. But as Moll struggles forward, the rattle of the cart and the rickety wheels almost fire us into the briars.

I don't know what's inside Daisy's head. But for me, this trip from the meadow has been an experience like nothing I've had before. I cling to the reins for grim life and Daisy is careful not to move an inch. By now, we have learnt how to balance ourselves against the sudden jolts of the cart.

Daisy whispers, 'I love the smell of the hay, Ned.'

I steal a look at her. A fresh breeze rustles the ribbon on her hair. Ahead of me, I can see the smoke rising up from Grannie's chimney before it fades away in curvy wisps.

The cart reaches the haggart and sways towards the far corner where the reek is going to be made. Moll clumps her way towards that spot. Not one bit of hay has she left behind her when passing under the trees.

271

Neither Daisy nor I want to get off. We bury our heads in the hay: two small children, a cloudless sky and the sunbeams winking gently down at us.

Rody, Tom and Denis have caught up. Their forks are again ready for work. But first, they must eat a few of Grannie's sandwiches and have a mug of her tea. She also gives each of them a few slices of rabbit and a small bottle of milk like yesterday.

They have no time to smoke their pipes but are anxious to begin building the reek before heading back to the meadow for the next two trams. After that, they will make three further journeys to bring back the rest of them. By that time, the reek will be building up nicely.

The site for building this year's reek is next to the remains of last year's reek. Jack has cut several branches from the haggart trees and laid them out in a long row to form the base of the reek. He brought a cartload of ferns from the wood to lay on top of the branches and on top of them, added a number of thin tree trunks to strengthen the ground covering. As in previous years, all this preparation will act as a seepage to soak up any water running down it during heavy rains.

It's not only Rody, Tom and Shy Denis who are on hand for building the reek. Fiddler Joe, along with Shawnee, Sweeney and Bucko, have spared a few days to add their forks to the work.

Jack directs Moll's cart as near as he can to the side of the reek. He starts forking in the hay: light forkfuls at first, ones he can pelt into the middle as he edges Moll along the side of the foundation. His friends are standing in the middle of the reek, directing forkfuls of hay round the base. There's a good deal of rasping voices as they put their hearts into the work.

The cackling hens have come into the haggart to see can they get hold of a few hayseeds as a side dish to Grannie's morning's mash. The little beggars cock their heads inquisitively at us. The men take no notice of them but if they get in their way, they'll give them a kick up the gable end with their boot.

On and on, cartload after cartload enters the haggart. By the end of the second day, the new reek is 4 ft deep thanks to the hard work of those pelting in the hay and those spreading it round the corners of the reek.

Fiddler Joe's sons are in their glory, standing on top of the reek and directing the hay as advised by him. They feel like real men and as the reek climbs higher, they are almost hidden from view midst its furrow and troughs. They raise their knees high in the soft mountains of hay. They stamp it down so that it's no longer loose but firm. It is now 6 ft high and taking on a new look as it begins to settle. The men make sure that the young lads keep the reek's corners well-loaded like the cornerstones of a house.

Shawnee is in charge of his brothers, whispering to them to stamp down the corners and to watch out for thistles, the sharpness of which can leave their feet in a mess. Jack and his friends send huge forkfuls to the boys to hold each corner firmly in place.

The lads are working harder than the men. It's a devil of a job to keep walking up and down on the reek and though their legs are aching like hell, they don't let on. Tramp, tramp, tramp, they keep marching the length of the reek to prevent it overheating and to let it settle down even more. They keep the edges sloping slightly outwards as it goes on getting higher, all under the direction of the men.

Before the end of the week, the reek will be 15 to 20 ft high. Meanwhile, the men have even harder work ahead of them. They stagger up the four wooden ladders and pelt more and more hay up to the boys so as to crown the reek's peak. When it's finally high enough and all the trams have been used in building it, the men join the boys and tidy up the reek by levelling off all its parts and covering the surface with ferns to consolidate the hay underneath.

Moll should be given one of Ellie's garlands for the arduous work she has done this day. Jack takes her down to the Bull Paddock as soon as he can and lets her drink from the river. Lightning races down to the river to greet her. He has been lonely without her.

Gret appears out of nowhere. So does Ellie and Mrs Fidget. The women wear knotted handkerchiefs on their heads against the hayseeds and midges. They have brought long rakes with them and are soon as busy as the men, combing all sides of the reek as good as a barber. Ah, the joy of an evening's raking: all working together as one as the women pace round the sides of the reek. Now you see them, now you don't.

The men don't speak to the women. The women don't speak to the men. The men are high up on the reek. So are the boys, their images humped against the afternoon sky.

Grannie brings out all the mugs and cups she can find and lays them along the potato-sack. She pours out the tea and silently gets busy before racing back home to fetch out more.

Jack has been down to Gerry's pub and brought back several bottles of stout. He hands them out to the men. He gives lemonade to the lads – also to Rody who hates strong liquor.

Grannie brings out a heap of cheese sandwiches, enough for a feast in a famine. Mouths (and then bellies) are soon full to explosion. For a while, there is silence, all eyes admiring the reek, admiring their handiwork. The top of the reek looks grand, sloped in tidily like a church roof with a slight peak down its middle. In this way, the hay will be protected from the rain and snow later on, the water shedding itself out over the edges of the reek.

Grannie gets up and walks round the reek, inspecting it like she did with the trams in the meadow. 'Good men yeerselves,' she cries. She's as pleased as punch. She then includes Gret and Mrs Fidget in her praises. Ellie is pleased to see the smile on her mother's face.

Grannie scuttles back into the yard to shoo the nosey hens into the hen house. The ducks are already fast asleep, mesmerised by the unusual commotion in the haggart.

Daisy and me, even Shawnee, Sweeney and Bucko, are amazed at the height of the reek. We can't help admiring the men and the women. We want to grow up and be like them. They don't talk to us. They are too tired to do so. They sit in silence along the side of the reek like starlings in a row, puffing on their pipes and filling the reek with smoke.

Much later, when I'm fast asleep and my dreams are full of me and Daisy wobbling all over the hay on top of Moll's cart,

Grannie and Jack are busy with the hay-twister abroad in the haggart. It's their last job, to make two long sugans, each one 70 ft long. They'll throw them over the reek from the lower end to the upper end and throw two more from the width, each of these 50 ft long.

Jack has to use one of the step ladders to get up to the top. With Grannie's help, he finally pegs down the reek, good and firm. All is now as safe as houses. The reek is a lovely sight and well-formed, much to the credit of Fiddler Joe's lads, who have given their all in forking the hay round each layer of the reek.

It is now pink twilight and soon the moon will curtain off the day. Shadows creep over the fields and the dusk gives the sun a last push out of the sky.

It's time for everyone to be asleep – even Grannie and Jack. The last rattling cartload of trams have gone up the lane, Old Tim sitting high at the front of his hay, a tired but happy man.

A great day has gone, never to come back, just one or two of the younger crows in Old Pat's rookery still muttering – the older ones scolding them before they're all fast asleep.

Jack prepares to lock the front door for the night. He looks out over the stream at the dusty lane. Wisps of hay are still dancing down along it. The first brown leaves upholster our flagstones. It'll soon be the end of summer and its big yellow sun – soon be the end of my childhood days in north Tipperary.

END OF PART SIX

RETURN TO THE RUINS

All good things come to an end. And in 1945, the World War was over. It was the moment Grannie and Jack had dreaded – me, leaving the two of them shuddering as they sat by the fire each evening. They always knew the day would come when I'd have to return to the parents I'd never set eyes on during these five long years.

They drove me with Moll and the cart into Nenagh Station where they introduced me to Kitty Kane, a distant cousin. She was returning to London to work as a nurse in Saint Mary's Hospital, Paddington – the place where I was born. She had been home throughout the war, tending to her aged mother.

I can still recall the day of my departure, the heartbreaking preparations as Grannie got me ready for my long journey to Dublin and out across the sea. I had no idea where I was going – to my mother and father and the ruined streets of London.

Many years later, I'd come to know the unspeakable grief of my two wartime guardians and how many tears they shed after tending to me all this time and then having to let me go. They must have spent days thinking of all that was happening to me. What must I be feeling other than embittered sorrow at being cast aside like this? By the time I reached Dublin, I felt lost and abandoned. The big yellow sun of recent years had slipped out of the sky and out of my life.

It was a Friday morning when Kitty Kane guided me down off of the train in Euston Station – her gloved hand holding tightly onto me. Did she think I might make a run down the platform to find my way back to Tipperary? It was never going to happen. I was five years old and my heart had been broken. No words can explain how much I missed Grannie and Jack!

There had been moments in my early childhood when I felt unsure of myself. 'The result of the bombing,' Jack said. But now I felt unsure of everything and everybody. Here I was in the biggest city on earth. Here to stay, here to start a new life with my unknown parents.

What a puzzle this railway station is (much bigger than
Nenagh Station) with all the noisy whistle of steam echoing off of
the station roof, the skilful horse-carts and taxis weaving in and out
– the big red buses back in circulation once more! There are more
people here than I ever knew existed.

From now on, there'll be flushed lavatories to replace the
dock-leaves that I've been trained to use behind the ditch. There'll
be gaslights in mantles down in my parents' basement to replace
the lamp that Grannie cleaned with brown paper and which Jack
filled with paraffin. There'll be no more candles that accompanied
Grannie and Jack when they needed extra light to read with.

There'll be water gushing from a tap in the scullery instead
of going daily to Brindley's well to bring back water for cooking,
washing and drinking tea. The well-hole, the lamp, the candles and
everything else that I was used to – all gone for good.

My new mother, Nell, is not a bit like Grannie. She is thirty
years of age. She is also thirty years younger than Grannie.
Grannie wears black clothes that reach down to her shins and like
many of the women of her age, she hasn't a tooth left in her head.
My mother's teeth are shiny and bright and she has a head of hair
that's wavy and black.

She has come to meet me here in Euston Station. She is
dressed in her twinset suit. She stands on the platform, gazing
down at my lonely, lost face. What thoughts must be in her head!

There's no sign of my father, Patsy. Money is scarce and at
this early hour of the morning, he is cycling along the Harrow
Road, his usual seven mile journey to Craven Park. What must be
in his mind? How will he welcome me this evening?

My mother does her best to put a smile on my face, hoping
I'll soon forget my past. I gaze up at her, taking in her lovely smile
and her attempts at laughter. It's all in vain. I have no idea who she
is, no idea where I am. My eyes are full of the many new wonders.
Tears suddenly roll down my cheeks, plain for my mother to see. It
must press dearly on her heart – a young mother seemingly
rejected by me.

I don't know it yet, but in later years, I'll come to understand things better. She has already made up her mind that she'll do her level best to bring me comfort. It'll be a long, hard task, however, before she can expect to take the place of Grannie and Jack and the only love I've ever known.

In the evening, Patsy returns from Craven Park. This is no ordinary evening. He's about to meet his estranged son for the first time and his mind is unsettled. He comes home smartly dressed and not in the work clothes that he's been wearing all day while helping to clear the bomb-site rubble into one of the countless flow of lorries.

He is a shy man, a proud man, just that little bit reserved. He doesn't like the neighbours seeing him badly dressed, doesn't like them knowing he's merely a labouring man. When he sees me, he doesn't make a mad rush towards me or twirl me round over his head like Jack used to do when we came out from Mass. He simply stands before me, not sure what his next move should be. He is like a frightened calf ready to make a bolt for the door and run out into the street. Poor Patsy. His mind is full of this new child, his only son.

A day later, I realise I have two little sisters: Breda, aged three and Margery, a few months old. This makes me even more unsure, just as uncertain as my father is. Above all, I feel lost and unwanted, like something strange that has flown in unexpectedly from round the corner.

Even before my sisters rise from sleep, my mother walks me round the basement to introduce me to my new surroundings. She shows me the staircase leading to the ground-floor flat where she and my father sleep in the room overlooking the back yard and where Margery sleeps in her cot beside them. I have never seen a staircase before, let alone attempted to climb one.

Excitedly, she leads me to the top of the stairs and silently opens the door to a small room. It must once have been used as a kitchen, for there is a deep sink in the corner next to the door. My sister Breda is sleeping here, dreaming her life away in her bed in the corner. My mother puts her finger to her lips, careful not to awaken her. The room overlooks the next garden belonging to Mr Bick, a retired policeman.

We return to the basement. She shows me the long passageway leading to the scullery. We pass the alcove with its protecting curtain on a pole. It houses a mishmash of clobber: my father's donkey jacket on a hook, his winter wellingtons for later on when the heavy snow will arrive, his garden rake, his shovel and spade and a thousand cobwebs.

Opposite the alcove is the lavatory. I have never seen such an obstacle before. Next to it is the door leading to the yard. There is wire netting above it to keep out the wildcats, who are constantly trying to get in and waylay the house cat, Whiskers, to whom I have yet to be introduced.

We make our way back along the passageway. On the left is the cupboard called the safe where my mother keeps her dried food (not the meat) as well as her porridge oats and self-rising flour. Sometimes, she has to throw away the packets of porridge oats when next-door's mice scratch their way through the walls and leave black-dotted droppings in the oats. Of late, Patsy has made a netted box to store things safely.

We trot back to the scullery where there is a low rimmed yellow sink. She shows me how to turn on and off the water that mysteriously comes out from a tap. In the centre of the scullery floor is a big obstacle called a copper boiler where my mother washes her sheets and towels. My father prepares this copper boiler once a week, bringing in coal from the coal cellar and shovelling it into the space below the wide opening that holds the clothes. As soon as the coal is ablaze, he will pour the water into the copper, a bucketful at a time, till the water is boiling hot and my mother can start her washing, prodding the clothes with a long pole, her face awash with soapy suds.

To dry the clothes, she shows me her metal mangle that she uses to rinse out the water from the washed clothes down onto a wide tray below.

All these bits of new information are too much for me to take in during this first morning in my strange new world. My mother is such a busy lady in her efforts to distract me from my sadness and interest me in all these novelties. Not once has she asked me about Grannie and Jack. She is far too frightened and apprehensive to start such a conversation. She is unsure of herself.

After that, she leads me to the front of the basement where there is a closed door. Behind it is hidden a dark and gloomy space with many pipes along the wall for gas to flow towards the house gaslights. It lies beneath the front steps of the house. Inside the door (says my mother, gabbling on), is the ghost of an old woman who died many years before. The place is haunted (she says) and the imprisoned ghost must never be let escape from inside there. I believe every word she says and from this day forth, it never crosses my mind to go in there.

A year later, my father will tell me the truth about the pipes in there being very loosely attached to the wall and if a child were to go in there and start swinging on them, they'd break asunder and gas would escape and cause a mighty explosion that would knock down the house. He'll scare the life out of me. Then, we'd have nothing left but a pile of old bricks and rubble. I am no fool: this hidden space will never be a place for me to explore.

Outside the front door of the basement lie two wide coal cellars – one for us and one for Nan-Nan, the old lady who lives above us. Coal is the replacement for the turf that I've been used to. Each month, six bags of it are delivered by Harry, the coal man, in his orange lorry. I have never seen coal before. In fact, I have never seen a lorry.

We climb the basement steps. For the first time since my arrival, I see another child. He is Johnnie Ridgeway. He's a good bit older than me, about Shawnee's age. I see him gingerly walking across the cut down railings that remain in front of our house. There isn't one complete set of railings left outside the other houses in our block, not even a half cut-off railing. All of them have been taken away and sold by the landlord in support of the war effort, sold to a Jewish gentleman who (rumour had it) has sold them overseas to the Germans to help them in their war effort.

'A Jew financing Hitler's Germany. Fancy that!' my father says. My mother doesn't believe this. It's too far-fetched.

We walk along the street. There isn't a car in sight. Nobody in our street owns a car and it's safe for us to stroll down the middle of the street.

I gaze around me at the huge houses, many of them taller than Grannie's church, more houses than I've ever imagined existed. I can't count them all and have to hold my chin up to see the chimneystacks on top of the houses that are still left standing. A number of them are bombed-out sites with only bits of their ruined frontage left untouched. They seem ready to topple down on top of us at any moment.

We stop walking when we come to the corner sixty yards away. There isn't any sign of a house there, just a huge hole in the ground. Bigger boys are armed with gas masks. They make frightening runs at little girls. They drag an Anderson air raid shelter out onto the middle of the street. It is built in two U-shaped halves that they can easily separate: one for the bigger girls and one for the bigger boys. I am once more mesmerised and transfixed, like I was a moment ago when I watched Johnnie Ridgeway tight-roping his way along the cut-away remains of our railings with his feet turned out in front of him.

I will stop writing now. It's over, the tale of my first five years on Earth.

E.F.H.

May 31st 2025

AFTERTHOUGHT

The Big Yellow Sun is based upon the reflections of my war-time guardians, Grannie and Jack, coupled with my own observations during return visits to them from London in the 1950s and 1960s - up to the time when I married my wife Joan in Kent. From that moment on, and after the birth of our three sons, my life was taken up with teaching in London's inner city and giving my full attention to my wife and our developing sons.

During my retirement years, however, I have found time to write an account of daily life in the years 1940 to 1945. That was the time when I spent the first five years of my life with my grandmother and uncle on their little farm in Tipperary after escaping from the London Blitz at the time of my birth.

I am most grateful to my two guardians for the book's details, especially regarding the first three years of my life with them.

I offer this memoir to my readers in good faith.

Yours truly,

E.F. Hickey

Please note:

Place names are true to life. Names of children in particular have been changed, though they themselves are true characters throughout my early years.

Printed in Great Britain
by Amazon

dbc715a0-e521-4029-a81b-882e79a9e251R01